LIZZIE DIDN'T DO IT!

by

William L. Masterton

BRANDEN PUBLISHING COMPANY

Boston

Library of Congress Cataloging-in-Publication Data

Masterton, William L., 1927-
  Lizzie didn't do it! / by William L. Masterton.
    p.cm.
  Includes bibliographical references and index.
  ISBN 0-8283-2052-7 (alk. paper)
  1. Borden, Lizzie, 1860-1927.
  2. Murder--Massachusetts--Fall River.
  I. Title.

HV6534.F2 M37 2000
364.15'23'0974485--dc21   99-088574

BRANDEN PUBLISHING COMPANY
17 Station Street
PO Box 843 Brookline Village
Boston, MA 02447

Dedication

*Dedicated to the memory of
Melvin Adams, a brilliant
lawyer who saw the truth
to which everyone else was blind
and, on a more personal level,
to my daughters-in-law:
Ilona, who nagged me
to write this book,
and Peggy, who didn't.*

Best Wishes. Jeannine
Bill Martin

CONTENT

FIGURES

6 William L. Masterton

SOURCES

1. *The Lizzie Borden Sourcebook*, David Kent and Robert Flynn, Branden Publishing Co., 1992
2. *Lizzie Borden, Did She: Or Didn't She?* Historical Briefs Inc., 1992. (This is a compilation of articles that appeared in the *New Bedford Evening Standard* between August 1892 and June 1893, dealing with the Borden case)
3. *Fall River Globe*, August 5, 1892
4. *Goodbye, Lizzie Borden*, Robert Sullivan, The Stephen Greene Press, 1974
5. *Forty Whacks*, David Kent, Yankee Press, 1992
6. Drawn by the author from a map supplied by Michael Martins, curator, Fall River Historical Society Museum
7. *Boston Globe*, August 31, 1892
8. *Lizzie Borden Quarterly,* Maynard Bertolet, Editor
9. Emery scrapbook
10. *Lizzie Borden*, Arnold Brown, Rutledge Hill Press, 1991
11. *Lizzie Borden, the Untold Story*, Edward Radin, Simon and Schuster, 1961
12. *Fall River Historical Society*, (Many of the photographs in references 1, 4, 5 and 8 came originally from this source.)
13. *Lizzie Borden*, Joyce Williams et al, 1980
14. *Forensic Medicine*, I Gordon and H. A. Shapiro, 1975
15. Horowitz, *Clin. Soc. 67* 216 (1984)
16. *Los Angeles Times*, June 15, 1995
17. *Fall River News*, June 15, 1893

PREFACE

U nravelling the Borden mystery is a project that has fascinated me throughout much of my life. A great many people have helped me with this project. The list starts with my great-aunt, **Minnie Masterton**, who lived in Fall River in 1892 when Andrew and Abby Borden were murdered. Conversations with her when I was a child convinced me, emotionally at least, of Lizzie's innocence. Sixty years ago Aunt Minnie argued that if her sister Emma knew Lizzie to be guilty she could never have lived with her for more than a decade after the crime. Could you?

In 1973, my older son **Fred R. Masterton**, then a college freshman, presented me with the most memorable Christmas gift I have ever received: a syllabus for a course on the Borden case offered at the University of Massachusetts. The readings recommended for that course convinced me that many of the commonly accepted "facts" of the case were flat-out wrong. For example, even though legend has it that the murder date, August 4, 1892, was the hottest day in the history of Fall River, newspaper weather reports proved otherwise. The temperature that day topped out at about 80°F.

When I retired from teaching chemistry at the University of Connecticut in 1987, I began searching in earnest for the solution to the Borden case. Among other things, I accumulated microfilm reels of several New England newspapers covering the events between August 4, 1892 and June 20, 1893, when Lizzie's trial ended in her acquittal. Among these was the Boston Globe, which gave the verbatim trial testimony. Though the courtesy of **Dan Lavering**, head librarian at the J.A.G. school at Charlottesville, VA, I was able to study these material at my leisure using the Cadillac of all microfilm readers.

In the summer of 1996, after another edition of my general chemistry text with Cecile Hurley had been put to bed, I began the final line of research that led to this book. Here I was helped greatly by several Fall River residents including:

•the staff of the Fall River Public Library, in particular **Patricia Redfearn** and **Dan Lelievre**, who generously allowed me to read microfilm copies of several Fall River publications of the 1890s, sometimes breaking the rules to do so.

• The staff of the Fall River Historical Society Museum, specifically **Michael Martins** (curator), **Dennis Binette** and **Jamelle Lyons**, who promptly and enthusiastically fulfilled my every request. Beyond that, they put out a series of publications which are invaluable to anyone studying the Borden mystery. Included among these is the testimony at the inquest and preliminary hearing and, most recently, the *Knowlton Papers*.

• **Len Rebello**, who perhaps knows more about the Borden case than anyone alive today. I was fortunate enough to have access to the first draft of his book, *"Lizzie Borden, Past and Present."*

The first draft of this book was reviewed, perhaps too kindly, by:

• my younger son, **Lt. Colonel R. Peter Masterton** of the J.A.G. Corps. He convinced me to make this less of a textbook and more of a "whodunit".

• a friend, **Gunnar Wengel**, whose enthusiasm for the manuscript convinced me I was on the right track.

• a fellow chemist, **Laddie Berka**, who knows far more about forensics than I do.

Many people have inspired me as I struggled with this book. I am particularly grateful to:

• my friend, **Maynard Bertolet**, editor of the *Lizzie Borden Quarterly*, who encouraged me to write about the Borden case.

• my publisher, **Adolph Caso**, who has the old-fashioned idea that quality is the bottom line in publishing. I hope he breaks even with this book, in which case I will too.

• my wife, **Loris Masterton**, who married me on the 60th anniversary of Lizzie's acquittal. (That's one way to remember your wedding date.) Loris loyally praised everything I wrote.

One person more than any other helped me turn a life-long dream into reality, **Bob Flynn** made available to me his collection of "Bordeniana," unquestionably the most extensive in the world. More important, he has been a sounding board, a counselor and a friend, sharing my moments of disappointment and exhilaration.

As you may have guessed by now, this is not your conventional true-crime book. If you anticipated blood and gore, perhaps you can still get your money back. I have concentrated, not on the horror of the Borden murders, but on the mystery that surrounds them. That is the feature of the Borden case that explains its enduring fascination.

The first half of this book presents what I hope is an unbiased account of the crime and the judicial proceedings that followed. The last half (Chapters 9-16) present my "solution" to the Borden mystery. Of course, I'm convinced that my analysis of what really happened in Fall River on August 4, 1892 is correct. It's just possible, though, that I might be wrong; that's happened before. For that reason, among others, I've gone to a great deal of trouble throughout the book to encourage you, the reader, to come to your own conclusions.

I sincerely hope that you have half as much fun reading this book as I did writing it. Enjoy!

William L. Masterton
Storrs, Connecticut

Chapter 1
DAY OF HORROR

August 4, 1892, was a pleasant midsummer day in Fall River, Massachusetts and indeed throughout most of New England. The sun was shining and the temperature was slightly below 80°F when, shortly after 11 A.M., Lizzie Borden left the barn to walk back to the house at 92 Second Street, where she lived with her father and stepmother. One report has it that on her way, Lizzie sang an aria from *Il Trovatore*, her favorite opera. This is almost certainly untrue; too bad, because it would have been appropriate. What Lizzie saw after entering the house became perhaps the most gruesome and certainly the most famous true crime story in nineteenth century America.

Andrew Borden, Lizzie's father, was lying on the sofa in the sitting room where she left him twenty minutes before. There was one important difference. When she went out to the barn, Andrew was asleep. When she came back he was dead; his head and face had been chopped to a bloody mass by someone wielding a hatchet. Frightened and horrified, Lizzie ran to the foot of the stairs and called out, "Come down quick, Maggie. Father's dead. Someone came in and killed him."

"Maggie" was Bridget Sullivan, the Borden's live-in maid (nobody knows why Lizzie called her Maggie). She had been sick that morning and was tired after spending a couple of hours washing windows. Shortly before 11 A.M., Bridget had climbed the stairs to her attic bedroom to take a brief rest before preparing dinner. When Lizzie called, Bridget hurried down and started to enter the sitting room. Lizzie stopped her, saying, "Don't go in there Maggie! I have to have a doctor. Go get Dr. Bowen."

Bridget ran across the street to Dr. Seabury Bowen's house. His wife, Phoebe Bowen, answered Bridget's frantic knock. Dr. Bowen was not home; he was making his rounds. (Remember, this was 1892; doctors still made house calls.) Mrs. Bowen promised to send her husband to the Borden house the moment he got home.

When Bridget returned with the disappointing news, Lizzie was standing as if in a trance at the screen door in the kitchen. At one point, Bridget said that Lizzie was crying; later she denied saying it. Lizzie told her, "I can't be alone. Go find Alice Russell and tell her to come over here." Alice Russell, a close friend of Lizzie, lived on Borden Street, a short distance away.

Fortunately, Miss Russell was at home and assured Bridget she would come to the Borden house to console Lizzie. First, though, she had to change her dress, which took perhaps five to ten minutes. You couldn't go calling on a neighbor in Fall River a hundred years ago wearing an ordinary house dress, no matter how urgent the call might be.

While all this was going on, a relatively young (fortyish) widow named Adelaide Churchill, who lived next door to the Bordens, was returning from downtown Fall River, where she had purchased the groceries for dinner. (Dinner, the principal meal of the day, was eaten at noon in most parts of the United States in 1892 and for many years thereafter.) She got back home just in time to see Bridget Sullivan hurrying back to 92 Second Street after her unsuccessful trip to Dr. Bowen's. Mrs. Churchill laid her purchases on the kitchen table and looked across to the Borden house twenty feet away. There she saw Lizzie standing alone at the screen door. Mrs. Churchill called out, "Lizzie, what's the matter?" Lizzie replied, "Oh, Addie, do come over; somebody has killed father."

Adelaide Churchill hurried over to the Borden house. There she asked Lizzie where she was when "it" happened. Lizzie said, "I went to the barn to get a piece of iron, came in and found the screen door open." In response to another question about her stepmother's whereabouts, Lizzie said, "She had a note to go see someone who is sick."

At Lizzie's request, Mrs. Churchill went out onto Second Street to find a doctor. She talked to several people, relating what had happened, and asking someone to locate a doctor or notify the police. A newsdealer named John Cunningham overheard the conversation but got it garbled. Cunningham phoned the police station to report that, "There's a row at the Borden house." It was a lot worse than that!

Marshal Hilliard, the head of the Fall River police force, received the call at 11:15 A.M. As it happened, about half of the policemen were attending a picnic at Rocky Point, a nearby amusement park. Nevertheless Hilliard was able to send a large contingent to 92 Second Street, which was only 400 yards from the police station.

The first officer to arrive at the Borden house, George Allen, had the presence of mind to station Charles Sawyer, a local painter, at the kitchen door with orders to admit no one except police officers. Sawyer carried out his duties faithfully. He remained on duty for seven hours, after which he asked to be relieved so he could go home to eat supper. His request was granted.

Dr. Bowen arrived home sometime between 11:15 and 11:30 and immediately crossed the street to the Borden house. There he examined Andrew's body. Later he described the gruesome scene.

"The blows extended from the eye and nose around the ear. In that small span there were 11 distinct cuts of about the same depth and general appearance. [A subsequent, more accurate count showed that Andrew had received 10 "whacks".] The cuts were about 4½ inches in length and one of them had severed the eyeball and socket . . . I could not inflict upon a dead dog the additional blows that were driven into Andrew Borden's head."

Partial List of Policemen Sent to the Borden House, August 4, 1892:

Who They Were	When They Came	What They Did
George Allen	11:20 AM	Reported back to Hilliard
Patrick Doherty	11:30	Searched house, talked to Lizzie
Francis Wixon	11:30	Searched premises
Michael Mullaly	11:40	Searched house, interrogated Lizzie
John Devine	11:40	Guarded house
John Fleet	11:50	Searched house, interrogated Lizzie
William Medley	11:50	Searched barn, interrogated Lizzie
Patrick Gillon	12:00	Guarded house
Philip Harrington	12:20 PM	Searched barn, interrogated Lizzie
Charles Wilson	1:00	Talked to Lizzie
John Minnehan	1:00	Searched house
John Riley	1:00	Not much, apparently
Rufus Hilliard	2:30	Searched premises
George Seaver	5:00	Searched house
Albert Chase	6:00	Guarded house
Joseph Hyde	?	Guarded house

Bowen, like Mrs. Churchill before him, asked Lizzie where she was when her father was murdered. She gave the same answer, that she had been out in the barn looking for some iron. (Bowen thought she said "irons" but that makes no sense.) Shortly afterward, Dr. Bowen went off to send a telegram to Lizzie's older sister, Emma Borden, who was visiting friends in a nearby resort town. Emma was unable to catch the noon train for Fall River; she got home at about 5 P.M.

From the telegraph office, Dr. Bowen went to a drugstore, perhaps to pick up a supply of sedatives. That afternoon he gave Lizzie two doses of bromocaffeine. Throughout the following week he prescribed a stronger sedative, morphine, to calm Lizzie's nerves.

By the time Bowen got back to 92 Second Street, a second body had been discovered. Adelaide Churchill and Bridget Sullivan found Lizzie's stepmother, Abby Borden, in the upstairs guest room. According to Bridget, they acted in response to Lizzie's suggestion; she told them, "I'm almost certain I heard her come in. Won't you go upstairs and see?" Bridget refused to go alone, so Mrs. Churchill accompanied her.

Abby, like her husband Andrew, had been slaughtered with a hatchet. Dr. Bowen examined this victim as well. He later gave a detailed description of the body.

"There was a large pool of blood under the dead woman's head as she lay face downward [on the floor] with her hands under her. Her head had been literally hacked to pieces and I easily made out 11 distinct gashes apparently the same size as those on her husband's face. [Bowen seemed to have a fixation on the number eleven; Mrs. Borden had received 19 whacks in all, 18 to the head.] One glancing blow cut off nearly two square inches of flesh from the side of her head."

Dr. Bowen went on to say that, with both Andrew and Abby Borden, he saw no sign of a struggle. No furniture was overturned, the victims' clothes were not disarranged, and Andrew's fists were not clenched. Bowen interpreted this to mean that Andrew was asleep when he was attacked and that Abby was taken by surprise. In both cases, death was virtually instantaneous.

Five people slept in the Borden house on the night before the murders. We've now accounted for four of them: Andrew Borden, Abby Borden, Lizzie Borden and Bridget Sullivan. The fifth was John Morse, brother-in-law and close friend of Andrew Borden. He had arrived from out of town on the afternoon of August 3 with no luggage, not even a toothbrush. As it turned out, his stay at 92 Second Street was considerably longer than he had anticipated. Morse spent most of the morning of August 4 visiting a niece in Fall River, a little more than a mile from the murder scene. At about 11:45 A.M. he returned, apparently to accept a dinner invitation offered earlier by Andrew.

For a man about to eat dinner, John Morse behaved a bit strangely. He took time out to eat a couple of pears before entering the house, where Bridget told him what had happened. Later Morse said he didn't notice the crowd of a hundred or more curious people milling around outside the Borden house.

FIGURE 1.1 Crowd surrounding the Borden house

Lizzie Borden, newly orphaned, quickly became the center of attention. Alice Russell, Adelaide Churchill and later Phoebe Bowen took turns fanning her and rubbing her hands. Lizzie protested that she wasn't about to faint or go into hysterics, but these well-meaning people continued their ministrations. They didn't know what else to do.

While this was going on, Lizzie also had to deal with a more hostile audience. At least four policemen interrogated her at some length. Not one of the people who came in contact with Lizzie that day saw even a single spot of blood on her person

THE CROWD GATHERED AT 92 SECOND STREET

From *Lizzie Borden Sourcebook*, p. 2

or her clothing. Several of her neighbors (and one policeman) so testified; the other police officers did so by implication.

In all of her interviews with the police, Lizzie told essentially the same story. She said that at about 9 A.M. that morning her stepmother received a note about a sick person. Shortly afterwards, her father went downtown; he returned at about 10:45 A.M. Lizzie said she helped Andrew assume a comfortable position on the sitting room sofa so he could take a nap. Shortly before 11 A.M., she went out to the barn; when she returned perhaps twenty minutes later, she found her father murdered.

Lizzie also told the police that she was sure neither Bridget Sullivan nor John Morse committed the murders. Responding to a rumor that a "Portuguese" at Andrew's farm in Swansea was involved, Lizzie denied it. She said that neither of the men who worked there would hurt her father.

Despite all this, Lizzie made a bad impression upon just about all of the policemen who talked with her. It was not what she said but how she said it that bothered them. When Assistant Marshal Fleet asked her if she knew who killed her father and mother, Lizzie replied sharply, "Mrs. Borden was not my mother; she was my stepmother. My mother died when I was a little girl." This might seem like a simple statement of fact, but Fleet interpreted it to mean that Lizzie disliked, perhaps even hated, Abby Borden.

Lizzie had even more trouble with Officer Philip Harrington. After interrogating her, he said, "[Lizzie] talked in the most calm and collected manner . . . There was not the slightest indication of agitation, no sign of sorrow or grief, no lamentation of the heart, no comment on the horrors of the crime and no expression of a wish that the criminal be caught." Later, Harrington told Marshal Hilliard, "I do not like that girl. She does not act in a manner to suit me; it is strange to say the least."

Besides interrogating Lizzie, the police spent considerable time Thursday morning and afternoon (August 4) searching the Borden house, barn and yard. They were looking, first and foremost, for the murderer. Needless to say, they didn't find him. They were also looking for bloody clothes; here again they drew a blank. Finally, the police searched for the murder weapon. Bridget Sullivan showed them two axes and two hatchets in the cellar. The axes and one of the hatchets, which had a peculiar claw hammer design, had suspicious looking stains on them. They were delivered to Dr. Edward Wood, professor of chemistry at Harvard Medical School, to be tested for the presence of blood.

Oh, yes, I almost forgot! Assistant Marshal Fleet came across a hatchet blade in a box on a high shelf in the cellar. Since one can't commit murder with a hatchet minus a handle, Fleet put the blade back in the box and forgot about it.

There were about as many doctors at the Borden house on Thursday, August 4, as there were policemen. A partial list includes:

John Abbott	William Dolan	William Learned
Seabury Bowen	Emanuel Dutra	John Leary
John Coughlin	Thomas Gunning	Anson Peckham
Albert Dedrick	? Hardy	J. Q. A. Tourtelott

Dr. Bowen, the Bordens' personal physician, was the first to examine their bodies. Dr. Coughlin was the mayor of Fall River, Dr. Dolan the medical examiner for the Fall River area of Bristol County. It is not at all obvious what the other gentlemen were doing. Perhaps they came for a lesson in human anatomy; it's not every day that you see head injuries of the type suffered by Andrew and Abby Borden. Reportedly Dr. Bowen, after viewing Andrew's body, suggested to Mrs. Churchill that she might like to look at what was left of her nextdoor neighbor. The good lady politely but firmly declined.

Dr. Dolan found out about the murders by accident; he happened to be passing 92 Second Street at about 11:45 A.M. His examination of the bodies was much more thorough than that of Dr. Bowen; it was Dolan who established that Andrew Borden had been struck 10 times, Abby 19. Later, at about 3:30 P.M., Dr. Dolan carried out what he called a "partial" autopsy. He removed the stomachs of the victims and sent them for analysis to the expert, Dr. Wood. This time you might say that Dr. Wood had his work cut out for him.

Legend has it that the calendar on the grandfather clock in the Borden house stopped on the day of the murders. A week later it still pointed to August 4, although the hours and minutes passed in the usual way. For the inhabitants of the house, August 4, 1892, must have seemed endless. It wasn't of course. The sun set at 7:00 P.M., exactly as predicted by the *Old Farmer's Almanac.* An hour or two later, Lizzie and Emma retired to their bedrooms on the second floor. John Morse, who must have been a remarkably unimaginative person, slept, as he had the night before, in the guest room where Abby Borden was murdered. Bridget Sullivan, with a much more active imagination, spent the night with a friend across the street. Alice Russell, a true friend in time of trouble, volunteered to stay with the Borden girls. On Thursday night, she used the room occupied by the elder Bordens the night before. Their bodies now lay on the dining room table, awaiting the arrival of the undertaker.

Officer Hyde, who was on guard at the Borden house, reported that sometime around 9 P.M., Alice Russell and Lizzie Borden made a trip to the cellar. Alice carried a kerosene lamp, Lizzie a chamber pot. Lizzie emptied the pot in either a sink (according to Hyde) or the water closet (according to Miss Russell). After that the two women went upstairs; fifteen minutes later Lizzie returned to the cellar alone. Hyde couldn't make out what she was doing this time. Perhaps she was using the water closet. Then again she might have been adding to a collection of menstrual pads soaking in a pail in the cellar; it was that time of the month for Lizzie. There is still another possibility; Lizzie could have added more sinister bloodstained objects such as a dress or undergarment to the pail. Apparently no one ever checked.

After Shocks

For many days after August 4, the Borden crime was the lead story on the front page of every newspaper in Fall River and vicinity. Early accounts of the crime were loaded with factual errors. The article shown below contains at least seven misstatements. The most interesting of these is the assertion that, "the murder suicide theory finds many supporters." So far as I know, no one has ever committed suicide with a hatchet.

FIGURE 1.2 Newspaper Article on Crime

On the other hand, newspaper accounts are the first place to look for insights

THE BORDEN MURDER.

Portuguese Farm Employe Suspected Assassin.

Daughter of Slain Couple First Discovered the Bodies.

Threads of Evidence Picked Up by the Police.

Mr. Borden Seen on the Street Shortly Before Found Dead.

No Trace of the Implements Used in the Commission of the Crime.

[By Associated Press.]

FALL RIVER, Aug. 4.—Andrew J. Borden and his wife were found at their home, 92 Second street, at 11 o'clock this forenoon, both dead. Both had been frightfully mutilated about the head and face with an axe, cleaver or a razor. Mr. Borden lay on a sofa in a room on the lower floor of the house. His head had been cut, and gashes from four to six inches long were found on his face and neck. Mrs. Borden was in her own chamber on the upper floor, and the condi-

tion of her face and head was the same as that of her husband. She lay face downward on the bed, which was a veritable pool of blood. The police were immediately notified and began an investigation. Up to the hour of writing no implements that could have been used in the commission of the crime had been found. This leads to the terrible suspicion that Mr. and Mrs. Borden were murdered. The murder and suicide theory is advanced and finds many supporters. Mr. Borden was a wealthy real estate owner and mill man, and was seen on the street half an hour before he was found dead.

There is hardly any doubt now that both were murdered. The daughter of the unfortunate couple was the first to make the discovery. She went up stairs after finding the body of her father and saw the form of her mother lying on the floor. She thought she had fallen in a swoon, but upon finding that she too was murdered, the girl fled down stairs and fainted. The police have searched in vain for any clew to the murderer. They are now after a Portuguese who runs the Borden farm at Gardner's Neck and who, it is said, was in the house a few minutes before the bodies were discovered.

It is reported that word was sent to Mrs. Borden this morning that a sick friend desired to see her to-day, but she didn't go out.

It is said that the servant, Bridget Sullivan, says she went into the room to make some inquiry of Mr. Borden about five minutes before Lizzie Borden gave the alarm. He was then sitting on the sofa reading a newspaper. Mr. Borden was on the streets and in several of the banks as late as 10 o'clock.

On the other hand, newspaper accounts are the first place to look for insights into the Borden case. They are full of intriguing suggestions that were never followed up, mostly because they contradicted the legend that gradually became frozen in place. For anyone hoping to solve the Borden mystery a hundred years later, the primary source has to be the local newspapers. In 1892 there were three dailies in Fall River. The *Evening News* was the most reliable and authoritative; it was also the dullest. At the other extreme was the provocative and often controversial *Globe*; the *Herald* was somewhere in between.

Two items of particular interest in the Fall River papers of Friday, August 5, are shown below. The reproduction at the left cites the reward offer made by Emma and Lizzie Borden, promising $5,000 for information leading to the arrest and conviction of the murderer. Although it appeared daily for over a year, no one ever claimed the reward. Sorry; it's too late now!

FIGURE 1.3 Two newspaper articles

$5,000
REWARD!
The above Reward will be paid to any one who may secure the

Arrest and Conviction
of the person or persons, who occasioned the death of

Mr. Andrew J. Borden and Wife.

EMMA J. BORDEN,
LIZZIE A. BORDEN.

DISCOVERY!
A Woman Inquired
for Poison.

Said That Drug Clerk
Identified Her.

Fall River Globe, Aug. 5, 1892. From *Lizzie Borden Sourcebook*, p. 11

The newspaper headline shown at the right refers to an article which first appeared in the *Fall River Globe*, a newspaper generally hostile to the Bordens. It relates to a statement made by a clerk named Eli Bence who worked at Smith's drugstore in Fall River. He said that on the day before the murders a young woman came to his store and attempted unsuccessfully to buy ten cents worth of prussic acid, a deadly poison. Bence identified this woman as Lizzie Borden.

On the morning of August 6 (Saturday), the double funeral of Andrew and Abby Borden was held in the sitting room where Andrew was murdered. The bodies were arranged so as to conceal the marks of violence; everyone agreed that undertaker Winwood had done a marvelous job. There were about 75 mourners present in the house; a crowd variously estimated at 1000-4000 people jostled around outside.

The services, in which the customary eulogy was omitted, were conducted jointly by Reverend Buck, Minister for Missions of the Central Congregational Church, and Reverend Adams of the First Congregational Church. Until quite recently, the entire Borden family had been members of Central Congregational. Andrew left in a cold fury when the deacons refused to meet his selling price for a piece of property. He bought a pew in First Congregational which he never used.

According to legend, Lizzie shocked Fall River society by refusing to appear in black for the funeral. The legend was wrong; two independent newspaper accounts said she wore a black lace dress. She and Emma were, of course, the principal mourners; they led the funeral procession to the Oak Grove cemetery where the Borden lot was located. At the cemetery there was a surprise that disappointed the curious onlookers. By order of Medical Examiner Dolan, there was no interment; the bodies were held in a receiving vault pending further examination.

On Saturday afternoon a second search was made of the Borden house. Six people took part: Marshal Hilliard, Assistant Marshal Fleet and Captain Desmond of the Fall River police department, Detective Seaver of the state police, Medical Examiner Dolan and Andrew Jennings, the Borden family lawyer. They had the complete cooperation of Lizzie and Emma Borden, who made it clear that they wanted the search to be as thorough as possible.

Indeed it was thorough. The *Providence Journal* reported, "Stoves, mattresses, bureau drawers, clothes, cupboards and shelves were examined. No place big enough to conceal a weapon as large as a table knife or clothing of the dimensions of a glove finger escaped the eyes of the officers."

One of the rooms searched was a secondfloor closet called a "clothes press" which contained dresses belonging to Lizzie and Emma. Detective Seaver took each dress off its hanger and examined it carefully. In a few cases, Assistant Marshal Fleet took a dress to a window to look at it in stronger light. They were looking for blood stains; they didn't find any.

The search started at 3 P.M. in Bridget's attic bedroom and ended at about 6:30 P.M. in the cellar. A further examination took place on Monday morning, starting in the cellar where a stone mason took a brick out of the chimney to make sure nothing was hidden there. The handleless hatchet was rediscovered; this time it got to the police station. The officers then went out into the yard where they probed an abandoned well and took apart a pile of lumber piece by piece. The search ended in the barn, where all the hay was moved and some of the floor boards torn up. Afterwards it was reported that, "Absolutely nothing was discovered which would lead to a clue or assist in any way in clearing up the mystery."

Suspects du Jour

To this point, we've concentrated upon what happened at 92 Second Street on August 4, 1892, and successive days. This account is based largely on contemporary newspaper reports corroborated later by court testimony. Actually the newspapers dealt mostly with speculations as to who committed the crime and how he or she did it. Public opinion on this subject changed from day to day.

Initially it was assumed that the murderer came in off the street to wield his hatchet. He could have hated or feared one or both of the victims, probably Andrew. Then again, considering the excess violence involved, he could have been a homicidal maniac striking at random. This is what people in Fall River feared. As a newspaper reporter put it, "It is not exactly reassuring to reflect that a maniac with an insatiable thirst for human blood may be at large, emboldened by his success and looking for additional victims."

There were several reports of suspects who behaved weirdly. A farmer named Joseph Lemay said that while walking through the woods near his house he heard someone say, "Poor Mrs. Borden." Looking around, Lemay saw a rough looking, unshaven man dressed in black sitting on a stone. The man had blood stains on his shirt. He picked up a small hatchet, shook it at Lemay, and began to grind his teeth (his own, not Lemay's). Then he got up, jumped a wall, and disappeared. Small wonder that the police were never able to locate this truly unique individual.

Within a day or two of the murders the police became convinced that Abby Borden died first, a considerable time before Andrew. Their conclusion was apparently based mostly on the fact that no one saw Abby after about 9 A.M. on Thursday morning. In contrast, Andrew Borden was seen as late as 10:45 A.M. The assumption of a time lapse between the murders virtually ruled out the possibility of an "outside job". A person coming in off the street to kill Abby Borden would have to conceal himself for an hour or two waiting for Andrew to show up. That, at least, was the way the police looked at it. Very early on they began to look within the Borden house for likely suspects.

The first insider to be suspected was John Morse. The police and the public were inclined to doubt that it was just a coincidence that the Bordens were killed less than twenty four hours after Morse came to visit them. Moreover, as we have pointed out, his behavior when he returned to 92 Second Street after the murders was peculiar to say the least. However, the police soon lost interest in Morse. His alibi, that he had been visiting his niece at the time of the murders, seemed solid.

FIGURE 1.4
John Morse
under suspicion

From *New Bedford Evening Standard*, Aug. 5, 1892

HAVE A CLEW!

Police in Pursuit of Assassin of the Bordens.

Finger of Suspicion Points to a Dartmouth Man.

Singular Stories Told by John W. Morse.

They Fail to Agree in Important Particulars.

Bridget Sullivan seems never to have been seriously considered as a suspect, although there was one inconsistency in her story. She originally told the police that she had been washing windows on the third floor at the time of Andrew's murder. Later she admitted that she had actually been resting in her third floor bedroom. One can well understand the motivation behind her original statement; for anyone, and especially a servant, to lie down during the day was considered downright immoral in 1892. One newspaper article stated primly, "The servant in the average Fall River family is much more likely to be found washing windows or making bread than in bed at 11 o'clock in the forenoon."

Within forty eight hours the police settled upon Lizzie Borden as the likely murderer; they never changed their mind. There seem to have been three principal reasons for suspecting Lizzie. First, Fleet and Harrington became suspicious of Lizzie when they interviewed her after the murders. She seemed altogether too calm and unconcerned, showing no signs of grief for her father and stepmother. Second, Lizzie's story about the note Abby Borden received was hard to believe. The note was never found and no one ever acknowledged sending it. Finally, Lizzie's attempt to buy prussic acid, a deadly poison, seemed incriminating.

On Saturday evening, Marshal Hilliard and Mayor Coughlin drove through crowds of curious onlookers to 92 Second Street to talk to Lizzie, Emma and John Morse. Coughlin started the conversation by saying, "I have a request to make and that is that [all of] you remain in the house for a few days, as I believe it would be better for all concerned if you do so." Lizzie asked, "Is there anybody in this house suspected?" After some hesitation, Mayor Coughlin replied, "Miss Borden, I must answer yes; you are suspected." A court later ruled that from that point on Lizzie Borden was, in effect, under arrest.

Chapter 2
PEOPLE AND PLACES

In this chapter, we will look at the principal characters in the Borden murders: Andrew Jackson Borden (aged 69), Abby Gray Borden (64), Lizzie Andrew Borden (32), John Vinnicum Morse (59), Emma Lenora Borden (41) and Bridget Sullivan (25?). Their lives prior to August 4, 1892, and their personalities may help us understand what happened that day. We'll also look at the place where the murders occurred, 92 Second Street in Fall River, Massachusetts.

The Victims: Andrew and Abby Borden

In 1892 Borden was a common name in Fall River, shared by about 400 people. There were at least four Andrew Bordens and two Andrew J. Bordens (the other one was a janitor). The family played a major role in the development of Fall River; distant relatives of "our" Andrew were instrumental in founding the cotton mills that became the city's largest industry.

Abraham Borden, Andrew's father, was a fish peddler who cried his wares from a pushcart in the streets. Andrew, growing up in impoverished circumstances in a shabby house on Ferry Street, vowed never to be poor again. In that respect he succeeded spectacularly, leaving an estate of $350,000, equivalent to perhaps five million dollars today.

Andrew Borden spent more than thirty years as an undertaker, where he prospered handsomely. Perhaps it was his money-back guarantee that attracted so many customers. Andrew promised that his caskets would preserve the remains of a loved one longer than those of his competitors. There is no record of anyone asking for his money back.

In 1878 Andrew retired from the undertaking business to pursue other financial interests. He became a stockholder in just about every profitable bank and cotton mill in Fall River. At the time of his death, he was president of the Union Savings Bank and a director of a host of institutions, including the First National Bank of Fall River, the B. M. C. Durfee Safe Deposit Trust Co., Globe Yarn Mills, Troy Cotton and

Woolen Manufacturing and the Merchants Manufacturing Company. Most of his energy was devoted to protecting the interests of these institutions and others in which he had a financial interest.

Andrew Borden had extensive holdings in real estate. His proudest possession was a three story commercial structure in downtown Fall River, built in 1890, which he modestly named the A. J. Borden building. Fifty years after his death it would be a major stop for every tourist bus that came to Fall River. Beyond that, Andrew owned several tenements. Reportedly he adjusted the rent to the financial status of the tenant, but only in one direction. Anyone who received a promotion or salary increase could look forward to having his rent raised.

Through foreclosures, Andrew picked up two farms in nearby Swansea. To make them more profitable, he sold farm produce on the streets of Fall River and even at 92 Second Street. Charles Sawyer, the man pressed into service as a guard on August 4, said he was familiar with the house because he had gone there to buy "vinegar and other stuff" from Andrew.

To state the obvious, Andrew Borden was obsessed with the acquisition and retention of money. The idea that spending money could be more enjoyable than making it never occurred to him. As a *Fall River Globe* article pointed out:

"He rarely, if ever, visited places of amusement; Providence and Boston were the limits of his traveling experience. He dressed poorly and, for a man of his means, shabbily . . . In his own peculiar way he undoubtedly derived much pleasure from [money]. His wealth was his theater, excursions and all kinds of amusements, embodied in the one thing. It was his pleasure to add to it, to scrape together, multiply, and see his great mass doubling and redoubling."

Andrew Borden's miserly ways made him many enemies. Among them was Hiram Harrington, married to Andrew's sister Lurana., who told the following story:

"Mr. Borden was an exceedingly hard man concerning money matters, determined and stubborn; when he got an idea nothing could change him. He was too hard for me. When his father died, he offered my wife the old homestead on Ferry Street for a certain sum of money. My wife preferred to take money from Andrew instead. After all the agreements were signed, he wanted my wife to pay an additional $3 for water tax upon the homestead."

Small wonder that three different authors, all of them Fall River natives, said that the predominant reaction in Fall River to Andrew Borden's death was, "Well, somebody did a good job!"

Figure 2.1 Andrew Borden

Andrew's first wife was Sarah Morse Borden, mother of Emma, Alice (who died at age 1) and Lizzie Borden. She was also the sister of John Morse. Sarah died of "uterine congestion" when Emma was twelve and Lizzie only two. Two years later, Andrew married Abby Durfee Gray, a thirty seven year old spinster. Andrew's second marriage was almost certainly one of convenience rather than love; he needed someone to raise his children. When Lizzie was asked under oath whether Andrew and Abby were happily married, she hesitated before answering, "Why I don't know but what they were."

Figure 2.2 Emma Borden and mother, Sarah

From *Forty Whacks*

From *Goodbye, Lizzie Borden,*

An early photograph of Abby Borden suggests that she was an attractive young woman. By 1892 she weighed over 200 pounds and her charms had faded; living with Andrew had taken its toll. However, she had something in common with Sara Lee confectioneries. "Nobody didn't like" Abby

Borden (except perhaps her stepdaughters; more about that later). A friend of Lizzie referred to Abby as "a kindhearted lovable woman who tried, but ineffectively, to win the love of her stepdaughters." Mrs. Southard Miller, who lived across the street, described Mrs. Borden as, "the best and most intimate neighbor I ever met." Bridget Sullivan said that when she considered going back to Ireland, Mrs. Borden said she would be lonely without her. "I didn't have the heart to leave her," Bridget added.

FIGURE 2.3 Abby Borden

The reaction to Abby's death differed considerably from Andrew's. Several people, including Joseph Lemay's weirdo (Chapter 1), referred to, "poor Mrs. Borden." No one mentioned, "poor Mr. Borden" which would have been the ultimate oxymoron. The same *Fall River* Globe article which took a dim view of Andrew had this to say about Abby Borden:

Mrs. Abby Durfee Gray Borden

From *Goodbye, Lizzie Borden*, p.19

"She had a kindly disposition . . . and was a model helpmate for her somewhat eccentric husband. She was opposed to pretentious appearances and dressed neatly and plainly; neither was she fond of amusement but rather preferred the surroundings of her home . . . Her memory will be cherished."

From the autopsy results, it appeared that Andrew and Abby Borden had been in excellent health. They did, however, have a severe gastrointestinal upset on Tuesday night before the murders. The next morning Abby went across the street to consult with Dr. Bowen. She told him that she and Andrew had vomited several times between 9 P.M. and midnight. Lizzie was less affected, Bridget apparently not at all.

Abby expressed to Dr. Bowen her fear that they had been poisoned, perhaps by some baker's bread they had eaten for supper. Bowen doubted that but advised a stiff dose of castor oil to be washed down with a little port wine. Later he decided that the neighborly thing to do was to go across to 92 Second Street and see how the Bordens were doing. Andrew greeted him with a warning that he didn't intend to pay for an unrequested house call. Same old Andrew, always looking for ulterior motives. Just for the record, Dr. Wood found later that the stomachs of the victims did not contain poison.

The Accused: Lizzie Borden

We really know very little about Lizzie's life prior to the murders. She was one month shy of being five years old when her father married Abby Gray. She had no recollection of her own mother, Sarah Morse Borden. As a child, Lizzie called Abby "mother"; later that changed. Lizzie said once, "I had never been to her as a mother in many things. I always went to my sister because she was older and had the care of me after my mother died."

Lizzie was an indifferent student, about average in intellectual ability. Teachers remembered her as a lonely girl with few friends at school. She dropped out of high school in her junior year, apparently for lack of interest. Lizzie gave her high school ring to her father; Andrew wore it on his little finger for the rest of his life.

In 1890 she crossed the Atlantic to tour Europe. No one knows what countries she visited or what impressions she brought back to Fall River. It has been suggested that Lizzie's trip abroad made her realize how dreary life was at home; that would be understandable.

About five years before the murders, Lizzie became active in the Central Congregational Church. She was the only member of her family to be involved in church work; in August 1892 she was secretary-treasurer of Christian Endeavor. As a member of the Fruit and Flower Mission, she visited the sick, the poor and the shut-ins. For several years she taught a mission class of Chinese men; later she worked with a group of young girls employed in the cotton mills.

For a woman, Lizzie was about average in height (5'4") and weight (135 lb). A photograph taken in the early 1890s suggests that she was attractive. No one ever called her beautiful, perhaps because of a certain "heaviness" in her lower face. Many said that Lizzie's best feature was

her hair; the phrases used to describe it ranged from "mousy brown" to "auburn tinged". There was disagreement about her eyes as well:
"She had dreadful eyes, colorless and soulless like those of a snake"
"Her large, light eyes were by far her most attractive feature"
"The eyes themselves were huge and protruding, the irises ice-blue"
"She had large brown eyes"

FIGURE 2.4 Lizzie Borden, circa 1892

What kind of a person was Lizzie Borden? That depends upon whom you listen to, the Lizzie lovers or the Lizzie haters. There are, however, some areas of agreement; we'll concentrate on those.

Lizzie resembled her father in many ways. She was stubborn, assertive in maintaining her rights, and forth-

From *Goodbye, Lizzie Borden*, p. 21

right in expressing her opinions. She was a stoical person who never (well, *almost* never) showed emotion in public. This was the quality that got Lizzie into trouble with Officers Fleet and Harrington and, through them, with the head of the Fall River police force, Marshal Hilliard. Her friends said that her calm demeanor after discovering her father's body was predictable; she always suppressed her emotions. Perhaps Lizzie herself said it best: "There is one thing that hurts me very much. They say I don't show any grief. Certainly I don't in public. I never did reveal my feelings and I cannot change my nature now."

In their attitudes toward money, Lizzie and Andrew were at opposite poles. Lizzie enjoyed spending money and did so every time she got a chance. While touring Europe she ran out of money; Andrew, much as it pained him, had to send her more. Her wardrobe was both expensive and extensive. Officers Fleet and Seaver examined the dresses in the

Borden sisters' clothes closet, about eighteen in number; of these, one belonged to Abby, a few to Emma and the rest to Lizzie. Most of Lizzie's dresses were blue, her favorite color.

There was another side to Lizzie's willingness to spend money. With less than one tenth of Andrew's income, she gave at least ten times as much to charity. When the mother of one of her former teachers needed a major operation and couldn't pay for it, Lizzie assumed all of the expenses. Somehow she paid the doctor and hospital bills out of her savings. Throughout her life, Lizzie did many, many kindnesses of this sort.

Lizzie was extraordinarily sensitive to rebuff or disapproval. Victoria Lincoln, a Fall River native, explained this by saying, "Her need to be loved outstripped her ability to love." Her uncle, Hiram Harrington, put it more critically. "Lizzie is of a repellant disposition and after an unsuccessful passage with her father would become sulky and refuse to speak to him for days at a time."

Again, let's give Lizzie the last word:

"One thing that hurts is the malignity that is directed against me. I have done much good to people who now desert me. In my own home there are hands stretched out against me that I have loaded with favors in the past. There is no one so humble that does not dare to condemn me."

An insight into the differing views of Lizzie's character comes from two stories. One appears in the book, *Lizzie Borden, the Untold Story* by Edward Radin, who was convinced of Lizzie's innocence. It seems that there was a group of boys in the neighborhood who lusted for the pears growing in the Borden backyard. One of them went to the door and, when Lizzie answered, asked if he and his friends could pick a few pears.

"She told me we could pick the fruit that had fallen to the ground but we must not climb the trees. We soon found a way to beat that. We would sneak into the yard and shake a big pile of pears off the trees. I'll never forget the first time we did it. Lizzie gave a start when she saw that mound of pears on the ground. She caught on immediately. Her eyes danced, her lips quirked up, and you could see she wanted to laugh out loud. After that, it became a game. I know she watched us through the window shaking the trees first, but she never spoiled the game for us by telling us outright that she knew. It made the pears taste even better and she must have realized it."

Agnes de Mille, who choreographed the ballet *Fall River Tragedy* and believed Lizzie to be guilty, told a quite different story.

"A workman once witnessed a curious scene in connection with the laying of some bricks. Miss Borden returned from shopping to find them cemented contrary to her instructions. She wheeled on the laborer and without a moment's warning flew into such a white fury that she seemed almost out of her mind. Her language and the violence of her physical demeanor were horrifying. The workman left and refused to return."

On the evening before the murders, Lizzie had a long and lugubrious conversation with Alice Russell. She described her parents' illness and Abby's fears, which Lizzie apparently shared, that they had been poisoned. She told of Dr. Bowen's visit and the rude reception Andrew gave him. As Lizzie put it, "I was so mortified." Lizzie went on to tell Alice about the trouble her father had with a man who came to the house to rent a store from Andrew. Her father turned him down, at which point they argued angrily. Finally, Andrew loudly ordered the man out of the house.

Throughout their conversation, Alice tried to persuade Lizzie that she was "making a mountain out of a molehill". However, Lizzie persisted, telling Alice that, "They have broken into the house in broad daylight, with Emma, Maggie and me there. Mrs. Borden's things were ransacked and they [broke into father's desk and] took a watch, money and streetcar tickets. Father reported it to the police but they didn't find anything." (The robbery occurred in June of 1891; Andrew told the police he was afraid they would not be able to find the real thief.)

Lizzie summarized her foreboding by saying, "I am afraid somebody will do something." Indeed within twenty four hours someone did do something awful. Perhaps Lizzie had a premonition; then again, perhaps her prophecy was self-fulfilled.

Significant Others: John, Emma and Bridget

John Vinnicum Morse, a bachelor, was the brother of Andrew's first wife. Born in Somerset, a town bordering Fall River, he migrated to the midwest at age twenty two. There he accumulated a tiny fortune raising cattle and horses, first in Illinois and later in Hastings, Iowa. Two years before the murders, he came back to New England. In August of 1892 he was living in South Dartmouth, Massachusetts with a butcher named Isaac Davis. He made frequent visits to the Borden house fifteen miles away, showing up in late June and again in mid July of 1892.

On Wednesday, August 3, after shaving his friend Davis (who was blind), Morse came to Fall River, arriving at the Borden house shortly after noon. The senior Bordens, who had just finished dinner, greeted him heartily. Abby invited him to sit down and eat, saying, "Everything is hot on the stove. It won't cost us a mite of trouble."

Later that afternoon, Morse rented a team of horses and drove to Andrew's farms in Swansea. There he arranged to take delivery of some cattle that Isaac Davis had bought from Andrew. Shortly before 9 P.M., Morse arrived back at 92 Second Street, carrying a basket of eggs that Andrew had requested. The two men talked in the darkness for about an hour and then went their separate ways to bed. Curiously, Lizzie didn't say hello to her uncle when she came back from Alice Russell's; indeed she didn't even see him on this visit until after the murders.

John Morse was six feet tall and weighed about two hundred pounds. According to the Fall *River Globe*, "His full beard of iron grey partially concealed a well tanned face, which is enlivened by two small, restless grey eyes, deeply set behind shaggy eyebrows. His appearance certainly is not inviting or prepossessing, and his mannerisms and habits are peculiar." (The *Globe* didn't much like any of the Borden family except Abby.)

FIGURE 2.5 John Morse

Clearly John Morse was a frugal, taciturn Yankee who did not make friends readily. Beyond that, opinions differed. Isaac Davis spoke up for him, saying, "No, sir, John V. Morse never committed that crime. Why, I would have trusted him with everything in the world and would as soon think of my own son doing the deed." Morse's Iowa neighbors were less complimentary. One person described him as, "selfish, close, hardfisted, but scrupu-

JOHN V. MORSE.

From *Lizzie Borden Sourcebook*, p. 34

lously honest." Another was sure that the suit Morse was wearing on the morning of the murders was the same one in which he left Iowa two years before. No wonder Andrew Borden and John Morse got along so well; they were "cut out of the same cloth".

Emma Borden, by general consensus, was a pale mirror image of her younger sister Lizzie. Emma was "plain" in appearance; Lizzie was "attractive". Emma had a weak jaw, Lizzie a strong one. The *Fall River Globe* was particularly cruel, referring to Emma's, "listless, expressionless face, indicating a person who is accustomed to obey the persuasion of a stronger mind." A reporter for the *Boston Globe* must have really hurt poor Emma when he said, "Lizzie looks six years younger than she is, Emma six years older." No wonder Emma seldom if ever posed for a portrait.

The contrast between Lizzie and Emma carried over to their personalities. Lizzie was "aggressive", Emma "submissive". Lizzie had a sense of humor; Emma never laughed (perhaps because she had very little to laugh about). Unlike Lizzie, Emma seldom strayed very far from 92 Second Street. Her two week visit to friends in Fairhaven, cut short by the murders, was highly unusual.

There is evidence, though, that Emma was not as meek and mild as legend has it. Lizzie referred to her stepmother first as "mother" and later as "Mrs. Borden". Emma called her "Abby" from day one, even though she was only a teenager when her father remarried. Perhaps Emma's disdain for Abby came from her own mother, Sarah Borden, who was brought up by a stepmother she intensely disliked.

Bridget Sullivan emigrated from Ireland in May of 1886. She worked in Newport, Rhode Island and South Bethlehem, Pennsylvania, before settling down in Fall River. In November of 1889 she went to work as a maid for the Bordens. She gave her age as twenty five at the time of the murders, but recent studies indicate she was born in March of 1864, which would make her twenty eight in August, 1892.

Regardless of how old she was, there is general agreement that Bridget Sullivan was a very good looking young woman. Newspaper sketches of Bridget suggest that she may have been a tad overweight by today's standards, but never mind. Joe Howard, a well-known reporter who covered the Borden case, said she was, "tall and spare, with an intelligent face, a good eye, a prominent nose, and a mouth indicating a love for the good things of life." The *Fall River Globe* was practically ecstatic about Bridget. After calling her "comely", the paper went on to say that she, "has a handsome complexion and always dresses neatly and tastily. In fact she appears to be the bestdressed member of the whole Borden family." Lizzie must have been infuriated by that comment.

FIGURE 2.6 Bridget (Maggie) Sullivan

To describe Bridget's personality, the word "excitable" comes to mind. Certainly she showed more emotion than Lizzie on the day of the murders. Charles Sawyer, the guard at the door, put it well. "The servant girl appeared to be somewhat frightened. I thought she acted as though she was considerably excited, although she talked intelligently." That night, Bridget refused to stay in the Borden house, even though all the doors were locked and police were standing guard outside. A few days later, when a policeman asked her what she thought about the murders, Bridget replied, "I'd be afraid to say anything at all. If I did, that terrible man that killed poor Mrs. Borden might come back and kill me too."

One of Bridget's duties at the Borden house was cooking. The meals she cooked shortly before the murders are listed below. (Several of the menus must be incomplete; otherwise the whole family would

BRIDGET SULLIVAN

From *Lizzie Borden Sourcebook* p. 38

have suffered from malnutrition.) Notice the preponderance of mutton, served three times in a row.

LE MENU, CHEZ BORDEN, AUGUST 1892

	BREAKFAST	DINNER	SUPPER
Tuesday Aug. 2	?	Swordfish (fried)	Swordfish (warmed) baker's bread, tea, milk cookies, cake
Wednesday Aug. 3	Pork steak Johnny cakes (1) pears, coffee milk	Mutton stew (2)	Mutton stew (warmed) bread, milk, cookies cake
Thursday Aug. 4	Mutton (cold) Mutton stew (warmed) Johnny cakes Bananas, coffee, milk	Mutton, warmed (3) Mutton stew	

(1) A small, inedible pancake made by frying corn meal
(2) John Morse thought it tasted like veal
(3) Warmed mutton was what Bridget Sullivan *would* have cooked for dinner if . . .

The final breakfast is a famous one. It has been said, not entirely in jest, that it must have been the catalyst if not the cause of the murders. Keep in mind, though, that hearty breakfasts such as this one were much more common in the "good old days" than they are today. Growing up in rural New Hampshire in the 1930s, I can remember eating warmed over steak for breakfast (it tasted a lot better than mutton).

House of Horror

The photograph, on the next page, shows the Borden property at 92 Second Street as it looked a few months after the murders. The narrow 2½ story house faces Second Street; the back of the property abuts houses on Third Street. The ornate picket fence at the front had two gates. The one shown at the right led directly to the front door; the other gate led to a side entrance located towards the back of the house. There was also an entrance in the rear (not shown) which opened into the cellar. It's not obvious from the photograph, but the entire property was enclosed by wooden fences which separated the Bordens from their neighbors.

FIGURE 2.7 Front view of Borden house, circa 1892

Behind the house you can see the two story barn, where Lizzie said she was when Andrew was murdered. Until a year or two before the murders, Andrew Borden kept a horse; in August of 1892 the barn served no useful purpose except as a storage area for articles no longer used but too valuable to throw away. To the right of the barn were several pear trees, which have been mentioned a couple of times already. Apparently everyone in the household except Bridget liked, or at least ate, pears.

From *Forty Whacks*

The Borden house was built in 1845 as a two-family tenement. The first and second floors were virtually identical at that time; each contained a kitchen, two medium sized rooms and two small rooms. When Andrew Borden bought the house in 1872, he converted the upstairs kitchen to a master bedroom. Downstairs, a partition between the two small rooms was removed to make a dining room. The resulting layouts of the two floors are shown in the diagram on the next page.

The downstairs parlor was almost never used. Had President Harrison come to visit, he would probably have been entertained there, but ordinary guests like John Morse made themselves comfortable in the sitting room. That was where Andrew and John talked in the darkness on the night of Wednesday, August 3. It was also where Andrew Borden was murdered on Thursday and where the funeral was held on Saturday.

The kitchen was where the "survivors" (Lizzie, Bridget, Adelaide Churchill, Alice Russell and Dr. Bowen) gathered after Andrew's body was discovered. Notice that in order to get from the kitchen to the front stairs, you had to pass through the sitting room. Perhaps that was why Bridget refused to go alone to look for Abby in the upstairs guest room; she had to pass by Andrew's body on the sitting room sofa.

FIGURE 2.8 Layout of the Borden house

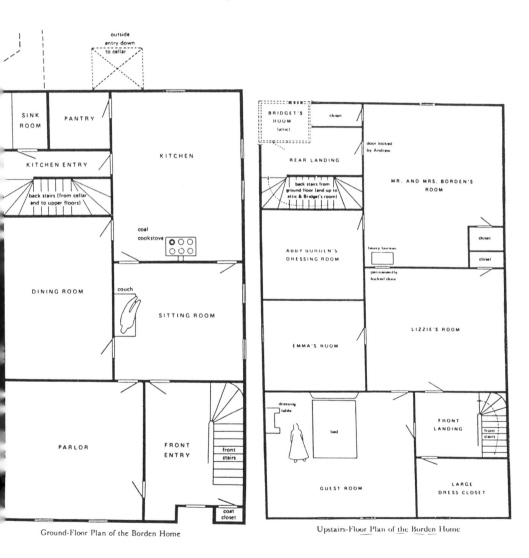

Ground-Floor Plan of the Borden Home

Upstairs-Floor Plan of the Borden Home

From *Goodye, Lizzie Borden*, pp. 14, 15

The second floor was effectively divided into two compartments. The two rooms toward the back (master bedroom, dressing room) were accessible only from the back staircase; the door to Lizzie's room was blocked by a heavy bureau. The three rooms at the front, facing Second Street (Lizzie's room, Emma's room, and the guest room) could be reached only from the front staircase. Notice that Emma's room was considerably smaller than Lizzie's. When the Bordens moved into the house, Emma, as the older sister, got the larger room. When Lizzie came back from Europe they switched. According to Emma, that was her own idea; maybe so, maybe not.

The back staircase went all the way from the cellar to the attic, where Bridget's room was located. Notice that she was far removed from the sitting room; given that and the street noise, it's hardly surprising that Bridget was unaware of Andrew's murder when it occurred.

The Borden house in 1892 had only one modern convenience, central heating furnished by a coal furnace. When city water became available in 1874, Andrew installed two cold water taps, one in the first floor sink room, the other in the laundry room in the cellar. Later he added a third faucet in the barn so he could water his horse. For all this, Andrew paid the city of Fall River $10 a year.

There was no convenient source of hot water in the Borden house. If you wanted to take a bath, you could start a fire under a large cast iron cauldron in the cellar; a couple of hours later you'd have ten gallons or more of hot water. Alternatively, you could heat smaller quantities of water to boiling on the kitchen stove, which burned wood or coal. (No wonder most people only bathed once a week a hundred years ago.)

There was only one toilet in the house, euphemistically called a "water closet"; it was located in the cellar. There was no water above the ground floor. Each bedroom was equipped with a receptacle called a chamber pot for nocturnal liquid waste. Andrew called his a "slop pail" and emptied it each morning in the back yard. The ladies of the household were more circumspect; they emptied their chamber pots in the water closet.

At the time of the murders, illuminating gas had been available in Fall River for several years; electric lights were just coming in. The Bordens had neither; Andrew was satisfied with kerosene lamps, which he used sparingly. Certainly, for a person of his means, the house was fitted out in a primitive way. Lizzie complained about this to her father, loudly and frequently, but to no avail.

Surprisingly, the Borden house has survived, almost unchanged structurally. The present owner, Martha McGinn, has restored the Victorian motif of a century ago and opened a bed and breakfast (telephone: 508 675 7333); tours are also available. Before staying there overnight, I checked on the number of toilets and the supply of hot water; both are more than adequate. The breakfast does not feature mutton of any kind. Otherwise it's pretty much as John Morse described it on that fateful morning in 1892; "plenty of it."

The Neighborhood

The surroundings of the Borden house are shown in the sketch below. Adelaide Churchill, the forty two year old widow who came over to console Lizzie on the morning of the murders, was her next door neighbor to the north. The two houses were only twenty feet apart but, because of the gate and fence arrangement, Mrs. Churchill had to walk considerably further to get from her front door to the side entrance of the Borden house. Dr. Kelly and his wife lived directly south of the Bordens; their house was somewhat more distant than Mrs. Churchill's.

Dr. Bowen, the family physician (age 52) lived across Second Street with his wife, Phoebe. They shared the house with Phoebe's parents, Mr. and Mrs. Southard Miller, perhaps the closest friends of Andrew and Abby Borden. The Crowe property contained a series of sheds and barns. John Crowe was a stone mason dealing in granite and marble. Several of his employees were working in the yard on the morning of the murders.

Figure 2.9 Surroundings of the Borden house

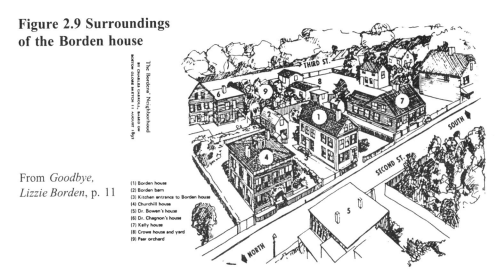

From *Goodbye, Lizzie Borden*, p. 11

(1) Borden house
(2) Borden barn
(3) Kitchen entrance to Borden house
(4) Churchill house
(5) Dr. Bowen's house
(6) Dr. Chagnon's house
(7) Kelly house
(8) Crowe house and yard
(9) Pear orchard

40 William L. Masterton

A map of Fall River where the action took place is shown below.
Dwelling houses or places of business are numbered. Alice Russell lived
about 200 yards northeast of the Borden house, on Borden Street. It
should have taken her only a few minutes to respond to Bridget's call.
Sarah Whitehead, Abby Borden's half-sister who was much younger than
Abby, lived at 45 Fourth Street, a short distance southeast of the Borden
home. She had two small children, George and Abby.

The A. J. Borden building, the Union Savings Bank of which Andrew
Borden was president, and several other major banks were all within easy
walking distance of the Borden house. Perhaps that explains why Andrew
Borden chose to live in this part of Fall River.

FIGURE 2.10 Fall River in 1892

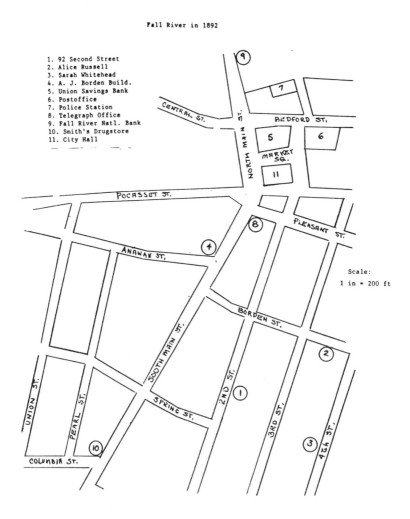

Beyond the range of this map is the house on Weybosset Street where John Morse visited his niece on the morning of the murders. It was a little more than a mile southeast of the Borden house. Also off the map is the Oak Grove Cemetery, where the Bordens are buried, about a mile northeast of where they lived.

The district known as "the Highlands" or, more commonly "the Hill" consisted of many elegant houses overlooking the Taunton River. It was centered about half-mile north of the Borden house. Included in this area, on Rock Street, is the Central Congregational Church which Lizzie attended.

Chapter 3
THE INQUEST

As pointed out in Chapter 1, the chief of police and the mayor of Fall River, Marshal Rufus Hilliard and Doctor John Coughlin, were convinced by Saturday, August 6, that Lizzie Borden murdered her father and stepmother. On Monday, August 8, they, along with Medical Examiner Dolan and Detective Seaver of the state police, held a conference to review the evidence against Lizzie. They were joined by Hosea Knowlton, District Attorney for Bristol County. Knowlton, shown at the right of the sketch below, was 45 years old. He was a short, stocky, squarefaced man known for his bulldog-like tenacity.

FIGURE 3.1 Jennings (left) and Knowlton (right)

The conference, which started at 5 P.M. and went on past midnight, was inconclusive. Knowlton cautioned against arresting Lizzie at this point. In the first place, there was no physical evidence linking her to the crime. The police search of the premises had failed to produce either a bloody hatchet or blood-stained clothing. Moreover, Lizzie was in effect under house arrest already; she had been told not to leave 92 Second Street.

The conference did agree upon one thing; Bridget Sullivan should be questioned more closely as to what she knew about the crime. She was summoned to the Fall River police station at

ATTORNEY JENNINGS AND
DIST. ATTY. KNOWLTON
VISIT THE BORDEN HOME

From *Lizzie Borden Sourcebook*, p. 217

10 A.M. on Tuesday, August 9. One thing led to another; what started as an interrogation of Bridget evolved into a formal inquest into the crime. This was presided over by Judge Josiah Blaisdell. The inquest was closed; no member of the press was allowed in the courtroom when Knowlton was examining witnesses.

Over the years, the testimony of all the witnesses except one has been made public. Bridget Sullivan's testimony seems to have disappeared; no one really knows what she had to say. Of the remaining witnesses, all except four (Lizzie Borden, Hiram Harrington, Augusta Tripp and Sarah Whitehead) testified later, either at the preliminary hearing (August to September, 1892) or the trial (June 1893). We'll concentrate here upon the four witnesses who never appeared upon the stand in open court, with particular emphasis, as you might expect, upon Lizzie Borden.

Augusta, Hiram and Sarah

Hiram Harrington, Andrew's brother-in-law (and least favorite relative) was a blacksmith. Sarah Whitehead, Abby's halfsister and closest confidante, was a young married woman (age 28) with two small children. Augusta Tripp was a friend of Lizzie and former schoolmate. All three of them were questioned as to the relationship between Abby and Lizzie. There was general agreement that the two women were not what you would call congenial. Augusta Tripp, who liked Lizzie, put it delicately:

Q. (Knowlton) "What can you tell us about the relations between Lizzie and her mother, so far as you observed it, and heard it from Lizzie?"

A. (Mrs. Tripp) "All I can tell you is that I don't think they were agreeable to each other."

Q. (Knowlton) "What made you think so?"

A. (Mrs. Tripp) "I have seen them together very little . . . They did not sit down, perhaps, and talk with each other as a mother and daughter might. They were very quiet."

Hiram Harrington, who didn't like Lizzie, was more critical:

Q. (Knowlton) "When Lizzie spoke about [Abby] last winter, what did she say?"

A. (Harrington) "I don't know as I could tell any more than to speak kind of sneeringly of Mrs. Borden. She always called her Mrs. Borden or Mrs. B. I don't know as I could remember anything to put together to make any sense."

Q. (Knowlton) "Did she speak in an unfriendly way of her?"

A. (Harrington) "Unfriendly, yes."

Q. (Knowlton) "It was understood that there was trouble in the family?"

A. (Harrington) "Oh, yes; there has been, I guess. For several years, I guess."

Curiously, Sarah Whitehead was non-committal about the relationship between Abby Borden and her stepdaughters:

Q. (Knowlton) "Did [Mrs. Borden] come to your house?"

A. (Mrs. Whitehead) "Yes, sir, she came very often."

Q. (Knowlton) "Did she seem to be on good terms with Emma and Lizzie?"

A. (Mrs. Whitehead) "She never seemed to say but very little about them; she was a woman who kept everything to herself."

Yet, outside the courtroom, Mrs. Whitehead told two police officers that Lizzie did not get along well with Mrs. Borden!

Hiram Harrington and Sarah Whitehead apparently decided that, as long as they were on the witness stand, they might as well get a few other things off their chests. Hiram got in one last dig at Andrew, pointing out that not only did he refuse to speak to his brother-in-law, he wouldn't even stay in the same room with him. Sarah Whitehead made it clear that she didn't like either Lizzie or Emma. "I always thought they felt above me," she said. She almost never went to the Borden house, "on account of those girls."

Incidentally, Alice Russell, in her inquest testimony, gave a very rational explanation of the strained relationship between Lizzie and Abby. She said, "Their tastes differed in every way; one liked one thing, the other liked another." She went on to talk about tension between the girls and their father. "Mr. Borden was a plain living man with rigid ideas and very set . . . He did not care for anything different . . . They would have liked to be cultured girls and would like to have had different advantages."

Lizzie's Story

At 2 P.M. on Tuesday, August 9, Lizzie Borden went to the Fall River police station to testify at the inquest. She went on the stand that afternoon, returned on Wednesday morning, and was recalled on Thursday, August 11. Before she testified, Andrew Jennings, the Borden family lawyer, shown at the left of Figure 3.1, asked that he be allowed to counsel Lizzie. Judge Blaisdell turned him down; the inquest was closed, particularly to lawyers. Jennings did, however, represent Lizzie in all subsequent court hearings on the Borden case.

It turned out that Lizzie could have used a lawyer at the inquest; she came close to breaking down a couple of times. Knowlton started out very mildly, establishing that her name was Lizzie, not Elizabeth, that Andrew Borden had only two living children, and other trivia. Then, during a tedious discussion of the dates at which John Morse had visited the Bordens, Knowlton suddenly turned sarcastic. Lizzie, in response to a question, asked him if he remembered the winter that the Taunton River froze over. Knowlton snapped, "I am not answering questions but asking them."

From that point on, Knowlton became an aggressive, relentless prosecutor. Lizzie seemed to lose her composure, frequently showing confusion. When Knowlton asked her where she was when her father came back from downtown on August 4, she couldn't remember whether she had been downstairs or upstairs. Knowlton pressed her on this matter, prompting Lizzie to exclaim:

"I don't know what I have said. I have answered so many questions and I am so confused that I don't know one thing from another. I am telling you just as nearly as I know how."

Later on, Knowlton seemed on the verge of losing his temper when the following exchange took place:

Q. (Knowlton) "Miss Borden, I am trying in good faith to get all the doings that morning of yourself and Miss Sullivan and I have not succeeded in doing so. Do you desire to give me any information or not?"

A. (Lizzie Borden) "I don't know it; I don't know what your name is."

Perhaps the worst moment for both of them came when District Attorney Knowlton, for some inexplicable reason, insisted that Lizzie describe her father's appearance when he lay dead on the sofa.

Q. (Knowlton) "You saw his face?"
A. (Lizzie Borden) "No, I did not see his face, because he was covered with blood."
Q. (Knowlton) "You saw where his face was bleeding."
A. (Lizzie Borden) "Yes, sir."
Q. (Knowlton) "You saw his face covered with blood?"
A. (Lizzie Borden) "Yes, sir."
Q. (Knowlton) "Did you see his eyeball hanging out?"
A. Lizzie Borden) "No, sir."
Q. (Knowlton) "See the gashes where his face was laid open?"
A. (Lizzie Borden) "No, sir."

When this interrogation finally ended, the stenographer entered the following statement into the court record: "Witness covers her face with her hand for a minute or two; then examination is resumed."

Altogether, Lizzie's inquest testimony filled more than forty single spaced pages. Here we'll concentrate on a few of the more relevant and interesting topics covered in the three days she was on the stand.

One thing that Knowlton asked Lizzie about was her relationship with Abby Borden:

Q. (Knowlton) "You have been on pleasant terms with your stepmother . . . ?"
A. (Lizzie Borden) "Yes, sir."
Q. (Knowlton) "Cordial?"
A. (Lizzie Borden) "It depends upon one's idea of cordiality, perhaps."
Q. (Knowlton) "Cordial according to your idea of cordiality?"
A. (Lizzie Borden) "Quite so."
Q. (Knowlton) "What do you mean by quite so?"
A. (Lizzie Borden) "Quite cordial. I do not mean the dearest of friends in the world, but very kindly feelings and pleasant. I do not know how to answer you any better than that."

Later on, near the end of her testimony, Lizzie described the incident, five years prior to the murders, that led her to call her stepmother "Mrs.

Borden" rather than "mother". It seems that Abby's half sister, Sarah Whitehead, owned the house at 45 Fourth Street jointly with her mother, Mrs. Oliver Gray. Mrs. Gray wanted to sell the house, which would have left Sarah homeless. To prevent that, Andrew Borden bought out Mrs. Gray's interest and gave it to Abby. Lizzie told Knowlton:

"I said if he gave that to her he ought to give us something; told Mrs. Borden so. We always thought she persuaded father to buy it. At any rate, he did buy it and I am quite sure she did persuade him. I said what he did for her people he ought to do for his own children. So he gave us grandfather's house." [That was the house on Ferry Street, where both Emma and Lizzie were born. On July 15, 1892, three weeks before the murders, Andrew bought it back from the girls, paying them $5000.]

According to Lizzie, that was all the trouble she ever had with Abby. When Knowlton asked her why, after this incident, she stopped calling Abby "mother", her answer was a simple one. "Because I wanted to", Lizzie said.

Lizzie testified that she last saw her father alive, resting on the sofa, at about 10:55 A.M. on the morning of August 4. At that point, she went to the barn in hopes of finding lead sinkers that she needed for a fishing trip with friends the following week. On the way to the barn, she picked up some pears that had fallen from the trees in the back yard.

While Andrew was being killed in the sitting room, Lizzie claimed she was rummaging through a box resting on a work bench in the barn loft. In the box, she found some nails, a doorknob and the thing she was searching for: flat pieces of lead suitable for sinkers. At more or less the same time, she was munching pears and occasionally looking out the window. Apparently she was in no hurry; as Lizzie put it, "I don't do things in a hurry."

Knowlton wasn't buying any of this. For one thing, Lizzie claimed earlier that she went to the barn to get a piece of iron, not lead. More important, he was convinced by now that she was in the house chopping up Andrew around 11 A.M., not in the barn loft. Knowlton hammered away at Lizzie's alibi, using a mixture of ridicule and exasperation. It didn't work; Lizzie stuck to her story. Consider the following exchange:

Q. (Knowlton) "The first thing in preparation for your fishing trip the next Monday was to go to the loft of that barn to find some old sinkers to put on some hooks and lines that you had not then bought?"

A. (Lizzie Borden) "I thought if I found no sinkers I would have to buy the sinkers when I bought the lines."

Q. (Knowlton) "You thought you would be saving something by hunting in the loft of the barn before you went to see whether you should need them or not?"

A. (Lizzie Borden) "I thought I would find out whether there were any sinkers before I bought the lines. If there was I should not have to buy any sinkers."

Q. (Knowlton) "You began the collection of your fishing apparatus by searching for the sinkers in the barn?"

A. (Lizzie Borden) "Yes, sir."

Q. (Knowlton) "You were searching in a box of old stuff in the loft of the barn?"

A. (Lizzie Borden) "Yes, sir; upstairs."

Q. (Knowlton) "That you had never looked at before?"

A. (Lizzie Borden) "I had seen them."

Again:

Q. (Knowlton) "You were then, when you were in that hot loft, looking out of the window and eating three pears, feeling better, were you not, than you were in the morning when you could not eat any breakfast?"

A. (Lizzie Borden) "I never eat any breakfast."

Q. (Knowlton) "You did not answer my question, and you will, if I have to put it all day. Were you then when you were eating those three pears in that hot loft, looking out of that closed window, feeling better than you were in the morning when you ate no breakfast?"

A. (Lizzie Borden) "I was feeling well enough to eat the pears."

At that point, Knowlton wisely changed his approach. Lizzie testified that she last saw her stepmother at about 9 A.M.; Abby was dusting in the dining room. In discussing their conversation, Lizzie introduced her story about the note:

Q. (Knowlton) "Had you any knowledge of [Abby] going out of the house?"

A. (Lizzie Borden) "She told me she had a note, somebody was sick, and said she was going to get the dinner on the way and asked me what I wanted for dinner."

Q. (Knowlton) "Did she tell you where she was going?"

A. (Lizzie Borden) "No, sir."

Q. (Knowlton) "Did she tell you who the note was from?"

A. (Lizzie Borden) "No, sir."

Q. (Knowlton) "Did you ever see the note?"

A. (Lizzie Borden) "No, sir."

Q. (Knowlton) "Do you know where it is now?"

A. (Lizzie Borden) "No, sir."

Q. (Knowlton) "She said she was going out that morning?"

A. (Lizzie Borden) "Yes, sir."

That was what Lizzie had to say about the note under oath. Earlier, she said it was delivered by "a boy".

One fragment of Lizzie's testimony that always baffled me was her statement that any blood spots on her undergarments could have come from flea bites. She went on to say that she told the police officers she had fleas. It turned out that Lizzie was using a Victorian euphemism; a woman going through a menstrual period, like Lizzie, was said to "have fleas".

Lizzie's Arrest

Lizzie completed her inquest testimony at 4 P.M. on Thursday, August 11. Three hours later she was arrested, charged with the murder of her father, Andrew Borden. For some curious reason, the warrant did not mention Abby Borden. It did, however, specify that the murder weapon was a hatchet. This must have disappointed several self-appointed experts who informed the police that Lizzie probably used a flatiron. (She was ironing handkerchiefs that morning and "everyone knows" that blood can be more easily washed off an iron than a hatchet).

There is some disagreement as to how Lizzie reacted to her arrest. A reporter for the *New York Times* said she took the news with surprising calmness. Yet, according to an account in the *New York Herald*, she , "fell into a fit of abject and pitiable terror." Take your pick!

At 9 A.M. on Friday, August 12, Lizzie Borden, accompanied by her lawyer, Andrew Jennings, appeared before Judge Blaisdell to answer the charge against her. When the clerk asked how she pleaded, she answered firmly, "not guilty." Blaisdell then scheduled a preliminary hearing for August 22, where he would preside as he had at the inquest. Jennings objected to this arrangement, saying among other things that:

"It is beyond human nature to suppose that Your Honor could have heard all the evidence at the inquest and not be prejudiced. I submit that Your Honor is acting in a double capacity and therefore you cannot be unbiased. This takes away from my client her constitutional right to be heard before a court of unprejudiced opinion."

The objection was overruled.

That same afternoon, Lizzie Borden was taken by train to the Bristol County jail at Taunton, fifteen miles north of Fall River. At Somerset, the train stopped briefly. On the platform there were about a dozen young women, one of whom somehow recognized Lizzie and cried out, "There she is; there's the murderess." All the women ran over to the car where she was sitting and peered in at her. According to a reporter on the train, Lizzie never moved a muscle. As Marshal Hilliard pointed out, "She is a remarkable woman possessed of wonderful power of fortitude." Lizzie's friend, Reverend Buck, put it more positively, "Her calmness is the calmness of innocence."

It was generally supposed that Lizzie would stay at the Taunton jail only until the preliminary hearing which, like the inquest, was to be held in Fall River. In practice, the jail was her "home" for the better part of ten months. Her cell was a small one, furnished with the bare necessities; a bed, a chair and a washbowl. She spent much if not most of her waking hours reading. Included were novels by Charles Dickens, religious tracts, and just about anything she could get her hands on. There was one exception; by her own request she did not receive a daily newspaper and so did not know what the press was saying about her. Lizzie's sister Emma frequently visited as did her minister and other members of the Central Congregational Church of Fall River.

The keeper of the Taunton jail was Sheriff Andrew Wright, who was at one time chief of police in Fall River. When he and his wife lived in Fall River, Lizzie was a little girl; she frequently came to their home to play with their daughter. Perhaps that explains why she was sometimes given special privileges at the jail. In particular, she was allowed to order meals sent in from a local hotel to supplement the meager and unappetizing prison fare. (A typical breakfast served to the inmates consisted of fish hash and bread; all things considered I might have preferred cold mutton and johnny cakes).

When Lizzie Borden was arrested, the predominant reaction in Fall River was one of relief. There was an almost palpable relaxation of the tension that had gripped the city for a week. No longer did people worry about a homicidal maniac invading their homes as he had the Borden house. The double murder was not, after all, a motiveless crime; instead it was an "inside job". In a weird kind of way, people wanted to believe that Lizzie was guilty. District Attorney Knowlton got letters demanding her conviction. Perhaps the most outspoken contained the following admonition:

"Do your Duty <u>without</u> fear. The whole world thinks Elizabeth Borden <u>murdered</u> her poor old <u>Father</u> and Stepmother. Elizabeth Borden chopped up those <u>two</u> poor old people, all for <u>money</u>, and <u>spite</u>, and <u>Hate</u>. She is a <u>Double Murderer</u> and should be hung <u>twice</u>. She committed <u>Two</u> murders and <u>chopped</u> up her poor old Father and his Wife in <u>cold blood</u>. She is a wicked wretch, a vile, <u>cruel</u> murderer. She is a child of the Devil. Do <u>not</u> let her off. She will chop up some one else if you let her off. Do your Duty and Hang her twice."

On the other hand, there were people who believed strongly in Lizzie's innocence. Someone sent Knowlton an abusive handwritten note:

"[You are a] Dirty Coward who attempts to destroy the reputation of an innocent woman. [Your face] should adorn the rogue's gallery instead of holding office in this commonwealth."

Lizzie's inquest testimony would haunt her for the rest of her life. Almost certainly it was directly responsible for her arrest. Her inconsistencies, both with her own prior statements and the testimony of others, persuaded many people that she was guilty.

Perhaps Lizzie's faltering performance at the inquest was caused by the morphine Dr. Bowen prescribed to calm her nerves. More likely, it was a result of District Attorney Knowlton's ferocious attack on her credibility. Nothing in Lizzie Borden's sheltered existence prior to August 4, 1892, prepared her for this type of confrontation. Toward Knowlton she felt fear bordering on terror. Never again would Lizzie Borden appear on the witness stand. One interrogation by a relentless prosecutor was enough for a lifetime.

Chapter 4
LIZZIE'S LONG ORDEAL

L izzie Borden was arrested on August 11, 1892; she did not come to trial until June 5, 1893. During that period there were two court proceedings. The first was a preliminary hearing, which was scheduled to start August 22. The purpose of such a hearing is to determine whether there is probable cause to believe the defendant guilty. The determination is made by the presiding judge, in this case Judge Blaisdell. The format of a preliminary hearing is similar to that of a trial; in particular, it is open to the press and both sides present their arguments. Perhaps that explains why it became, in Lizzie's case, a dress rehearsal for the trial; both Knowlton and Jennings used it to test strategies which were later refined or abandoned.

Massachusetts law in 1892 required that, if a judge at a preliminary hearing found probable cause of guilt (as Blaisdell did with Lizzie) the case must then go to a jury. In Lizzie's case, the grand jury consisted of twenty one men whose task was to determine whether there was enough evidence to bring her to trial. The grand jury hearing was secret; we can only speculate as to how they reached their conclusion.

This chapter will explore a few of the highlights of these hearings and a couple of related questions that arose in the ten months between Lizzie's arrest and her trial.

"You Gave Me Away, Emma"

On August 22, Lizzie Borden was taken by rail from the Taunton jail to the Fall River District Court where the preliminary hearing was to be held. As it turned out, District Attorney Knowlton was not ready to present his case, so the hearing was postponed to Thursday, August 25. Instead of going back to Taunton, Lizzie chose to stay in Fall River for those three days. She occupied the private quarters of the matron of the Fall River jail, Mrs. Hannah Reagan.

On the afternoon of Wednesday, August 24, a confusing incident occurred at the Fall River jail when Emma was visiting Lizzie. Allegedly, Mrs. Reagan overheard a quarrel between the two sisters in which Lizzie said, "You gave me away", to which Emma replied, "No, Lizzie, I only told Mr. Jennings what he ought to know for your defense."

The *Fall River Globe*, a newspaper hostile to Lizzie, interpreted this incident to mean that Emma had confessed Lizzie's guilt to Attorney Jennings. The *Fall River Evening News*, which was friendly to Lizzie, told quite a different story.

According to that article, Mrs. Reagan wanted to repudiate the story but was prevented from doing so by Marshal Hilliard, who said she would tell her story in court. Indeed she did, although not at the preliminary hearing.

Figure 4.1 Newspaper headline
Hosea Knowlton for the Prosecution

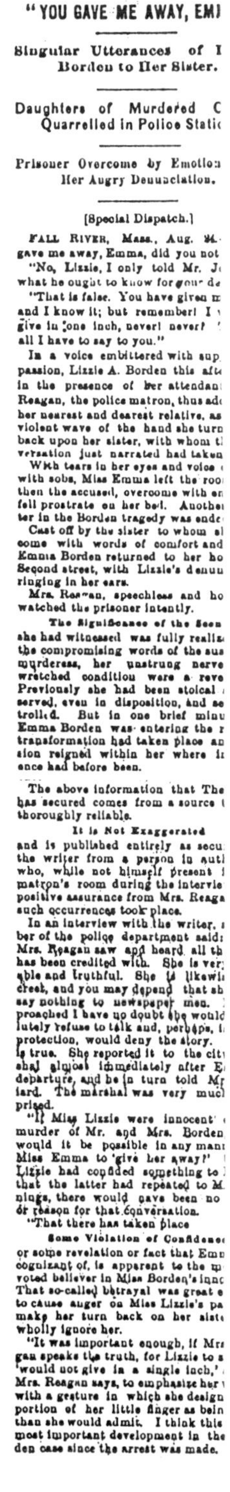

To convince Judge Blaisdell that Lizzie Borden was probably guilty of murdering her parents, District Attorney Knowlton emphasized two points. He argued that Lizzie had exclusive opportunity and that she lied repeatedly about her activities related to the murders.

To show exclusive opportunity, Knowlton sought to prove that Abby Borden was killed 1 - 2 hours before Andrew, i.e., between 9 and 10 A.M. During that interval, according to Knowlton, Lizzie was alone with her stepmother inside the house. Bridget Sullivan was outside washing windows, John Morse was visiting his niece on Weybosset Street and Andrew Borden was in downtown Fall River. Even supposing someone sneaked into the house to kill Abby, it's hard to believe that Lizzie could have failed to hear a two hundred pound woman crash to the floor.

Knowlton's argument for the time lapse depended primarily on the testimony of Dr.

From *New Bedford Evening Standard*, Aug. 25, 1892

"YOU GAVE ME AWAY, EMI

Singular Utterances of I Borden to Her Sister.

Daughters of Murdered C Quarrelled in Police Static

Prisoner Overcome by Emotion Her Angry Denunciation.

[Special Dispatch.]

FALL RIVER, Mass., Aug. 24—gave me away, Emma, did you not "No, Lizzie, I only told Mr. J; what he ought to know for your de "That is false. You have given m and I know it; but remember! I v give in 'one inch, never! never? all I have to say to you."

In a voice embittered with sup passion, Lizzie A. Borden this aft in the presence of her attendan Reagan, the police matron, thus ad her nearest and dearest relative, as violent wave of the turn back upon her sister, with whom t versation just narrated had taken. With tears in her eyes and voice with sobs, Miss Emma left the roo then the accused, overcome with an fell prostrate on her bed. Another ter in the Borden tragedy was end Cast off by the sister to whom el come with words of comfort and Emma Borden returned to her ho Second street, with Lizzie's denun ringing in her ears. Mrs. Reagan, speechless and ho watched the prisoner intently.

The significance of the Scen she had witnessed was fully realiz the compromising words of the sus murderess, her unstrung nerve wretched condition were a reve Previously she had been stoical : served, even in disposition, and so trolled. But in one brief minu Emma Borden was entering the r transformation had taken place an sion reigned within her where in ance had before been.

The above information that The has secured comes from a source t thoroughly reliable.

It is Not Exaggerated and is published entirely as secu the writer from a person in auth who, while not himself present : matron's room during the intervie positive assurance from Mrs. Reaga such occurrences took place.

In an interview with the writer, : ber of the police department said: Mrs. Reagan saw and heard all th has been credited with. She is very able and truthful. She is likewis creek, and you may depend that sh say nothing to newspaper men. proached I have no doubt she would lutely refuse to talk and, perhaps, i protection, would deny the story. is true. She reported it to the city ahal almost immediately after E: departure, and he in turn told Mr iard. The marshal was very muc prized.

"If Miss Lizzie were innocent' murder of Mr. and Mrs. Borden would it be possible in any mani Miss Emma to 'give her away?' Lizzie had confided something to that the latter had repeated to M nings, there would have been no or reason for that conversation. "That there has taken place Some Violation of Confidence or some revelation or fact that Emn cognizant of, is apparent to the m voted believer in Miss Borden's innoc That so-called betrayal was great e to cause anger on Miss Lizzie's pa make her turn back on her siste wholly ignore her.

"It was important enough, if Mr gan speaks the truth, for Lizzie to s 'would not give in a single inch,' Mrs. Reagan says, to emphasize her with a gesture in which she design portion of her little finger as bein than she would admit. I think this most important development in the den case since the arrest was made.

Wood, who concluded that digestion had proceeded 12 hours further with Andrew as compared to Abby Borden. To corroborate the priority of Abby's death, Knowlton relied on the testimony of Dr. Dolan, who said that when he examined the two bodies, Abby's was colder and her blood had coagulated to a greater extent.

Knowlton further argued that, in her inquest testimony, Lizzie had lied concerning at least three important matters. For one thing, he was convinced that Lizzie's story about her trip to the barn was a fabrication designed to provide an alibi for her father's murder. Again, he argued that her story about the note Abby received was a lie made up to explain to Andrew why his wife wasn't there to greet him when he came home. Finally, Knowlton attempted to show that Lizzie tried to purchase a lethal poison the day before the murders, even though she denied doing so at the inquest. To prove this, Knowlton put on the stand Eli Bence, the drugstore clerk who identified Lizzie as the woman who tried to buy ten cents worth of prussic acid.

Throughout the preliminary hearing, District Attorney Knowlton relied heavily on the testimony of police officers. All in all, he put seven of them on the stand. One of the most interesting of these, in a weird sort of way, was a young man named Philip Harrington, who seemed to have a compulsion for dwelling on irrelevant details. After describing his conversation with Lizzie following her father's murder, he went on to give his impression of Alice Russell's countenance as she consoled Lizzie. Knowlton cut him off, saying dryly, "I don't know as I care for Miss Russell's appearance. What did you do then?" Harrington had a long, involved answer for that question:

A. (Harrington) "I went downstairs through the front hall, through the sitting room, and into the kitchen. Dr. Bowen stood there close by the stove. I walked by him to the east.

Q. (Knowlton) "This does not in any way affect Dr. Bowen . . . What did you see in the stove?"

A. (Harrington) "I was going to tell what he had in his hand. When he took the cover off the stove . . . there was . . . something that appeared to be burnt paper and it appeared to be quite large. I should say quite large, judging from the size of the stove comparatively speaking."

Believe it or not, that's the end of the story, at least as Harrington told it at the preliminary hearing. What do you suppose the "burnt paper" was? The missing note? No, it was much larger than that. Andrew's morning newspaper? Wrong again; that ordinarily wound up in the water closet for one reason or another. Sorry; you'll just have to wait until Chapter 6 to find out the significance, if any, of the burnt paper.

Andrew Jennings and Melvin Adams for the Defense

Lizzie Borden's defense consisted largely of refuting the prosecution's case. There were stories of suspicious strangers seen in the vicinity of the Borden house. Beyond that, the defense raised a few embarrassing questions of its own. Where was the bloodstained murder weapon? the bloodstained dress that Lizzie wore to commit the murders? Above all, why did no one see even a trace of blood on Lizzie herself?

For the preliminary hearing, Andrew Jennings added a second member to Lizzie's defense team. He chose a former classmate at Boston University Law School, Melvin Adams. Among the least of Adams' distinctions was that he had a state, Ohio, for his middle name.

Figure 4.2 Melvin Adams (standing)

Of all the lawyers with the Borden case, Adams is my favorite. He had a quick mind, could think on his feet, and was always prepared. Often it seemed that he knew more about the subject under discussion than the expert witness he was questioning. Adams was effective in cross examination, where his aggressiveness was leavened by a sense of humor. (Actually, I have a special reason for appreciating Melvin Adams which you may be able to deduce before this chapter is over.)

Emma.   Mr. Jennings.   Lizzie.   M. O. Adams.
MR. ADAMS CROSS-EXAMINING FOR THE DEFENCE.

From *New Bedford Evening Standard*, pp. 4-3

Bridget Sullivan was the first witness at the preliminary hearing. Early in his cross-examination, Adams drew from her a damaging admission.

Q. (Adams) "Did [the prosecution] have any testimony or anything written out, or any paper which they showed you last night?"
A. (Bridget Sullivan) "Mr. Knowlton showed me a little paper."
Q. (Adams) "Was he talking about that paper when he showed it to you?"
A. (Bridget Sullivan) "No, sir. He said a little of it."
Q. (Adams) "How much did he read to you, quite a little?"
A. (Bridget Sullivan) "About half a dozen words, I should judge."
Q. (Adams) "What were those half a dozen words?"
A. (Bridget Sullivan) "I don't know."

The clear implication was that Bridget had been coached in some part of her testimony. This tended to diminish the impact of anything negative Bridget said about Lizzie.

With the next witness for the prosecution, Medical Examiner Dolan, Adams played hardball. Dolan, on August 11, had performed an autopsy on the victims, during which he removed their heads. These were "cleaned" (you don't want to know the details) to produce skulls which were later exhibited in court. Six days later, on August 17, the headless bodies of Andrew and Abby Borden were finally laid to rest in Oak Grove Cemetery. Adams took a dim view of this whole macabre procedure.

Q. (Adams) "Do you mean to say that these bodies are now buried without the heads?"
A. (Dolan) "Yes, sir."
Q. (Adams) "Has it been said to any member of the family, or any friend, that these people were buried without their heads?"
A. (Dolan) "I do not know."
Q. (Adams) "Have you said it or caused it to be said?"
A. (Dolan) "No, sir."

A year later, in a speech he gave to the Massachusetts Medico-Legal Association, Dolan defended his postmortem surgery, pointing out that the skulls were essential to identifying the murder weapon. He could have avoided a great deal of criticism had he pointed this out on the witness stand.

At one point Adams brought up the subject of the murder weapon. Dr. Dolan had suggested it might be the claw hammer hatchet found in the Borden cellar. He saw what looked like blood spots and human hairs on the hatchet. Subsequently, Professor Wood showed that the "blood spots" were really rust or varnish; the hair came from an animal, probably a cow. Dolan insisted the claw hammer hatchet could still be the murder weapon.

Q. (Adams) "In your opinion, would that [claw hammer] hatchet furnish an adequate cause of these wounds?"
A. (Dolan) "Yes, sir."
Q. (Adams) "The wounds in both [victims]
A. (Dolan) "Yes, sir."

After the preliminary hearing, the claw hammer hatchet was eliminated because it did not fit certain of the wounds in the skulls Dolan had prepared.

Adams was not convinced that there was a significant time lapse between the two murders. He brought up this topic again and again at the preliminary hearing. When Professor Wood testified that digestion had proceeded considerably further with Andrew Borden than with Abby, Adams got him to admit that the stomach upset suffered by both of them a couple of days earlier could affect the rate of digestion. When Dolan said that Andrew's blood was bright red where Abby's was dark and coagulated, Adams put Professor Draper of Harvard, an authority in this field, on the stand.

Melvin Adams asked him a couple of seeming innocuous questions. As indicated in the newspaper headline (Figure 4.3), Draper's answers were devastating. He pointed out that, in essence, time of death cannot be estimated from the extent of coagulation of the blood. Finally, when Dr. Dolan said that Andrew Borden's body was warmer than that of his wife Abby when he examined them, Melvin Adams pointed out that Dolan failed to use a thermometer here, relying instead on his sense of touch.

Figure 4.3 Defense witness Draper

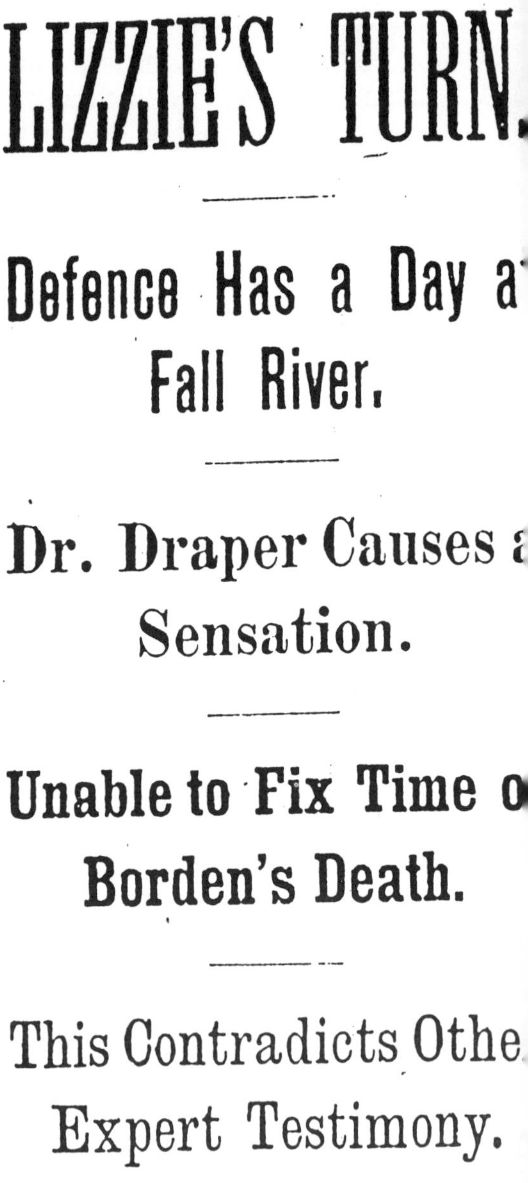

Andrew's Trip Downtown

At the preliminary hearing, the prosecution put on six different witnesses to trace Andrew Borden's movements in downtown Fall River on the morning of August 4.

Three of these (Abram Hart, John Burrell and Everett Cook) were bank employees. They testified that Andrew showed up that morning at the Union Savings Bank, the National Union Bank and the First National Bank in that order. He was president of the first bank named, a stockholder and depositor in the second, and a director of the third.

Once Andrew disposed of his financial business, he turned to his real estate interests. Specifically, he conferred with a businessman named Jonathan Clegg who was about to rent a store from Andrew. Clegg began his testimony by admitting that he was hard of hearing. His interrogators, Knowlton for the prosecution and Jennings for the defense, compensated for his deafness by speaking more loudly than normal.

LIZZIE'S TURN

Defence Has a Day at Fall River.

Dr. Draper Causes a Sensation.

Unable to Fix Time of Borden's Death.

This Contradicts Other Expert Testimony.

From the *Boston Globe*, Aug. 31, 1892

Clegg, whose store was located on North Main Street, had met Andrew there two days earlier, on Tuesday afternoon. At that time, he had made tentative arrangements to move into the A. J. Borden building on South Main Street. Now, on the morning of the murders at 10:20 A.M., he called Andrew over to his store to confirm these arrangements.

According to Clegg, his conversation with Andrew Borden lasted exactly nine minutes. When Andrew departed at 10:29 A.M., he went to the A. J. Borden building. There he talked to two carpenters, Joseph Shortsleeves and James Mather, who were remodeling the new store that Clegg had just rented. According to Mather, Andrew Borden spent several minutes upstairs in the store, then came down, picked up an old broken lock, and left at 10:40 A.M. Assuming that's correct, he probably got back to 92 Second Street at about quarter to eleven.

Figure 4.4 North Main Street, Fall River, in the 1890s

From *Forty Whacks*
Probably Guilty

District Attorney Knowlton closed the prosecution's case at the preliminary hearing by reading Lizzie's inquest testimony into the record, thereby making it public for the first time. The hearing itself ended on September 1, 1892, after summations by Andrew Jennings for the defense and Hosea Knowlton for the prosecution. According to newspaper reports, both men made eloquent presentations. When Knowlton finished, Judge Blaisdell arose and delivered his verdict in what was described as a low and tremulous voice.

"After this protracted examination, there is only one thing to perform. It is for the magistrate to render his decision. Sympathy would constrain me to say: not probably guilty. But I must face the stern realities and pass upon the evidence thus presented and thus discussed.

"Supposing for a single moment that instead of a woman the defendant was a man and he was found close by that guest chamber which to Mrs. Borden was the chamber of death; then supposing that he was the last to see Mr. Borden alive and the first to find his body, and that the only account he could give of himself was the unreasonable account that during the time of the murder he was out in the barn looking for sinkers, would there be any question in mind as to what should be done with such a one found under such circumstances and environment:

"There is only one thing to be done, however painful it may be. In the judgment of the court, the defendant is probably guilty."

No one seems to have objected to the obvious sexism of Blaisdell's remarks. Neither did anyone chastise him for what may have been the longest sentence (104 words) ever delivered in the Fall River courtroom. Curiously though, for reasons which had nothing to do with the Borden case, Judge Blaisdell was brought up on charges before the Fall River Bar Association in March of 1893, whereupon he resigned his office.

The reaction to the verdict was mixed. Knowlton was pleased; Lizzie wasn't. The *Providence Journal* approved: "The decision of Judge Blaisdell in the Borden hearing . . . was exactly what everyone who has followed the testimony carefully and without prejudice must have anticipated." The *Boston Post* was unhappy and sarcastic: "Now that Lizzie Borden has been held for trial on the charge of murdering her father, it would be a good thing for the police to go to work and see if they cannot find the real murderer."

Was Lizzie Insane?

As pointed out earlier, Fall River's initial reaction to Lizzie's arrest was one of relief. However, as time passed, many people had second thoughts. Here was a young woman, Lizzie Borden, who prior to August 4, 1892, had a completely unblemished character. Indeed, that's an understatement; Lizzie was a devoted church member, actively involved in all kinds of good works. How could such a person suddenly slaughter her parents, with a hatchet no less?

A disturbing idea must have occurred to some of the more well-to-do members of Fall River society. Expressed in words: "What is the world coming to? You can't trust anyone nowadays. People you love, members of your own family, can suddenly turn against you. Do you suppose that my daughter . . . my son . . . my heir . . . could do what Lizzie did?"

There was a simple way to banish such frightening thoughts from one's mind. Suppose Lizzie was insane? That would explain her sudden reversal of character. And heaven knows, there was good reason to believe that the murders were the act of a maniac. The hatchet kept falling long after Andrew and Abby were dead. What better evidence for insanity could there be?

Even before Lizzie was arrested, there were rumors that the Fall River police believed her to be insane when she committed the murders. After the preliminary hearing, the insanity issue was discussed openly, as indicated in the newspaper.

Figure 4.5 Article on Lizzie's sanity

Sometime in the late autumn of 1892, the Attorney General of Massachusetts, Albert Pillsbury, became a believer. Pillsbury was an ambitious politician, contemplating a run for governor in 1893. He was well aware that prosecuting Lizzie Borden was a no-win situation politically. No matter how it came out, a lot of voters would be alienated. But, just think! If Lizzie were found to be insane, no further court proceedings would be necessary. She would be committed to a mental hospital; after a decent interval she could be released as "cured" and resume a normal life. Here was a way to make everybody happy: the police, the prosecution, the people of Fall River

INSANITY INDICATED.

Strong Doubts If Miss Borden Is Ever Tried.

An Official Thinks An Asylum May Be Her Lot.

A Pawtucket Woman Saw a Man Leave the Borden Yard.

One of the prosecuting officials of the Borden case is quoted by the Boston *Globe* as saying authoritatively on condition that his name be withheld from publication:

"On the day of the murder and very frequently since that time, I have talked with Lizzie A. Borden and have watched her closely. During her entire examination I sat in a position to command a full view of her face. At the inquest I heard her testimony, I believe I have observed her more closely than any other person connected with the prosecution."

"What do I think?"

"In answering that question I will first explain my reasons for framing my opinion of her. During 14 years official work for the State I have seen and dealt with many cases of insanity. I have been brought in constant contact frequently with the inmates of the Taunton Insane Hospital and of the Worcester asylum. I consider myself as well qualified to judge a case of mental irregularity as any man who is not an expert on insanity or a physician accustomed to the treatment of brain diseases.

With such experience, basing my opinion on what I have seen of Lizzie's eyes and movements, her physical make-up and mannerisms, I am loth to believe her a victim of mania.

Her eyes have been very unnatural, and the way she has used them is identical with that of a person mentally deranged. This has been noted where her countenance was in repose, when it was not possibly assumed. The expression I have seen her wear time after time has been surely indicative of mental disturbance.

She has looked wilder and more irresponsible half of the time the past fortnight than any person I have seen in the Taunton hospital for months. My opinion has been corroborated by an expert who was led out of curiosity to attend the hearing one day and observe her.

As firmly as I believe she committed the murder, just so firmly do I think it the work of one insane. People may say, why doesn't she show signs of disturbance now? It is a well known fact that a person may be comparatively sound on all matters but one. That is the way I think it is with Lizzie.

When she has been locked up a few weeks, and the excitement of the examination is off, I shall look for a mental collapse and more definite signs of her trouble. In the event of my prediction coming true, it would be only necessary to procure two doctors to examine her, and then, without more ado, an order could be given for her removal to the insane hospital, and that would be the end of the prosecution of the Borden murder case.

This I really believe will be the ultimate result.

If Lizzie's condition is what I really think it is such as and will be certain.

If she is mentally sound, and her counsel appreciates the true strength of the government's case, with comparatively little trouble the same methods could be adopted with the same results. In either case I would not be the least surprised if Lizzie Borden never came to trial."

New Bedford Evening Standard, Sept. 3, 1892

and perhaps even Lizzie herself, who would be removed from the shadow of the gallows.

The insanity argument seemed almost too good to be true. As a matter of fact, it was. Pillsbury persuaded Knowlton, against his better judgment, to feel out Andrew Jennings on the idea of testing Lizzie's sanity. Jennings didn't buy the idea. In a letter dated November 22, 1892, he said:

. . . "I have been seriously considering your proposition and have come to the conclusion that I cannot consent to unite with you in the examination proposed. I asked Adams' opinion on the advisability of the course proposed without expressing any opinion of my own . . . [We] came to the same conclusion that in view of all the circumstances we could not do anything which suggested a doubt of her innocence and that the course would not be wise or expedient on our part." (Apparently no one bothered to ask Lizzie Borden for her opinion, but then, she was only a client.)

Knowlton gloomily reported back to Pillsbury:

"I could do nothing whatever with Jennings. He took exactly the position I feared he would, and seemed to regard it as some sort of surrender if he consented to anything. We can make some investigations into family matters without him, but it will not be so thorough as it would be if we had his assistance."

Knowlton did indeed make inquiries about Lizzie's sanity. Nobody thought she was insane, but some of the comments were interesting. Captain James C. Stafford of New Bedford said, "I used to know quite well the mother of Lizzie Borden; her name was Sarah Morse . . . She had a very bad temper . . . never heard of any of the Morses or Bordens [being] insane or anything like it."

Southard Miller, a next-door neighbor, said: "I have lived in Fall River 64 years. Andrew Borden used to work for me. I know the Bordens and all of the Morses . . . I never knew or heard that any of the Morses is or was insane. I saw Mr. Borden a little while before the murders . . . I did not want anything to do with it and I did not go near the house."

Another neighbor, Rescom Case, commented, "I have my opinion about Lizzie Borden and I hope they will get more evidence. My wife don't know any more than I do about the Bordens or Morses. We never heard that any of them is or ever was insane, but I think that some of them are worse than insane."

Along these lines, Sarah Whitehead didn't think Lizzie was insane, but she was ugly. It's not clear whether Mrs. Whitehead was referring to Lizzie's appearance or her personality. At any rate, she didn't want Lizzie to get off by claiming insanity.

The only family member who commented publicly on this issue was John Morse. He said he always found Lizzie to be as sane as he was. Presumably that meant she was sane; people called John Morse a lot of things but no one ever called him crazy.

So much for the insanity ploy; it was abandoned. Incidentally, Albert Pillsbury dropped out of the race for governor in 1893. Hosea Knowlton succeeded him as Attorney General of Massachusetts. You'll never guess who succeeded Knowlton as District Attorney: Andrew Jennings (in 1894). All three men were Republicans.

Lizzie Indicted

The grand jury met in Taunton on November 15, 1892 to consider the Borden case. Their deliberations were supposed to be secret, so we should have no idea of what transpired. However, as might be expected with more than twenty jurors, one or more of them leaked. One thing we know is that the prosecution came up with a "new" hatchet, which fit the wounds in the victims' skulls better than the claw hammer hatchet. The weapon of choice was now the hatchet without a handle found by Assistant Marshal Fleet in the Borden cellar on the day of the murders. You may wonder how Lizzie Borden, or anyone else for that matter, managed to kill two people with a bare hatchet blade. Sorry; you'll just have to wait until Chapter 6, where we'll have a lot more to say about the handleless hatchet.

On November 21 the grand jury adjourned for ten days. No one really knows why they did this, but there were a couple of theories. Many people speculated that the jury found the case against Lizzie too weak to indict her, but gave Hosea Knowlton ten days to produce more convincing evidence. Another possibility is that Knowlton wanted time to consider the question of Lizzie's sanity. Knowlton denied that, but it seems a singular coincidence that all of his correspondence on this issue came during the adjournment period.

When the grand jury returned on December 1, they heard additional testimony from Alice Russell. It seems that Miss Russell had seen Lizzie burn a dress in the kitchen stove the day after she was accused of having murdered her parents. Although Miss Russell testified at both the inquest and preliminary hearing, she said nothing about the incident at those court appearances. However, her conscience bothered her; she sought advice from a lawyer who suggested she tell the story to the grand jury.

Apparently the grand jury found that information incriminating enough to return an indictment against Lizzie Borden on the following day, December 2. Reportedly, this action was supported by twenty out of twenty one jurors voting; the minimum number required was twelve. This time around, Lizzie was charged with the murders of both Andrew and Abby Borden. Curiously, the indictment did not identify the weapon used as a hatchet. It was described as a "sharp cutting instrument" which in principle could have been anything from a penknife to a machete.

After the grand jury's action, it seemed that Lizzie Borden's ordeal was rapidly approaching a climax. All that remained was the final act: a Superior Court trial for her life. That was generally expected to take place early in the new year, 1893. Andrew Jennings made a bet with a friend that the trial would start by the beginning of February. He lost a hat on that wager. More than six months passed between the grand jury indictment and the trial. Lizzie spent that time in the Taunton jail, watching, waiting and wondering. If she was guilty, she had plenty of time for regret and remorse. If innocent, the six months must have seemed an endless nightmare.

Chapter 5
THE TRIAL: DID LIZZIE LIE?

L izzie Borden went to trial for the murder of her father and stepmother on June 5, 1893. The trial was held in New Bedford, ten miles east of Fall River. The two cities were settled in the 17th century, New Bedford in 1640, Fall River in 1656. Fall River grew faster; its population in 1893 was 83,000 as compared to 47,000 for New Bedford. There were other differences. Fall River was a mill city, New Bedford a whaling port. It was Herman Melville (in *Moby Dick*) who made New Bedford famous, not Lizzie Borden.

In 1893 and ever since then, Lizzie's final ordeal was often referred to as "the trial of the century". Mostly this reflected the intense interest shown by the press. Major newspapers in the country and quite a few minor ones insisted on having its own reporter at the trial. Two of the better known reporters were Joe Howard, a flamboyant, verbose writer representing several newspapers including the *Boston Globe*, and Julian Ralph, the distinguished correspondent for the *New York Sun*. While Howard was the more famous of the two, Ralph was more respected by his peers. Their contrasting styles are shown by their descriptions of Lizzie, contained in their columns on the first day of the trial.

"Life here has a face. [Lizzie's] dark brown hair was modestly coiled behind. Her full forehead was very pale, her wide apart eyes had an unpleasant stare. Her cheeks, which are over full, hang down below the line of the chin making a pronounced mark on either side of the face, carrying the line from the lower part of the ear a long distance down to the point of an obstinate and stubborn chin.

"But to return to Lizzie. Outside in a neighboring field was a most demonstrative cow, whose mooing was almost continuous, frequently interrupting the learned judge, often drowning the responses of mild mannered witnesses, and causing as far as eye could see the one and only smile that changed the impassiveness of the Borden countenance from morning until night."

Joseph Howard

"Those who saw Miss Borden for the first time were very much astonished. Her newspaper portraits have done her no justice at all. Some have made her out a hard and hideous fright and others have flattered her. She is, in truth, a very plainlooking old maid. She may be likened to a typical school marm, plain, practical, and with a face that shows the deep lines of either care or habitual low spirits.

"And now the difficult thing is to describe her face. Like her dress, it was that of a lady. She has large, brown eyes and a fine high forehead, but her nose is a tilting one and her cheek bones are so prominent that the lower part of her countenance is greatly overweighted. Her head is broadest at the ears. Her cheeks are very plump, and her jaws are strong and conspicuous. She is no Medusa or Gorgon. There is nothing wicked, criminal or hard in her features. Her manner in public has often been described as if she were callous or brazen. It was not so today."

Julian Ralph

This chapter and the three that follow are devoted to the Borden trial. Instead of following the conventional, chronological approach covering the complete testimony of each witness in succession, we will use a topical approach. All of the testimony relevant to a given topic will be considered at one time. This should enable you to analyze the trial testimony to decide for yourself whether Lizzie was innocent or guilty. First though, let's set the scene by introducing the courtroom personnel who, starting on June 5, 1893, determined Lizzie's fate.

Lawyers, Jurors and Judges

In February of 1893, Andrew Jennings and Melvin Adams added a third member to Lizzie's defense team. This was George Robinson, who had served three consecutive one year terms as (Republican) governor of Massachusetts (1883-886). Governor Robinson at age 59 was the senior member of the team; Andrew Jennings was 44, Melvin Adams 42. Robinson became the workhorse for the defense at the trial. He cross-examined most of the prosecution witnesses, prepared briefs on points of law, and gave the closing argument.

Robinson had very little experience as a trial lawyer, and it showed. His briefs contained more bombast than logic and he was much less adept at cross-examination than Adams. Robinson's principal contribution came out of his political background. His homespun, down-to-earth manner of speaking gave him instant credibility with the jurors; he knew exactly what to say and how to say it when he addressed them.

FIGURE 5.1 Governor Robinson

Lizzie Borden had a closer relationship with Robinson than with either Jennings or Adams. It started when Robinson visited her in jail a few months before the trial and said, "It's all right, little girl", patting her on the arm. From that point on, Lizzie saw Robinson as a father figure, at least until she received his bill. He charged $25,000 for a fifteen day trial for which the other defense lawyers had done all the preparation. By comparison, the judges who presided at the trial earned annual salaries of $5,000.

EX-GOVERNOR ROBINSON
QUIZZES MISS RUSSELL

From *Lizzie Borden Sourcebook*, p. 238

In addition to her lawyers, Lizzie was accompanied in the courtroom by one or both of the ministers associated with her church, Reverends Edwin Augustus Buck and William Walker Jubb. Both men were convinced of Lizzie's innocence and were frequently quoted to that effect in the press.

Figure 5.2 Left to right (front row) Emma, Lizzie and Rev. Buck
(Next page)

Ordinarily, in a case of this importance, the lead prosecutor would be the Attorney General of the state. However, Albert Pillsbury begged off, citing ill health. "Conventional wisdom" has long considered this a lame excuse, suggesting his real reasons were political. The facts show other-

From *Lizzie Borden Sourcebook*, p. 125

wise. In December of 1892, Pillsbury came down with diphtheria, a bacterial disease for which, in the days before antibiotics, there was no effective treatment. Pillsbury was lucky enough to survive, but his doctors insisted he stay out of the Borden trial.

To assist Hosea Knowlton for the prosecution, Pillsbury chose William Moody, District Attorney of Essex County. At age 40, Moody was the youngest attorney at the Borden trial; he also became the most prestigious. In 1906 his friend, President Theodore Roosevelt, chose William Moody to be an Associate Justice of the Supreme Court of the United States.

Figure 5.3 William Moody

For a time it seemed that Moody *was* the prosecution, all by himself. He gave the opening statement, prepared legal briefs, and examined virtually all the prosecution witnesses. Perhaps this reflected the fact that, three weeks before the trial started, Knowlton's three year old daughter came down with scarlet fever, a disease every bit as deadly as diphtheria. Then again, Knowlton was never very enthusiastic about prosecuting Lizzie Borden. In a letter to Pillsbury dated April 24, 1893, Knowlton wrote:

DISTRICT ATTORNEY MOODY

"Personally, I would like very much to get rid of the trial of

From *Lizzie Borden Sourcebook*, p. 254

the case and feel that my own feelings in that direction may have influenced my better judgment. I feel this all the more upon your not unexpected announcement that the burden of the trial would come upon me . . . .

"The case has proceeded so far . . . that it does not seem to me that we ought to take the responsibility of discharging her without trial, even though there is every reasonable expectation of a verdict of not guilty. I am unable to concur fully in your views as to the probable result. I think it may well be that the jury might disagree upon the case. But even in my most sanguine moments I have scarcely expected a verdict of guilty."

The Borden jurors were relatively well paid by the standards of a century ago. They received $3 a day, more than twice the average wage of mill workers in Fall River. The composition of the jury is given below. The comments were collected to aid the prosecution in jury selection. Looking over the list of jurors it would seem that, to get on a jury in Massachusetts a hundred years ago, it helped to be a "good man"; women could not serve on a jury. It also helped to be middle-aged or older; the average age of the jurors was 53. Notice also that most of the jurors were Republicans, which is hardly surprising; Massachusetts was a strongly Republican state in the 1890s. In 1896 the unsuccessful Democratic candidate for president, William Jennings Bryan, received 47% of the popular vote nationally; in Massachusetts he was held to only 26%.

The jury was sequestered in a hotel near the New Bedford courtroom. They could communicate with the outside world by letter, but all of their mail was censored. Newspapers were forbidden. The deputy sheriffs accompanied the jurors to the hotel dining room. On Sunday the judges made special arrangements for jurors to listen to a nondenominational service. This idea fell through when Augustus Swift refused to attend; he didn't like the minister. Despite all this, one of the jurors (Allen Wordell) said many years later, "We were a jolly crowd; we enjoyed ourselves while we lived together during the two weeks of the trial and we had many a good time afterwards." Indeed, for at least ten years after the trial, the "twelve jolly jurors" had annual reunions.

BORDEN JURORS

Name	Age	Politics	Prosecution Comments
Frank Cole	49	Rep.	Jeweler; intelligent, reads the papers
William Dean	54	Rep.	Farmer; good man
John Finn	?	Dem.	Very intelligent Irishman
Louis Hodges	59	Rep.	Iron moulder; all right
George Potter	54	Rep.	Limited education; good common sense

*Charles Richards	64	Rep.	Realtor; will try to get excused
Augustus Swift	62	Rep.	Doesn't believe in circumstantial evidence
William Westcott	48	Ind.	Married to second wife; good man
+Frederick Wilbur	36	Rep.	Says she's guilty; good, fair man
John Wilbur	60	Rep.	Farmer; good, square man
Lemuel Wilbur	56	?	Doesn't believe in capital punishment
Allen Wordell	45	Rep.	Sells farm tools in New Bedford

* Foreman
+ Wilbur was a very common name in Bristol County in the 1890s; Frederick, John and Lemuel appear to have been unrelated.

In Massachusetts in 1893 every capital case was presided over by a panel of three Superior Court justices appointed by the Chief Justice. For the Borden trial, the panel consisted of Chief Justice Albert Mason (age 57) and the two associate justices whom he chose: Caleb Blodgett (age 61) and Justin Dewey (age 57). Of the three, Dewey was the only one who achieved notoriety through the Borden trial. He did this by giving a controversial charge to the jury (Chapter 8). Dewey was appointed to the Superior Court by then Governor Robinson in 1886.

Decisions of the Court

During the trial, the three judge panel made several rulings on the admissibility of testimony. Two decisions towered over all the others in importance. The first of these was the admissibility of Lizzie Borden's inquest testimony. It was this testimony that convinced Hosea Knowlton of Lizzie's guilt. He felt that the jury would react the same way he did.

Midway through the prosecution's case, William Moody moved to have Lizzie's testimony read to the jury; Governor Robinson immediately objected. To help the judges decide the matter, the prosecution and defense drew up a factual statement. They agreed that Lizzie was not under arrest when she testified, but had been told by Mayor Coughlin and Marshal Hilliard that she was suspected. From that point on, she was under constant observation by the police. The statement further stipulated that Lizzie's request to be represented by counsel during the inquest was denied; however, Jennings conferred with her before she testified. Neither

District Attorney Knowlton nor Judge Blaisdell cautioned her that she need not testify to anything that might incriminate her.

Moody, in his argument to the court, emphasized that the key question was whether Lizzie's testimony was given voluntarily. If so, it was admissible, regardless of the circumstances under which it was given. Robinson's argument for the defense was an emotional one:

"The practice resorted to was to put her really in the custody of [Marshal Hilliard] . . . keeping her with the hand upon the shoulder she, a woman, could not run covering her at every moment, surrounding her at every instant . . . Denied counsel to tell her that she ought not to testify to anything that might tend to criminate herself, she stood alone, a defenseless woman . . . If that is freedom, God save the Commonwealth of Massachusetts." To this, Moody replied, "I say of [Robinson's] argument generally: it is magnificent but it is not law."

The decision of the court was delivered by Chief Justice Mason:

"We are of the opinion, based upon principle and authority, that if the accused was at the time of such testimony under arrest . . . the statements so made are not voluntary and are inadmissible at the trial. The common law regards substance more than form. The principle involved cannot be evaded by avoiding the form of arrest if the witness at the time of such testimony is practically in custody. We are all of the opinion that this consideration is decisive and the evidence is excluded."

As you can see from the headline below, this ruling was considered a major victory for the defense. However, the effect was not quite as sweeping as it seemed at the time. As the *Fall River Globe* pointed out, the prosecution got in much of Lizzie's inquest testimony through police officers and others who talked with her on the day of the murders.

Figure 5.4 Exclusion of inquest testimony

First reactions to the court's decision to exclude Lizzie's inquest testimony were generally favorable. The *Providence Journal* put it well: "For the judges at New Bedford to have admitted as evidence the testimony of Miss Borden before the

From *Lizzie Borden Sourcebook*, p. 264

LIZZIE WEPT

But Her Tears Were Those of Joy

Signal Victory Won by the Defense.

Inquest Testimony Ruled Out by the Court.

Damaging Statements Are Thus Excluded.

Prisoner Breaks Down

inquest would have been to establish a most dangerous precedent. It was a sensible judicial decision."

Later, there were second thoughts, particularly among legal authorities. In November of 1893, Professor John Wigmore published an article in the *American Law Review* in which he criticized the Court's ruling:

"Is there any lawyer in these United States who has a scintilla of doubt that her counsel fully informed the accused of her rights? . . . and that he allowed her to go on the stand because he deliberately concluded that it was the best policy for her, by so doing, to avoid all appearance of concealment or guilt?"

Another important judicial decision involved the admissibility of the prussic acid testimony (Chapters 1, 4). You will recall that Eli Bence, a clerk at Smith's drugstore in Fall River, identified Lizzie Borden as the woman who attempted to buy prussic acid from him, supposedly to use on a fur piece.

On the ninth day of the trial, the prosecution put Bence on the stand. Governor Robinson objected, whereupon the judges sent the jury out of the courtroom. They then listened to arguments by Moody for the prosecution and Robinson for the defense as to whether the testimony should be allowed.

When Moody and Robinson concluded, Chief Justice Mason told them politely that their arguments were irrelevant. The Court's decision on this matter would hinge on the answer to a simple question. Was it possible that the woman who tried to buy prussic acid intended to use it for an innocent purpose, e.g., to treat furs? If not, the story about the fur piece must have been a ruse designed to obtain a deadly poison, and it made sense to put Eli Bence on the stand to see if he could positively identify that woman as Lizzie Borden.

On the morning of Thursday, June 15, the prosecution put on three witnesses to testify to the properties and uses of prussic acid. The first was Charles Lawton, a New Bedford druggist. He told District Attorney Knowlton what he wanted to hear.

Q. (Knowlton) "Do you know of any use for which prussic acid is put other than for the purpose of a medicine?"
A. (Lawton) "Not that I know of; no sir."

The next witness, a New Bedford furrier named H. H. Tilson, went a step further, saying that prussic acid was never used to preserve furs. He was followed by Nathaniel Hathaway, an analytical chemist. On direct examination Hathaway appeared to corroborate the two earlier witnesses. However, Robinson, in his cross-examination of Hathaway, found that the chemist had, the night before, done some research on the properties of prussic acid. Specifically, Hathaway had studied the effect of prussic acid on ants and, as he quaintly put it, "various other nondescript bugs." They all died instantly.

Robinson, sensing an opening, pushed ahead eagerly:

Q. (Robinson) "Well, now, the result of all your experiments (is] that the two percent solution . . . will kill flies, moths and ants?"
A. (Hathaway) "Yes, sir."
Q. (Robinson) There is nothing in prussic acid that makes it unsuitable to use to kill moths on furs?"
A. (Hathaway) "Leaving out the effect on the person, [there is] no objection."

That did it. Apparently the court was convinced by Hathaway's research that prussic acid could be used for an innocent purpose. Chief Justice Mason gave the ruling: "It is the opinion of the court that the preliminary proceedings have not been sufficient. [Translation: the prosecution has not shown conclusively that prussic acid cannot be legitimately used to preserve furs]. The evidence is excluded."

Reportedly, Moody was furious at the ruling. In his opening statement at the trial, he had referred to the prussic acid incident at some length. At a minimum, the jurors must have been puzzled to have heard nothing about this topic in open court. Moody wanted to drop the case when the judges excluded the prussic acid evidence, letting Lizzie Borden go free. Knowlton refused to go that far. He did, however, abruptly and to everyone's surprise, rest the prosecution's case.

Figure 5.5 Exclusion of prussic acid testimony

It is interesting to speculate as to how present-day courts would rule on the admissibility of these two critical lines of evidence. The ruling on Lizzie's inquest testimony would very likely be the same today as it was in 1893; it would be excluded. Involuntary statements have long been

New Bedford Evening

Standard p. 1

DEFENSE!

———

A Bright Day for Lizzie Borden.

———

Collapse of Commonwealth's Case.

———

The Prussic Acid Story Not Allowed.

———

That Ended Evidence for Prosecution,

held to be inadmissible in a criminal trial. Chief Justice Mason essentially held that Lizzie's testimony was involuntary because she was in custody at the time. His ruling foreshadowed that of the United States Supreme Court nearly seventy years later in *Miranda vs. Arizona*. There, the Court held that the police are required to inform a suspect of his or her rights during custodial interrogation. In a modern criminal trial, Lizzie's inquest testimony would be excluded because she was not properly informed of her "Miranda" rights.

In contrast, the prussic acid evidence almost certainly would be allowed under today's legal standards. In a modern criminal trial, evidence of this sort is generally admissible as long as it is relevant to the defendant's guilt or innocence. Certainly Lizzie's attempt to purchase a deadly poison shortly before her parents were found butchered makes it more likely that she had murder on her mind. This was indeed the argument that Moody used a hundred years ago; a court today would undoubtedly agree with him.

Did Lizzie Lie about her Feelings for Abby?

You will recall (Chapter 3) that in her inquest testimony Lizzie used the words "cordial", "kindly" and "pleasant" to describe how she felt about her stepmother. Other people at the inquest described the relationship in more harsh terms. Augusta Tripp didn't think they were "agreeable"; Alice Russell said they were not "congenial". Hiram Harrington said that Lizzie was "unfriendly" toward Abby.

District Attorney Knowlton was convinced that Lizzie murdered her stepmother because she hated her. Assistant Marshal Fleet apparently agreed with him. At the trial he recounted a conversation with Lizzie on the day of the murders in which she said, "Mrs. Borden was not my mother; she was my stepmother."

One prosecution witness at the trial went further than any other in expressing Lizzie's dislike for Abby. This was Mrs. Hannah Gifford, who made dresses for the Borden women.

Q. (Moody) "Now, Mrs. Gifford, will you state the talk [you had with Lizzie], what you said and what she said?"

A. (Mrs. Gifford) "I was speaking to her of a garment I had made for Mrs. Borden and instead of saying 'Mrs. Borden' I said, 'Mother' and she said, 'Don't say that to me, for she is a mean, good-for-nothing thing.' I said, 'Oh, Lizzie, you don't mean that!' And she said, 'Yes, I don't have much to do with her: I stay in my room most of the time.' I asked her if she didn't go downstairs to her meals and she said she didn't eat with them any more than she could help."

At the other extreme, Emma Borden, under cross-examination at the trial, supported Lizzie's version of her relationship with Abby.

Q. (Knowlton) "Do you still say that the relations between your stepmother and your sister Lizzie were cordial?"
A. (Emma Borden) "The last two or three years they were."
Q. (Knowlton) "Notwithstanding that she never used the term mother?"
A. (Emma Borden) "Yes, sir."

Next to Emma, Bridget Sullivan was probably more aware of Lizzie's true feelings toward Abby than anyone else. Moreover, she was a prosecution witness, presumably not prejudiced in Lizzie's favor. Under cross-examination by Robinson, she tended, at least at first, to confirm Lizzie's inquest testimony.

Q. (Robinson) "You never saw any conflict in the family?"
A. (Bridget Sullivan) "No, sir."
Q. (Robinson) "Never saw the least--any quarreling or anything of that kind?"
A. (Bridget Sullivan) "No, sir, I did not."

Robinson should have quit while he was ahead; instead he made the mistake of bringing up the meal habits of the Borden family.

Q. (Robinson) "Now, Miss Emma and Miss Lizzie usually came to the table, did they not, as the father and mother did?"
A. (Bridget Sullivan) "No, sir, they did not."
Q. (Robinson) "What?"
A. (Bridget Sullivan) "Most of the time they did not eat with their mother and father."

Finally, Robinson retreated to safer (and more relevant) ground.

Q. (Robinson) "Didn't [Lizzie and Abby] talk in the sitting room [on the morning of the murders]?"

A. (Bridget Sullivan) "I heard [Lizzie] talk as she came along."

Q. (Robinson) "Talking in the sitting room?"

A. (Bridget Sullivan) "Mrs. Borden asked some questions and Lizzie answered very civilly."

Q. (Robinson) "There was not, as far as you know, any trouble that morning?"

A. (Bridget Sullivan) "No, sir, I did not see any trouble with the family."

SOMETHING TO THINK ABOUT

Of all the witnesses who testified at the inquest, preliminary hearing or trial, Hannah Gifford was the only one who suggested that Lizzie truly hated her stepmother, saying that Lizzie called Abby a "mean, good-for-nothing thing." In evaluating that statement, consider what Justice Dewey had to say about it in his charge to the jury.

"Take Mrs. Gifford's [conversation] just as she gave it and consider whether or not it will fairly amount to the significance attached to it, remembering that it is the language of a young woman and not of a philosopher or juror. What, according to common observation, is the habit of young women in the use of language? Consider whether or not they do not often use words which go far beyond their real meaning."

And yet one wonders if other witnesses were holding something back when they described the relationship between Lizzie and Abby. No one likes to gossip about bad feelings within a family, particularly if it tends to incriminate a friend. Augusta Tripp, Alice Russell and Bridget Sullivan all found themselves in that position. Did they perhaps understate the animosity Lizzie felt for her stepmother?

Did Lizzie Lie About the Note?

When Andrew Borden came home on the morning of August 4, 1892, Lizzie told him that her stepmother had gone out in response to a note which referred to a sick person. Afterwards she told several other people about the note, including Bridget Sullivan, Alice Russell, Mrs. Churchill and Dr. Bowen. For once, Lizzie was consistent, telling the same story to everyone.

The prosecution was convinced that the story about the note was a lie. District Attorney Knowlton went so far as to say that he would stake his whole case on that premise. His reasoning was based on at least three facts. In the first place, no one ever acknowledged sending the note. Moreover, no one besides Abby ever saw the note. Emma Borden testified that she couldn't find the note in Abby's pocketbook or work basket. Alice Russell told a confusing story about its possible whereabouts.

Q. (Moody) "Miss Russell, do you know anything about a search for a note by Dr. Bowen?"

A. (Alice Russell) "Yes, sir."

Q. (Moody) "State what there was about that."

A. (Alice Russell) "Dr. Bowen came in and said, 'Lizzie, do you know anything about the note your mother had?' She hesitated and said, well, no, she didn't. He said, 'Have you looked in the waste basket?' and I think I said no. He said 'Have you looked in her pocket?' and I think I said then, 'Well, then, she must have put it in the fire.' And Lizzie said, 'Yes, she must have put it in the fire.'"

Alice Russell's testimony is ordinarily interpreted to mean that Dr. Bowen couldn't find the note either in the waste basket or the pocket of the dress Abby was wearing, whereupon Alice suggested that Abby probably burned the note and Lizzie agreed. Quite possibly that was what Miss Russell was trying to say in her cautious, circuitous way.

Finally, the prosecution claimed that no one corroborated Lizzie's story about the note. The only person in a position to do that was Bridget Sullivan, who talked with Abby that morning. Here was what Bridget had to say.

Q. (Moody) "Up to the time when Miss Lizzie Borden told her father and told you, had you heard anything about [the note] from anyone?"

A. (Bridget Sullivan) "No, sir, I never did."

This implies that Abby did not tell Bridget about the note. Indeed, at the preliminary hearing, Bridget said specifically that, "Mrs. Borden did not say anything to me about the note." That would settle the matter, but it doesn't. Consider what Adelaide Churchill had to say at the trial:

Q. (Robinson) "What did Bridget tell you about Mrs. Borden having a note?"
A. (Mrs. Churchill) "She said Mrs. Borden had a note to see someone who was sick and she was dusting the sitting room and she hurried off. [Bridget] said that Abby didn't tell her where she was going; she generally did."

This puts quite a different interpretation on Bridget's testimony. Moody tried to clarify the issue on re-direct examination, but he didn't ask the right question.

Q. (Moody) "Lest there be any mistake, Mrs. Churchill, you didn't speak of the talk with Bridget with reference to the note as in substitution but in addition to what Lizzie Borden told you?"
A. (Mrs. Churchill) "It was after Lizzie had told me."

This tells us absolutely nothing. Unfortunately, no one ever asked Bridget the crucial question: "Did you see Mrs. Borden interrupt what she was doing and hurry off?"

SOME THINGS TO THINK ABOUT
The trial testimony is not particularly helpful here. The only person who knew whether a note was delivered was Abby Borden and it was too late to ask her about it. To decide this matter for yourself, you may want to think about the following questions.

What reason could the author of the note have had for not coming forward? Given that Abby was a shy, somewhat reclusive person whose only close friend was her sister Sarah Whitehead, does it seem likely that she would have gone out to visit a sick person? On the other hand, why would Lizzie have made up a complex, verifiable lie when a simpler one would have sufficed? Moreover, why didn't Andrew question Lizzie's story about the note?

Did Lizzie Lie About her Trip to the Barn?

According to her inquest testimony, Lizzie Borden spent the time between 11:00 and 11:15 A.M. on August 4, 1892, in the loft of the Borden barn, looking for sinkers and eating pears. The prosecution, on the other hand, believed that she spent that time in the sitting room, chopping up her father and concealing the evidence.

There were at least two reasons for doubting Lizzie's story. In the first place, she changed her mind a couple of times as to the purpose of her trip to the barn loft. She told Dr. Bowen she went there to find "some iron". She told Alice Russell she was looking for "a piece of tin or iron" to fix a screen. Later Lizzie settled on a story about a search for sinkers, which Knowlton found ridiculous.

Beyond that, the prosecution claimed that the barn loft must have been extremely uncomfortable on a warm August morning. Moody, in his opening statement, put it this way: "August 4, 1892, was one of the hottest days of the last summer in this vicinity. The loft of the barn was almost stifling in the intensity of its heat." Later, Knowlton said, "There is not a man of you that does not remember that that day was hot to a degree by which this day is cool and comfortable in comparison. And you are asked to believe that [Lizzie] went out of the house and up to that barn, to the hottest place in Fall River."

The prosecution's star witness here was Officer William Medley of the Fall River police force. He testified that he arrived at the Borden house at about 11:40 A.M. and interrogated Lizzie. Suspicious of her story, Medley went out to the barn to check it.

Q. (Moody) "After you went into the barn, what did you do?"
A. (Medley) "I went upstairs until I reached about three or four steps from the top, and while there part of my body was above the level of the floor and I looked around the barn to see if there was any evidence of anything being disturbed and I didn't notice anything. I stooped down low to see if I could discern any marks on the floor . . . I didn't see any, and reached out my hand to see if I could make any impression on the floor of the barn and I did make an impression."
Q. (Moody) "Describe what there was on or about the floor by which you made an impression."
A. (Medley) "Seemed to be accumulated hay dust and other dust."

Medley went on to say that he took four or five steps on the floor and could see his footsteps in the dust.

Q. (Moody) "Did you see any footsteps in that dust other than the ones you made yourself?"
A. (Medley) "No, sir."

The implication was, of course, that Lizzie couldn't have gone to the barn loft that morning, since she left no footprints. Medley went on to comment about the temperature.

Q. (Moody) "Did you notice the temperature of the loft when you went up?"
A. (Medley) "Well, I know it was hot, that is all, very hot, you know it was a hot day.

Medley estimated that he spent about ten minutes in the Borden house before going into the barn. He arrived at the house at 11:40; therefore he must have started his experiments in the barn loft at about 11:50 A.M. Remember that time; it's important!

To refute Medley's testimony, the defense put several witnesses on the stand who claimed to have walked around in the barn loft that morning before Medley got there. The reasoning here was straightforward; if Medley couldn't see their footprints, he couldn't have seen Lizzie's either. One of the more credible witnesses was Alfred Clarkson, a "steam engineer" (whatever that is or was).

Q. (Jennings) "What time did you get [to the Borden house] on the morning of the murders?"
A. (Clarkson) "I should say 11:30."
Q. (Jennings) "How soon after you got there (did you go to the barn]?"
A. (Clarkson) "Seven or eight minutes."
Q. (Jennings) "Did you get in the upper part of the barn?"
A. (Clarkson) "Yes, sir."
Q. (Jennings) "Was there anyone else up there when you were there?"
A. (Clarkson) "There were three [other people]."
Q. (Jennings) "Was [Officer Medley] there when you got there?"
A. (Clarkson) "No, sir, I didn't see him."

In effect, Clarkson said that he and three other people were in the barn loft ten minutes or more before Medley came on the scene. However, the impact of his testimony was diminished by Knowlton on cross-examination. He pointed out that at the preliminary hearing Clarkson said he arrived at the Borden house at 11:40 instead of 11:30.

The defense put on one witness who directly corroborated Lizzie's story. This was Hyman Lubinsky, an ice cream peddler who drove a team of horses past the Borden house on the morning of the murders.

Q. (Jennings) "Can you tell me about what time it was when you left the stable?"

A. (Lubinsky) "Well, a few minutes after 11."

Q. (Jennings) "When you got to the Borden house, did you see anybody?"

A. (Lubinsky) "I saw a lady come out . . . from the barn right to the stairs back of the house."

This was, of course, the path that Lizzie Borden said she took at about the time Lubinsky passed the house. Lubinsky could not identify the woman he saw, but he said it was not Bridget, whom he knew by sight.

Lubinsky was a Russian immigrant with a limited knowledge of English; Knowlton gave him a very hard time. The reporter Julian Ralph put it well. "Never did a lawyer try harder to confuse a witness than did Mr. Knowlton on this occasion. He walked up and down between the witness and his desk, prodding him with rapid questions. He was nervous, querulous and scolding in his tone."

And yet, on the whole, Lubinsky gave as good as he got.

Q. (Knowlton) "Did you look at any other yard besides the Borden yard?"

A. (Lubinsky) "I looked all over the yard."

Q. (Knowlton) "What were you looking round for?"

A. (Lubinsky) "Because I am acquainted with looking around."

Q. (Knowlton) "Do you remember seeing anyone in the Borden yard any other day before that day?"

A. (Lubinsky) "I don't remember."

Q. (Knowlton) "You didn't take any notice any other day?"

A. (Lubinsky) "Something made me look at it that day. What has a person got eyes for but to look with?"

If you're confused by some of the time discrepancies referred to in this section, you're not alone. Even today people don't always agree as to when an event took place; a hundred years ago it was far worse. The basic problem was that there was no primary standard of time. Today you and I can turn on TV or radio and get the official time. If we synchronize our watches, the chances are they will read the same within seconds six months later. In 1892, that wasn't possible. Residents of Fall River set their time pieces by various arbitrary standards such as the city hall clock or the one in the railroad station, which seldom agreed with each other.

It's difficult to say how much confidence to place in the times testified to by Medley, Clarkson, Lubinsky or other witnesses. Discrepancies up to five minutes are common; larger errors are entirely possible. For example, Mrs. Caroline Kelly testified that she saw Andrew Borden return home that morning at 10:32 A.M. by her clock. That was eight minutes *before* another witness, James Mather, relying on the city hall clock, saw Andrew leave downtown Fall River!

A more extreme example involves the newsdealer John Cunningham, who phoned the police to report Andrew Borden's murder. Cunningham said that, according to the clock in the store where the phone was located, he placed the call at 10:50 A.M. According to the clock in the police station, the call came in at 11:15!

SOME THINGS TO THINK ABOUT

To evaluate Lizzie's story about her trip to the barn, you may want to consider some of the points raised by District Attorney Knowlton in his closing argument. "[Lizzie] told her friend Alice that she went [to the barn] to get a piece of iron to fix her screen. Why couldn't somebody have told us what screen needed fixing? She told [the police] that she went out into the barn to get some sinkers. Show us the fish line that those sinkers went on."

To judge the testimony of William Medley and Hyman Lubinsky, you may want to think about the following questions. Do you leave footprints when you cross a dusty floor? Could the woman Lubinsky saw have been someone other than Lizzie or Bridget? Might Lizzie have gone to the barn after her father was killed rather than before?

We've now considered three instances where the prosecution argued that Lizzie lied in her inquest testimony: her feelings toward her stepmother, her story about the note and her trip to the barn. You'll have to decide for yourself, taking account of the evidence presented at the trial, whether Lizzie told the truth about these matters (and others).

If you feel she lied in one or more cases, you need to go one step further and decide how much significance to attribute to it. Certainly lying suggests guilt, but it doesn't prove it. Innocent people often lie when they feel that the truth would embarrass or incriminate them. Bridget Sullivan told a "white" lie when she said she was washing windows on the third floor when Andrew Borden was murdered. Later she admitted she was taking a nap in her bedroom instead. Other people involved in the Borden case very likely lied on the witness stand, including Emma Borden (to protect Lizzie) and John Morse (to protect himself, Chapter 9).

The Hottest Day

According to legend, August 4, 1892, was a scorching hot day in Fall River. For a hundred years, everyone who wrote about the Borden case embellished the legend; it got hotter and hotter as time passed.

Edwin Porter (1893) "the hot sunshine of an exceptionally warm midsummer day"
Edmund Pearson (1937) "a sultry day of typical August weather; a day, as the hours advanced toward noon, of almost intolerable heat"
Frank Spiering, (1984) "In Fall River, temperatures were hotter than anyone remembered, well over 100°."

Once again, the legend is wrong. At 11 A.M., when Andrew Borden was murdered, the temperature was approximately 78°F. This is based on observations by the United States Signal Service and on weather reports from two Fall River newspapers, the *Herald* and the *Evening News*. August 4, 1892, might be described as a "hot day" compared to Christmas. It would be better to call it a "typical midsummer day"; the normal high in Fall River in early August is 82°.

The legend originated with the statements of Moody and Knowlton. As might be expected, police officers agreed with the prosecution. Curiously, Lizzie did too; at the inquest she agreed with Knowlton that the barn loft was "very hot." The only dissenters were two young men, Thomas Barlow and Everett Brown, who claimed (Chapter 10) to have been in the barn loft that morning before Medley. Barlow in particular said that the loft was relatively cool.

The myth that August 4, 1892, was the "hottest day" is only one of many concerning the Borden case. However, it seems as if such a brutal, shocking crime should have been accompanied by extreme weather, even though it wasn't. Had the murders occurred in September or December, they should have taken place in a hurricane or a blizzard respectively.

Chapter 6
THE TRIAL:
COULD LIZZIE HAVE DONE IT?

In his closing argument to the jury, District Attorney Knowlton commented at some length on the fact that the evidence against Lizzie Borden was circumstantial. No one saw her kill her father or stepmother. That is hardly unusual; murderers usually prefer to operate in private. (John Wilkes Booth was a notable exception).

The unusual feature of the Borden case was the absence of any physical evidence linking Lizzie to the murders. She left no "bloody glove" or other personal memento at the scene of the crime. Perhaps that explains why the prosecution seemed to be struggling from behind through so much of the trial. Knowlton and Moody found themselves trying to convince the jury, not that Lizzie committed the crime, but that she could have done so. They had to address the following questions, among others:

How did she chop up her parents without getting blood on herself?
What did she do with the dress she was wearing at the time?
Where was the murder weapon she used?

In this chapter, we'll concentrate upon the trial testimony related to these three topics.

The Absence of Blood

Several people came in close contact with Lizzie shortly after the discovery of her father's body. None of them saw any blood on her face, her hands, her hair or her dress. The testimony of Adelaide Churchill was typical.

Q. (Robinson) "You afterwards saw [Lizzie] with Miss Russell, and she was lying on the lounge?"

A.   (Mrs. Churchill) "Yes, sir."
Q.   (Robinson) "At that time, did you see a particle of blood on her dress?"
A.   (Mrs. Churchill) "No, sir."
Q.   (Robinson) "On her hands?"
A.   (Mrs. Churchhill) "No, sir."
Q.   (Robinson) "On her face?"
A.   (Mrs. Churchill) "No, sir."
Q.   (Robinson) "Or any disarrangement of her hair?"
A.   (Mrs. Churchill) "No, sir."

(Had Lizzie gotten blood on her hair, she presumably would have washed it out, causing a "disarrangement".)

Governor Robinson asked the same questions to Bridget Sullivan, Alice Russell, Charles Sawyer and Phoebe Bowen. All of them gave the same answers as Mrs. Churchill, although Bridget hedged a little.

Q.   (Robinson) "You didn't see any blood on Lizzie?"
A.   (Bridget Sullivan) "No, sir, I don't remember seeing any blood."
Q.   (Robinson) "Face or hands or anywhere?"
A.   (Bridget Sullivan) "No, sir, I didn't."
Q.   (Robinson) "And her hair, was that all in order properly?"
A.   (Bridget Sullivan) "As far as I can remember."

Having pretty well established the absence of blood on Lizzie, the defense tried to go a step further and show that the murderer, whoever he or she may have been, had to be stained by blood. With this objective in mind, Melvin Adams cross-examined four of the prosecution's expert witnesses, starting with Dr. Dolan. At first Dolan seemed inclined to argue with Adams, but eventually he conceded the point.

Q.   (Adams) "Would it not have been natural that the assailant [of Andrew Borden] would have been covered with blood or would have been spattered and sprinkled with blood?"
A.   (Dolan) "Not necessarily."
Q.   (Adams) "How do you explain that they would not have been?"
A.   (Dolan) "Because it [might] not spurt . . . in the direction of the assailant.

Q. (Adams) "But when the hatchet goes into the wound, doesn't it get covered with blood, particularly the edge of it?"

A. (Dolan) "Yes, sir."

Q. (Adams) "And when a hatchet is covered with blood which is fresh and warm, isn't it liable to come off in a swinging blow?"

A. (Dolan) "Yes, sir."

Q. (Adams) "And wouldn't you say it would be probable that the assailant would be covered with blood, or have spatters upon him?"

A. (Dolan) "He would have spatters, yes, sir."

Dolan was followed to the stand by three professors at Harvard Medical School, all of whom were practicing physicians: Edward Wood, Frank Draper and David Cheever. Wood readily agreed with Adams that the murderer must have been spattered with blood.

Q. (Adams) "Assuming that the assailant stood behind Mr. Borden when these injuries were given and received, have you formed any opinion as to whether he would be spattered by blood to any extent?"

A. (Wood) "I don't see how he could avoid being spattered from the waist up."

Q. (Adams) "Assuming that the assailant stood over Mrs. Borden when she was lying down on the floor . . . have you formed an opinion as to whether her assailant would be spattered with blood?"

A. (Wood) "I don't see how the assailant could avoid being spattered . . . from the lower portion of the body upwards."

Draper essentially agreed with Wood, but expressed his opinion more cautiously.

Q. (Adams) "In your opinion, would the assailant [of Mr. Borden] of necessity receive some spatters of blood upon his clothes or person?"

A. (Draper) "I should think so."

Q. (Adams) "Would not the assailant of [Mrs. Borden] have been spattered with blood?

A. (Draper) "I should think so."

Of the four expert witnesses, Professor Cheever was the only surgeon. He had direct knowledge of how blood spurts or spatters from an incision.

Q. (Adams) "When you perform an operation, your face and hands [get covered with blood], I suppose?"
A. (Cheever) "Very often."
Q. (Adams) "And hair?"
A. (Cheever) "Not so much."
Q. (Adams) "Is there in the head a temporal artery, where these injuries were disclosed on the head of Mr. Borden?"
A. (Cheever) "Yes, sir. Two of the cuts would go through it."
Q. (Adams) "Would you expect a spurting (of blood] from such cuts?"
A. (Cheever) "Yes, sir . . . extending several feet."
Q. (Adams) "Would not the assailant have been spattered with blood?"
A. (Cheever) "I think he would."
Q. (Adams) "To what extent?"
A. (Cheever) "Very considerably."
Q. (Adams) "Would he not have been spattered, probably in the face and about the head?"
A. (Cheever) "He would be likely to be."
Q. (Adams) "In your opinion would the assailant of [Mrs. Borden] have been spattered?"
A. (Cheever) "I think he or she would be."

SOMETHING TO THINK ABOUT
From the testimony just described, it's safe to say that:
* *no one saw any blood on Lizzie's person or clothes.*
* *the murderer must have been spattered with blood;*
  how much blood we don't know.

Taken together, these statements suggest Lizzie's innocence but certainly don't prove it. Could Lizzie have taken a bath after the murders? Did she change her clothes?

Lizzie's Clothes

In my wife's opinion, Lizzie Borden had a great many dresses. Most of them were blue, her favorite color. Two of her dresses were discussed at some length during the trial. The first of these was the dress Lizzie turned over to the police, saying it was the one she wore on the morning of

August 4, 1892. In the trial transcript this dress was described as being dark blue. At the inquest Lizzie called it, "navy blue, sort of a Bengaline silk with a navy blue blouse." Webster's dictionary a century ago defined Bengaline silk as a "corded fabric of silk and wool." Lizzie agreed except that she said the main component was linen rather than wool. Knowlton insisted on referring to it as a "silk dress", probably because he felt no juror would believe that a God-fearing young woman would wear silk in the morning.

At the trial, several people who saw Lizzie after 11A.M. testified as to whether or not she was wearing the Bengaline silk. Two witnesses, Bridget Sullivan and Alice Russell, said they didn't notice what dress she was wearing; they were more concerned about other matters. Dr. Bowen described her dress as "drab"; this led to a long, tedious discussion as to what color he meant. Finally, in exasperation, Bowen said, "It was an ordinary, unattractive, common dress that I did not notice especially."

Dr. Bowen's wife Phoebe seems to have been more observant than he. She said Lizzie was wearing a "dark dress which had a blue waist with a white design on it." When Andrew Jennings held up the Bengaline silk, Mrs. Bowen said, "I would say it was the [dress] she had on. That was what she usually wore in the morning."

Adelaide Churchill disagreed with Phoebe Bowen.

Q. (Moody) "Will you describe the dress [Lizzie] had on while you were there?"

A. (Mrs. Churchill) "It looked like a light blue and white groundwork. It seemed like a calico or cambric with a dark navy blue diamond printed on it."

Q. (Moody, holding up the Bengaline silk) "Was this the dress she had on that morning?"

A. (Mrs. Churchill) "It does not look like it."

Officer Doherty, who talked to Lizzie shortly after she discovered her father's body, testified as follows:

Q. (Moody) "Can you give any description of the dress [Lizzie] had on?"

A. (Doherty) "I thought she had a light blue dress. That is all I can say about it."

Q. (Moody, holding up the Bengaline silk) "I would ask you if it was that dress?"
A. (Doherty) "No, I don't think so."

On cross-examination, Doherty admitted that he really didn't notice much about the dress.

One thing we can say for sure about the Bengaline silk is that there was no blood on it. Questioned on this point, Professor Wood said flatly, "The dress was thoroughly examined and there is not even a suspicion of a blood stain on it." Wood also tested the stockings, shoes and white underskirt that Lizzie turned over to the police along with the Bengaline silk. He found no blood upon the shoes or stockings, but he testified that:

"The white [under]skirt contains a small blood spot on it. The blood spot was about 1/16 inch in diameter, about the size of the head of a small pin. The size of the blood corpuscles is consistent with it being human blood. It probably came onto the skirt from the outside and not from the inside."

Under cross-examination, Wood agreed with Adams that the blood spot was at the back of the underskirt rather than the front. That being the case, it's hard to see how the blood could have spattered from either of the victims.

Another dress discussed at great length during the trial was the one Lizzie burned, in the presence of her sister Emma and Alice Russell, on Sunday morning, August 7, three days after the murders. At the trial, Miss Russell described the dress as follows:

Q. (Moody) "Give us a description of the dress that she burned."
A. (Alice Russell) "It was a cheap, cotton Bedford cord."
Q. (Moody) "What was the color?"
A. (Alice Russell) "Light blue ground with a small dark figure."

In case you're curious, Webster's dictionary referred to Bedford cord as "a firm cloth with heavy ribs running lengthwise in the fabric." On cross-examination, Alice Russell said that she did not see any blood on the dress, but it was soiled on the bottom edge.

Mrs. Mary Raymond testified that she made the Bedford cord dress for Lizzie in the spring of 1892. Her description of the dress agreed with that of Alice Russell; she referred to it as "a cheap cotton dress, light blue with a dark figure." Mrs. Raymond explained how the dress got soiled.

The Borden house was being painted at the time she made the dress; Lizzie got paint on the bottom of it. To make matters worse, the blue color faded or wore off. The Bedford cord must have been a very cheap dress.

Miss Russell described the dress-burning incident in some detail.

Q. (Moody) "Will you state what you saw after you returned [on Sunday morning]?"

A. (Alice Russell) "I went into the kitchen . . . Miss Lizzie was at the stove and she had a skirt in her hand and her sister turned and said, 'What are you going to do?' and Lizzie said, 'I am going to burn this old thing up; it is covered with paint.'"

Q. (Moody) "What did you see then?"

A. (Alice Russell) "Miss Lizzie appeared to be either ripping something down or tearing part of the garment . . . I said to her, 'I wouldn't let anyone see me do that, Lizzie.' She didn't make any answer. I left the room." Alice Russell went on to say that while Lizzie was burning the Bedford cord, there were police officers outside the house.

Figure 6.1 Alice Russell, Prosecution Witness

Emma Borden, testifying for the defense, gave a somewhat different version of the dress-burning episode. Recall (Chapter 1) that the police, accompanied by Andrew Jennings and Dr. Dolan, thoroughly searched the Borden house on the afternoon of Saturday, August 6. Among the rooms searched was the "clothes press", an upstairs closet where Lizzie kept her dresses. At the trial, Jennings questioned Emma on this point.

MISS RUSSELL

Q. (Jennings) "What, if anything, did Dr. Dolan say as to the nature of the search that had been made [on Saturday afternoon]?"

From *Lizzie Borden Sourcebook*, p. 147

A. (Emma Borden) "He told me the search had been as thorough as could be made unless the paper was torn from the walls and the carpets taken from the floors."

Q. (Jennings) "Now where was that dress, if you know, on Saturday, the day of the search?"

A. (Emma Borden) "I saw it hanging in the clothes press over the front entry . . . I said (to Lizzie], 'You have not destroyed that old dress yet; why don't you?"

Figure 6.2 Emma Borden, Defense Witness

Throughout her testimony, Emma insisted that burning the Bedford cord was her idea. Consider, for example, her account of what happened on Sunday morning.

Q. (Jennings) "Now will you tell the court and the jury all that you saw or heard [Sunday] morning?"

A. (Emma Borden) "I was washing dishes and I heard my sister's voice. I turned round and saw she was standing between the foot of the stove and the dining roan door. This dress was hanging on her arm and she said, 'I think I shall burn this old dress up.' I said, 'Why don't you?' or 'You had better' or 'I would if I were you.'"

EMMA BORDEN ON THE STAND

From *Lizzie Borden Sourcebook*, p. 291

The prosecution maintained that, on the morning of August 4, Lizzie wore the Bedford cord rather than the Bengaline silk she gave the police. Knowlton pointed out that in her testimony Adelaide Churchill said Lizzie wore a light blue dress with a white background. That sounds like the Bedford cord, as Alice Russell and Mrs. Raymond described it. Remember, though, that Mrs. Churchill went on to say, "It seemed like a calico or cambric." Governor Robinson questioned Alice Russell on this point.

Q. (Robinson) "You called [the dress Lizzie burned] a Bedford cord?"
A. (Alice Russell) "Yes, sir."
Q. (Robinson) "Is that what we call a calico?"
A. (Alice Russell) "No, sir."
Q. (Robinson) "And is it a cambric?"
A. (Alice Russell) "No, sir."

SOME THINGS TO THINK ABOUT

Throughout this section we have sought answers to two questions. The first is: did Lizzie tell the truth when she claimed to have worn the Bengaline silk dress on the morning of the murders? The evidence here seems conflicting; Phoebe Bowen voted "yes" while Adelaide Churchill and probably Officer Doherty voted no . Surprisingly though, their descriptions of the dress Lizzie wore resemble each other closely. The distinction between "light blue" and "dark blue" seems a rather subtle one. By the same token, the Bengaline silk and the Bedford cord (as Alice Russell and Mary Raymond described it) have a lot in common. Both were blue; both were made from a corded fabric.

The more important question is: why did Lizzie burn the Bedford cord? The prosecution thought she did it because she feared that Professor Wood would find bloodstains on it that her friends didn't notice. The defense argued that the incident was an innocent act committed simply to get rid of a garment too badly soiled to be worn. Perhaps so, but why didn't Lizzie burn the dress before the murders rather than after? Then again, if she was worried about bloodstains, why didn't she burn it before the police searched the house?

On a lighter note, why do you suppose Emma and Lizzie kept referring to the Bedford cord as an "old dress?" It was made in May and burned in August, three months later. That doesn't sound old to me; I have suits that date back twenty years or more. You never can tell when they'll come back into fashion.

The Handleless Hatchet

By the time of the trial, the prosecution had pretty much decided that the handleless hatchet shown below was the murder weapon. Moody put it this way: "The Government does not insist that the homicides were committed by the handleless hatchet. It *may* have been the weapon. It may well have been the weapon."

Figure 6.3 The handleless hatchet

Goodbye Lizzie Borden, p. 114

It was the contention of the prosecution that Lizzie used this weapon (with the handle attached) to kill her father and stepmother. After the murders, she broke off the handle, for unknown reasons, and somehow disposed of it. What remained was the hatchet head shown in the photo.

The handleless hatchet was an old one; the blade, which had a cutting edge of 3½ inches, was covered with rust. The piece of wood left when the handle was broken extended perhaps 1½ inches below the head of the hatchet; the rest of the handle was missing. Notice from the photo that there was a peculiar slot or notch about a quarter of an inch wide on the lower edge of the hatchet head.

This weapon was found in the cellar of the Borden house by Assistant Marshal Fleet on the day of the murders. It was in a box along with several other old tools. At the trial, Fleet described its condition as follows:

> Q. (Moody) "Mr. Fleet, will you describe everything in respect to the appearance of that hatchet, if you can?"
>
> A. (Fleet) "The hatchet was covered with a heavy dust or ashes."
>
> Q. (Moody) "Describe the ashes as best you can."
>
> A. (Fleet) "It was covered with white ashes . . . on both sides."

Fleet went on to say that the other tools in the box were covered with a fine dust, much finer than that on the hatchet. Then Moody questioned him about the break in the handle.

> Q. (Moody) "At that time, Mr. Fleet, did you observe anything as to the point of breaking of the handle?"
>
> A. (Fleet) "I recognized this was apparently a new break."

All the policemen who examined the hatchet in the days immediately following the murders (Mullaly, Seaver, Medley and Desmond) agreed with Fleet that the blade of the handleless hatchet was covered with ashes on both sides and that the break in the handle appeared to be a fresh one. Detective Seaver conceded, on cross-examination, that he couldn't tell within three months when the break occurred.

Everything seemed to be going smoothly for the prosecution until Mullaly, who was with Fleet when he found the handleless hatchet, testified under cross examination, where he surprised everyone.

> Q. (Robinson) "Nothing else was taken out of the box while you were there?"
>
> A. (Mullaly) "Nothing but the hatchet and parts of the handle."
>
> Q. (Robinson) "Well, parts? That piece (referring to the small piece of wood in the hatchet head)?"
>
> A. (Mullaly) "Yes, and there was another piece of the handle."
>
> Q. (Robinson) "The rest of the handle?"
>
> A. (Mullaly) "Yes, sir. It was a piece with a sharp break in it."
>
> Q. (Robinson) "Who took it out of the box?"
>
> A. (Mullaly) "Mr. Fleet took it out."

Knowlton and Moody told Robinson that they had never heard of the existence of such a handle, let alone seen it. Fleet, recalled to the witness stand, denied he had seen the handle in the box, let alone taken it out. Nevertheless, thanks to Mullaly, the damage was done. At best, the Fall River police looked ridiculous, as indicated by the newspaper headline below. At worst, they had conspired with the prosecution to conceal evidence. Reporters started referring to the handleless hatchet as the "hoodoo (bad luck) hatchet".

Figure 6.4 Fleet vs Mullaly

Professor Wood testified as to the chemical tests he had carried out on the hatchet. He said that he scraped off some of the rust that covered both sides of the head and tested it for blood; he found none. Then he took the small piece of wood out of the head and soaked it for several days in water. The solution tested negative for blood.

On direct examination, Wood implied that it would be quite easy to wash all the blood off the hatchet before it was broken.

Q. (Knowlton) "Assuming the hatchet to have been used for in-

Big Sensation in Borden Case.

Officer Fleet Gets Sadly Twisted.

Did Not Mention All He Found at First.

Mullaly Contradicts Fleet's Story.

Says Hatchet Handle Was in Box.

Government Unable to Produce It In Court.

From *Lizzie Borden Sourcebook*, p. 243

flicting the wounds and then subjected to some kind of cleaning process . . . could this have occurred without your having discovered traces of blood on the hatchet or the handle?"

A. (Wood) "Before the handle was broken, not after."

Q. (Knowlton) "Why do you make that distinction?"

A. (Wood) "Because it would have been very difficult to wash blood off that broken end. It might have been done by a thorough cleaning, but that would also stain the fracture."

Q. (Knowlton) "Why do you give the other answer before the hatchet was broken?"

A. (Wood) "That hatchet handle fitted very tightly into the head and was a smooth handle, so far as I could tell from the part remaining."

On cross-examination, Wood conceded that washing all the blood off the hatchet might not be all that easy after all.

Q. (Adams) "This slot on the inner edge of the head [recall Figure 6.3.] It furnishes a good refuge for any blood to gather?"

A. (Wood) "Yes, sir."

Q. (Adams) "And it would have been quite a place to clean, assuming any blood got on it?"

A. (Wood) "It would and there is white dust in there."

The prosecution sought to establish through medical testimony that Lizzie could have used the handleless hatchet to murder her parents. The first witness to be queried on this point was Medical Examiner Dolan.

Q. (Knowlton) "In your opinion were the wounds that you found . . . such as could be inflicted with a hatchet by a woman of ordinary strength?"

A. (Dolan) "Yes, sir."

Knowlton then asked Dolan to explain how the handleless hatchet, with a 3½ inch cutting edge, could have produced wounds varying in length all the way from ½ inch to five inches.

Q. (Knowlton) "How could a 3½ inch hatchet make a two inch wound?"

A. (Dolan) "Because the whole cutting edge wouldn't be brought into play at once."

Q. (Knowlton) "And how can a 3½ inch hatchet make a four inch wound?"

A. (Dolan) "By sliding and by going in underneath."

Dr. Draper agreed with Dolan that the wounds could have been made, "with an ordinary hatchet in the hands of a woman of ordinary strength." He went on to express an opinion as to how long the cutting edge of the hatchet must have been, based on a deep wound in front of Andrew Borden's left ear.

Q. (Knowlton) "What do you say the [length of the edge of the hatchet] must have been?"

A. (Draper) "3½ inches."

To show the jury how he reached that conclusion, Draper made use of Andrew Borden's skull, which Dr. Dolan had so thoughtfully prepared for him. He placed a stiff piece of tin 3½ inches long into the wound mentioned above; it fit perfectly. In contrast, a four inch piece of tin would not enter the wound. Then Draper repeated the demonstration with the handleless hatchet; it fit both the length and width of the wound. The spectators, and presumably the jurors, were suitably impressed.

Figure 6.5 Draper fits the hachet to Andrew's skull

THE HANDLELESS HATCHET FITTED IN THE SKULL.

New Bedford Evening Standard p. 3

On cross-examination, Melvin Adams gambled and failed. He was convinced that any hatchet with a cutting edge of about 3½ inches would fit the wound referred to by Dr. Draper. Accordingly, he asked Draper to test a cheap, new hatchet. It didn't fit; it was too wide. The effect here was similar to Mullaly's "discovery" of the missing handle; this time it was the defense that was embarrassed. All in all, Draper's testimony was a triumph for the prosecution.

The final medical witness was another Harvard professor, Dr. Cheever. On direct examination, he gave the answers Knowlton was looking for.

Q. (Knowlton) "What is your opinion as to whether [the handleless hatchet] could have caused the wounds you found?"
A. (Cheever) "I think it could."
Q. (Knowlton) "I will ask whether or not these wounds could have been inflicted by a woman of ordinary strength with a hatchet of that size and cutting edge?"
A. (Cheever) "With a handle . . . twelve to fourteen inches long, they could."

In his cross-examination, Adams picked up on a statement by Cheever that the cutting edge of the hatchet could not have exceeded 3½ inches.

Q. (Adams) "Could not an instrument [with a cutting edge] less than 3½ inches get in?"
A. (Cheever) "Yes, sir."
Q. (Adams) "Don't you think upon consideration that a hatchet head less than 3½ inches in width, say three inches, might have been used?"
A. (Cheever) "Yes, sir."
Q. (Adams) "Possibly 2¾ inches?"
A. (Cheever) "Possibly, but I think not."

SOME THINGS TO THINK ABOUT
Either accidentally or by design, the prosecution was vague as to what Lizzie did with the handleless hatchet after the murders. The implication was that she washed the hatchet, deliberately broke the handle, rubbed the hatchet head in ashes and hid it in the box in the cellar. But neither Knowlton nor anyone else suggested why she broke it or why she rubbed it in ashes. Above all, one might ask, why didn't

Lizzie leave the hatchet at the scene of the crime? Was there something about the hatchet or the missing handle that tied it to her? (In case you're thinking of fingerprints, try again; they weren't used for crime detection in the United States until well after 1900.)

Mullaly's testimony struck at the heart of the prosecution's theory. It would make no sense for Lizzie to break the handle and then put it back in the box with the hatchet head. If Mullaly was mistaken, and he may well have been, what did Lizzie do with the missing handle? The prosecution didn't even speculate on that.

The crucial question, of course, was whether the handleless hatchet was the murder weapon. Professor Wood's failure to find any blood on it argued against its use for that purpose. Wood did say, though, that it could have been cleaned readily, except for the slot in the edge of the head. Incidentally, what was the "white dust" he found in the slot and how long had it been there?

Dr. Draper's demonstration showing that the handleless hatchet, and only that hatchet, fit the deep wound in Andrew's skull was the strongest evidence that it was the murder weapon. However, the impact of his testimony was considerably diminished when Dr. Cheever said the cutting edge could have been less than 3½ inches. Earlier, at the preliminary hearing, Dr. Dolan said that another hatchet with a cutting edge of 4½ inches could have been the murder weapon.

Regardless of what the experts had to say, the public seems never to have accepted the handleless hatchet as the murder weapon. Over the years several other hatchets have turned up, causing at least a temporary sensation. One was found in 1929 when the Borden barn was torn down. It turned out to be a cooper's hammer rather than a hatchet. Another showed up twenty years later when the house was being remodeled. The suspicious stains on this hatchet proved not to be blood but aluminum paint, which didn't exist in the 1890s.

The only plausible alternative to the handleless hatchet was found by a boy on a neighbor's roof in June of 1893, while Lizzie's trial was in progress. We'll have more to say about that hatchet in Chapter 15. Ironically, it seems never to have been tested for blood and no one seems to have the faintest idea where it is today.

The Naked Lady and the Bloodstained Coat

Over the years, a great many people have suggested how Lizzie Borden might have avoided getting blood on her person or clothes while slaughtering her father and stepmother. One risque idea is that Lizzie stripped naked before picking up the hatchet. This theory was popularized in the movie *The Legend of Lizzie Borden*, starring Elizabeth Montgomery.

Certainly if Lizzie stripped to the buff, she would not have gotten blood on her clothing. However, that solves only half of the problem; why did no one see any blood on her person? Remember, Lizzie had at most fifteen minutes (10:55 A.M.--11:10 A.M.) to kill her father and conceal the evidence. She couldn't walk into a shower to wash off the blood; the Borden house didn't even have a bathtub. Lizzie would have had to wash off the blood bit by bit at a cold water faucet. To do that, carefully clean her hair, dispose of the washcloth and towel used, and get dressed again would have taken more than fifteen minutes all by itself. Besides, several witnesses testified that her hair was not even disarranged, let alone wet (there was no such thing as an electric hairdrier in 1892!)

An alternative explanation of how Lizzie avoided bloodstains involves Andrew Borden's Prince Albert coat, a long frock coat which he had worn downtown that morning. When the murder scene was investigated, that coat was found wedged under his head against the sofa. It has been suggested that Lizzie wore the coat while she wielded the hatchet. Put on backwards, it might have protected her clothing (but not her person) from blood. So far, so good; now comes the hard part. How do you suppose Lizzie got the coat back under Andrew's head without getting herself soaked with blood?

The most bizarre explanation of all was suggested, in an offhand way, by Hosea Knowlton in his closing argument. He cited the testimony of Officer Philip Harrington, who reported seeing a large amount of burnt paper in the kitchen stove. Knowlton speculated:

"I can think, in my coarse masculine way, of many ways in which the person, the upper part of the person, could have been protected, easily protected, while [the murders] took place. Paper would have done it. Burnt paper was found and no attempt was made to explain it."

What in the world did Knowlton have in mind? Was he implying that Lizzie put a paper bag over her head before swinging the hatchet! Did she maybe take off her clothes and hang a paper window shade around her neck to absorb the blood? Or did Lizzie fashion a dress out of newspapers to wear for this special occasion?

Let's face it. If Lizzie committed the murders, she disposed of the dress she wore in the simple, obvious way; she hid it. Perhaps this was the dress she burned a few days later. Then again, maybe the remnants of a bloodstained dress will show up some day at 92 Second Street.

Chapter 7
THE TRIAL
Could Someone Else
Have Done It?

The task of the defense at the Borden trial was to convince the jury that there was reasonable doubt of Lizzie's guilt. To do that, they had to offer a plausible explanation as to how someone else could have committed the murders. Lizzie made their task more difficult by eliminating the two most likely suspects. She told Assistant Marshal Fleet that John Morse must be innocent because he left the Borden house that morning while both Andrew and Abby were alive and didn't return until after they were dead. Lizzie went on to exonerate Bridget Sullivan because she was napping upstairs when Andrew was killed.

The only suspect Lizzie could come up with was a man who had come to the front door a couple of weeks before the crime. She overheard a heated discussion between him and her father about renting a store in a building that Andrew Borden owned. At the trial, the defense produced several witnesses who talked about "mysterious strangers" they had seen in the vicinity of the Borden house before the murders. The most convincing testimony here was given by Dr. Benjamin Handy, a former neighbor of the Bordens now living on "the Hill" at Rock Street.

The prosecution ridiculed the idea of an intruder coming in off the street to commit the murders. First off, they insisted that he couldn't have gotten into the Borden house unobserved; as District Attorney Knowlton put it, "Everything was locked up. It was the most zealously guarded house I ever heard of." More important, assuming a time lapse between the murders, how could the intruder have escaped observation by Lizzie, Bridget or either of the murder victims for one to two hours? Finally, no one in the neighborhood saw a hatchet-carrying, bloodstained stranger leaving the Borden house after the murders.

In this chapter, we'll look at the testimony offered at the trial by the defense and the prosecution as to whether or not Lizzie Borden had "exclusive opportunity" to commit the murders.

Stranger(s) at the Borden House

At the inquest, Lizzie described a loud, angry confrontation her father had with a man who wanted to rent a store in the A. J. Borden building.

Q. (Knowlton) "Tell all you saw and heard."
A. (Lizzie Borden) "I did not see anything. I heard the bell ring and father went to the door and let him in. I heard the man say, 'I would like to have that store.' Father said, 'I am not willing to let your business go in there.' And the man said, 'I thought with your reputation for liking money, you would let your store for anything.' Father said, 'You are mistaken.' Then they talked for a while and then their voices were louder and I heard father order him out."

The police made no effort whatsoever to locate or identify this man. There is some reason to believe that he may have shown up again at 92 Second Street on the morning of the murders. Assistant Marshal Fleet testified at the trial that Lizzie told him a man came to the front door at about 9 A.M. She heard him talking to her father about a store. According to Lizzie, the stranger spoke with an English accent.

Dr. Handy, a defense witness at the trial, described a man behaving strangely near the Borden house on the morning of the murders.

Figure 7.1 Second Street looking south, 1892

Second Street Looking South in 1892
From *Lizzie Borden Quarterly*, p. 5

Q. (Jennings) "Did you go by [the Borden house] on the morning of the murders?"

A. (Handy) "Yes, sir."

Q. (Jennings) "What time?"

A. (Handy) "About 10:30."

Q. (Jennings) "Well, tell us what took place."

A. (Handy) "I saw a medium sized young man of very pale complexion with his eyes fixed upon the sidewalk, passing slowly toward the south."

Q. (Jennings) "What, if anything, attracted your attention to him?"

A. (Handy) "In the first place, he was a very pale individual, paler than common."

Q. (Jennings) "Anything else?"

A. (Handy) " . . . I cannot describe very well what he [was doing], but he was acting strangely."

Q. (Jennings) "In consequence of his appearance, did you do anything?"

A. (Handy) "I turned in my carriage to watch him as I drove by."

Q. (Jennings) "Did you ever see him before?"

A. (Handy) "I have a faint idea that I had seen him on Second Street some days before."

Q. (Jennings) "Can you describe the man more fully?"

A. (Handy) "He was well dressed in a light suit, collar and necktie."

On cross-examination, Dr. Handy expanded on his description.

Q. (Knowlton) "Won't you describe more particularly what you meant when you said he was acting strangely?"

A. (Handy) "I can't put it into words, sir. *He was acting differently than I ever saw any individual on the street in my life.* He seemed to be agitated . . . "

Q. (Knowlton) "In what way did he show he was mentally agitated?"

A. (Handy) "The intense expression on his face and his not observing anything that was about him . . . His eyes were fixed upon the ground."

Q. (Knowlton) "He didn't appear to be intoxicated at all?"

A. (Handy) "No, sir."

SOMETHING TO THINK ABOUT
The police, believing Lizzie to be guilty, never took seriously the
"mysterious stranger" she talked about. Dr. Handy's "wild-eyed man,
as he was referred to by the press, was another matter altogether.
Anyone who could make such a profound impression on a trained
observer such as a physician has to be taken seriously. The police
searched for him but were never able to find anyone who came close
to fitting Handy's description.

Doors, Locked and Unlocked

There were three doors which, in principle at least, could have been used by an intruder to enter the Borden house before the murders. One of these was the cellar door, at the back of the house. This could be fastened from the inside by a bolt which slid horizontally into an open cylinder attached to the door casing. With the bolt in place, there was no way to open the door from the outside.

Bridget testified that she bolted the cellar door two days before the murders, after hanging the laundry outside to dry, and that it stayed bolted.

> Q. (Moody) Did you notice any change in that door down to and after the time of the deaths of Mr. and Mrs. Borden?"
>
> A. (Bridget Sullivan) "No, sir, I did not."

Since Bridget was the only person who ordinarily used the cellar door, she would most likely make sure it was bolted. Moreover, her account was confirmed by George Allen, the first policeman to enter the Borden house after the murders. He testified that the cellar door was bolted on the inside when he got there. It's a safe bet that no one entered or left the Borden house on the morning of the murders through the cellar door. Indeed, Governor Robinson, in his final argument to the jury, agreed with the prosecution on that point.

A more plausible entrance for an intruder would be the front door, leading out to Second Street. Here there were three fastenings. One was a spring lock, opened from the outside by a key, from the inside by turning a lever. Then there was a bolt similar to the one on the cellar door. Finally, there was an ordinary mortise lock, in which a metal plug slides in and out of an opening in the door casing. This required a key to be unlocked from either the outside or inside.

According to Emma Borden, the bolt and the mortise lock were used only at night. In the morning, either Emma or Lizzie unlocked these two fastenings, leaving only the spring lock to secure the front door. According to John Morse, the spring lock was defective; it wouldn't "catch" unless you slammed the door hard. This was confirmed by the testimony of Jerome Borden, a business associate and relative of Andrew Borden.

All this suggests an intruder could have entered the Borden house through the front door, assuming he had only to get past the spring lock. However, it appears that, contrary to custom, all three of the front door fastenings were locked on the morning of the murders. When Andrew Borden returned from downtown at about 10:45 A.M., he couldn't get into the house, even though he had a key to the spring lock. Andrew expressed his displeasure by yelling for assistance; Bridget answered his call.

Q. (Moody) "When you got to the front door, what did you find the conditions of the locks [to be]?"

A. (Bridget Sullivan) "I went to open it, [opened] the spring lock as usual and found the door was [still] locked. I unbolted it and found that [the mortise lock] was locked with a key."

Q. (Moody) "What did you do with reference to the [mortise] lock?"

A. (Bridget Sullivan) "I unlocked it [with a key]. As I unlocked it, I said, 'Oh pshaw', and Miss Lizzie laughed upstairs."

Legend has it that Bridget said something stronger than "pshaw", most likely "pshit", although she vigorously denied it. At any rate, Lizzie found the whole incident to be hilarious. Andrew Borden, on the other hand, was not amused.

The most likely entrance for an intruder was the kitchen, or side door, facing Mrs. Churchill's house. Here there was a wooden door which everyone agreed was open all the time on the morning of the murders. Outside that was a screen door which could be fastened to the casing by a simple hook and eye.

The diagram on p.109 shows the status of the screen door at various times on the morning of the murders. Notice that prior to about nine o'clock, the door was looked except for a few brief intervals when it would have been virtually impossible for an intruder to have entered. After that, the situation changed considerably. Between nine and nine thirty, the screen door was unhooked about half the time; after nine thirty, it was unhooked most of the time.

Figure 7.2 Side entrance to the Borden house

Side entrance, 92nd Street
Forty Whacks

Status of Kitchen Screen Door, Aug. 4, 1892

Time	Action	Witness
6:30 AM	Bridget unhooked door to bring in milk; hooked door when she came back	Bridget Sullivan
7:00 AM	Andrew Borden unhooked door to empty slop pail; probably hooked it when he returned	Bridget Sullivan
9:00 AM	Andrew unhooked door to let John Morse out; hooked it when he returned	John Morse
9:10 AM	Bridget unhooked door to enter yard to vomit; probably hooked it when she returned 15 minutes later	Bridget Sullivan
9:30 AM	Bridget unhooked door to wash	Bridget Sullivan

	windows outside	
10:30 AM	Bridget hooked door when she came inside to wash windows	Bridget Sullivan
10:55 AM	Lizzie unhooked door to go to barn; found door open when she returned	Lizzie Borden (at inquest)

SOME THINGS TO THINK ABOUT

It's curious, to say the least, that the front door was triple locked on the morning of August 4. Bridget testified that, as far as she knew, Andrew Borden had never been locked out of the house before. District Attorney Knowlton, in his closing argument, suggested that Lizzie locked the door to ensure privacy while she chopped up her stepmother. Governor Robinson, on the other hand, thought it was the "mysterious intruder" who triple locked the front door after he entered the house. To put it mildly, that doesn't make a great deal of sense.

All this is interesting but basically irrelevant, since the kitchen door was open most of the time after 9:30. In principle at least, an intruder could have entered through that door, committed the murders, and left the same way.

Notice that the intruder could have entered the house during either of two time periods. Assuming a time lapse between the murders, he would have had to come in between 9:30 and 10:30 A.M. while Bridget was washing windows outside and Lizzie was engaged in various activities within the house. To do that undetected would have been difficult. If, on the other hand, you agree with Melvin Adams that there was no time lapse (Chapter 4), the intruder's task would have been much simpler. He could enter shortly before 11 A.M., while Lizzie was in the barn loft and Bridget was napping in her room. After committing both murders in rapid succession, he could then leave through the same door he entered.

The Time Lapse: Real or Imaginary?

At the trial, as at the preliminary hearing, the prosecution tried hard to prove that Abby Borden was murdered considerably earlier (1 - 2 hours) than her husband. In this way, they hoped to convince the jury, once and for all, that an intruder could not have come in off the street to commit the murders.

A total of nine prosecution witnesses testified about time of death evidence. They included three policemen (Deputy Sheriff Wixon, Assistant Marshal Fleet, Officer Doherty) all of whom emphasized the difference in appearance of the blood surrounding the two bodies. In Andrew's case, the blood was said to be "bright", "thin" and "fresh". Abby's blood was "dark", "thick" or "hard" (whatever that means). The implication was that, since Mrs. Borden's blood was coagulated to a greater extent than her husband's, she must have died earlier.

Two bystanders (George Pettee, Albert Dedrick) whose examination of the bodies was their sole connection with the case, also testified to the priority of Abby's death. Pettee was a lifelong friend of Andrew Borden which perhaps explains why Dr. Bowen gave him a tour of the slaughter-house, lifting off the sheets that covered the bodies. Pettee said he could detect "movement" in Andrew's blood, while Abby's blood was stationary. Dedrick was a physician who wandered into the Borden house at 2 P.M., three hours after Andrew's murder. He concluded, for no obvious reason, that Abby died "several hours" before Andrew.

Four expert medical witnesses (Medical Examiner Dolan, Professor Wood, Dr. Draper, Dr. Cheever) testified as to the time of death. Dr. Dolan was a key witness; he was the only one of the four who examined the bodies on the day of the murders, at about noon. Moreover, he conducted two autopsies on the victims, the first on August 4, the other a week later on August 11.

Dr. Dolan testified at the trial that he believed Mrs. Borden died before her husband; he estimated a time lapse of about 1½ hours. This conclusion was based on three observations. The first of these was the difference in coagulation of the blood, referred to previously. Then there was the difference in contents of the victims' intestines. Mrs. Borden had undigested food in the upper part of her intestines; her husband did not. This implied that digestion was still going on when Abby Borden died; in Andrew's case it had been completed.

Finally, and most important from Dolan's point of view, was the difference in temperature between the two bodies:

Q. (Knowlton) "Now turning to the body of Mrs. Borden, did you make any observations as to the bodily heat?"
A. (Dolan) "Yes, sir."
Q. (Knowlton) "What was the result?"

A. (Dolan) "I felt the body with my hand and it was much colder than that of Mr. Borden."

You may recall that Melvin Adams tore into Dr. Dolan's testimony at the preliminary hearing; he did it again at the trial. Adams first established an inconsistency in Dolan's testimony.

Q. (Adams) "Well, didn't you say [at the preliminary hearing] that in your opinion Mrs. Borden died about an hour and a half before you saw her?"
A. (Dolan) "I don't know whether I said it that way or whether I said an hour and a half before Mr. Borden." [Actually, he said it both ways at different times!]
Q. (Adams) "And you saw her in the vicinity of 12 o'clock?"
A. (Dolan) "Yes, sir."
Q. (Adams) "So the opinion which you formed then was that she died somewhere from half past ten to eleven o'clock?"
A. (Dolan) "According to that statement, yes, sir."

Adams went on to dispute the evidence upon which Dr. Dolan based his present opinion of a significant time lapse between the murders.

Q. (Adams) "How soon does blood that is separated from the body begin to coagulate?"
A. (Dolan) "Various authors differ on that. The time is generally put down from three to ten minutes."

[This author has found that when he cuts himself shaving, the bleeding stops, due to coagulation, after about five minutes. Of course, I don't use a hatchet.]

Q. (Adams) "After fifteen minutes, you wouldn't dare to express any opinion as to . . . the time that the person had been dead, based upon the appearance of the blood?"
A. (Dolan) "Solely, no, sir."
Q. (Adams) "Was there some other factor, the factor of digestion, that came into your opinion?"
A. (Dolan) "Yes, sir."

Q. (Adams) "Assuming that one has been more ill than the other, would it make any difference in the digestion?"
A. (Dolan) "It would, yes, sir."
Q. (Adams) "So that you have nothing left but the temperature?"
A. (Dolan) "Yes, sir."
Q. (Adams) "And that is tested simply by touch?"
A. (Dolan) "Yes, sir."

As Dr. Dolan left the witness stand he must have breathed a sigh of relief. Never again would he have to go through the ordeal of cross-examination by Melvin Adams.

Professor Wood examined the victims' stomachs, sent him by Dr. Dolan on August 4. He testified that Mrs. Borden's stomach contained a considerable amount of solid food, while her husband's was nearly empty. On this basis he concluded that digestion had been going on for about 2-3 hours in Abby's case, 3½-4½ hours in Andrew's.

Q. (Knowlton) "Assuming that the two persons whose stomachs you examined ate breakfast at the same time and partook of the same breakfast substantially, what difference in the time of their deaths would be indicated, assuming the digestion to have gone on normally?"
A. (Wood) "Assuming the digestion to have gone on naturally in both cases, the difference would be somewhere in the neighborhood of an hour and a half, more or less."

Adams, on cross-examination, got Wood to agree that a stomach upset could affect the time required for digestion. Nevertheless, Wood repeated his belief that Abby Borden probably died between 9 and 10 A.M., one to two hours before Andrew.

The two remaining medical witnesses, Dr. Draper and Dr. Cheever, based their opinions about times of death on the testimony they heard, as spectators at the trial, from Professor Wood and Dr. Dolan. Both doctors concluded that Abby Borden died one to two hours before Andrew. The way they reached that conclusion is illustrated in Cheever's testimony.

Q. (Knowlton) "Will you state what [evidence] you have listened to that seemed to be significant [with regards to the priority and time of death]?"

A.   (Cheever) "The fact that Mrs. Borden's body was sensibly cooler than Mr. Borden's, the fact that the blood was coagulated to a certain degree . . . about the person of Mrs. Borden and was . . . dripping from the wounds of Mr. Borden, and the fact that in Mrs. Borden's case digestion was still going on and that in Mr. Borden's case it was apparently completed. All these things taken together convinced me that Mrs. Borden died first and probably by a considerable interval."

Q.   (Knowlton) "What interval . . . ?"

A.   (Cheever) "The minimum I should place at about an hour; the maximum . . . two hours."

SOME THINGS TO THINK ABOUT

The sheer volume of testimony to the effect that Mrs. Borden died before her husband is impressive. Most convincing are the opinions of Drs. Wood, Draper and Cheever. All of them were acknowledged experts in forensic studies (to the extent that there was such a thing as a forensic expert a century ago!)

Yet doubts remain; a couple of them were raised by Adams in his cross-examination of Medical Examiner Dolan. What significance, if any, does the difference in appearance of the blood have? How reliable is a difference in body temperature measured by touch? Notice also, from Knowlton's question to Wood (p. 113) all the assumptions that have to be made to interpret the digestion evidence (they ate the same amount . . . of the same food . . . at the same time . . . that digestion occurred naturally . . .).

The Invisible Murderer

If a stranger came in off the street to murder Andrew and Abby Borden, he must have escaped undetected afterwards. That wouldn't have been easy; his bloodstained clothing alone would have drawn attention, to say nothing of a bloody hatchet. To drive this point home, the prosecution put on the stand a motley group of people all of whom testified they had seen no such person leaving the Borden house that morning at the crucial time, i.e., 11:00-11:15. These witnesses included a young woman (Lucy Collet), who was housesitting in the neighborhood. The impact of her testimony was diminished when she became confused as to whether she arrived on the scene at quarter of eleven or quarter past eleven. Then there was a neighbor (Mrs. Aruba Kirby), who looked out of her kitchen window at about 11:30 and didn't see any suspicious person fleeing the Borden home. That's hardly surprising; by 11:30 most of the traffic was entering 92 Second Street, not leaving it.

Three other witnesses were equally unconvincing. A workman, Joseph Desrosiers, insisted that he heard about the murders at 10 A.M., while Andrew Borden was making his rounds in downtown Fall River. Another workman who testified that he didn't see any mysterious stranger, Patrick McGowan, admitted he left the neighborhood at 10:30 A.M. Finally there was Thomas Bowles, an employee of Mrs. Churchill, who was washing a carriage sometime that morning, maybe around 11 A.M.; he couldn't be sure.

The only witness in the group who had his times straight was a stonecutter, John Denny. He arrived in Crowe's yard, diagonally across from the Borden house, at 6:45 A.M. and worked steadily until 11:45, when someone told him about the murders.

Q. (Moody) "[Between 10:45 and 11:45], did you see anyone come from the Borden premises and go out into Third Street?"
A. (Denny) "No, sir."
Q. (Moody) "Had you seen anyone taking the contrary course?"
A. (Denny) "No, sir."

There is a fatal flaw in the testimony of all of these witnesses, including that of John Denny. Consider the sketch on the next page. It shows the locations of various individual (letters B to M) that morning relative to the Borden house. Notice that none of them were in a position to see what was going on at 92 Second Street. Their vision was blocked by fences, buildings or trees. If a bloodstained stranger carrying a hatchet had run past John Denny, for example, he would have been seen. If, however, he had walked through the open kitchen door and out onto Second Street, he would have been invisible to all these witnesses.

Figure 7.3 Diagram showing location of witnesses
(See next page)

The Borden Neighborhood

(B) Bowles (C) Collet (Dn) Denny (Ds) Desrosiers (K) Kirby (M) McGowan
(1) Borden House (2) Borden barn (3) Kitchen entrance to Borden hosue (4)
Churchill house (5) Dr. Bowen's house (6) Dr. Chagnon's house (7)
Kelly house (8) Crowe house and yard (9) Pear orchard

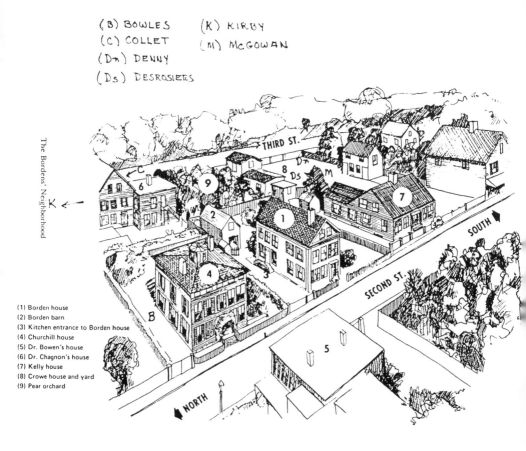

(1) Borden house
(2) Borden barn
(3) Kitchen entrance to Borden house
(4) Churchill house
(5) Dr. Bowen's house
(6) Dr. Chagnon's house
(7) Kelly house
(8) Crowe house and yard
(9) Pear orchard

Constructed from *Sullivan*, p. 11

SOMETHING TO THINK ABOUT
Looking at Figure 7.3, it would seem that there were three people ideally situated to see what was going on at 92 Second Street that morning. These were the women who were the immediate neighbors of the Bordens: Mrs. Churchill to the north, Mrs. Kelly to the south, and Mrs. Bowen across the street. They were all witnesses at the trial. Why didn't the prosecution ask them if they saw a mysterious stranger fleeing the Borden house between 11:00 and 11:15 A.M.?

These ladies weren't interrogated on this point for good reason. Mrs. Churchill went "downstreet" to buy meat for dinner shortly before 11 A.M. She didn't return until after Andrew's murder had been discovered. Mrs. Kelly was on her way to a dentist's appointment when she met Andrew on the street at about 10:45 A.M. When she got home an hour later, the action was all over. Mrs. Bowen couldn't see the Borden house that morning because the shutters were closed on her windows facing Second Street and the Borden house.

It would seem that the murderous intruder, if indeed there was one, picked exactly the right time to finish the job. Neither the neighbors nor the people who lived at 92 Second Street were in a position to witness his departure. (Lizzie was in the barn, Bridget on the third floor). How lucky can you get?

Andrew Borden's Small White Package

Three people saw Andrew Borden return to 92 Second Street from downtown Fall River on the morning of the murders. The first of these was his next door neighbor, Mrs. Kelly. On her way to a dental appointment, she saw Andrew fumbling with the front door lock, trying to enter the house. It was Bridget Sullivan who unlocked the door to let him in. The last person to see Andrew on that fateful morning was Lizzie Borden. According to her inquest testimony, she talked to him for several minutes before she went out to the barn at about 10:55 A.M.

Curiously, all three of these women said that when Andrew Borden returned that morning, he carried a package in his hand. Lizzie told Officer Harrington that her father, "had a small package in his hand when he came home." Bridget Sullivan testified that when Mr. Borden cam home, "he had a white package in his hand." Mrs. Kelly said that Andrew carried a "*small white* package in his hand." She went on to estimate the dimensions; the package was, "about five inches square and about an inch thick."

In the century that has passed since the murders, there has been a great deal of speculation as to what was in the package. Depending upon how you count them, there have been two or three popular theories. One assumes that the package contained a broken lock. As mentioned in Chapter 4, two carpenters testified that they saw Andrew Borden pick up a broken, discarded, worthless lock from the floor of the A. J. Borden building in downtown Fall River. This theory assumes that Andrew stopped at the post office on the way home to buy a white envelope into which he put this valuable lock, presumably to protect it from dust, humidity and pickpockets.

Other people have suggested that the package contained a legal document which precipitated the murders. Depending upon who is telling the story, the document was either a will, leaving most of his fortune to his beloved wife Abby and cutting off Lizzie and Emma with a mere pittance, or a deed made out to Abby for a farm in Swansea where Lizzie had spent many happy days as a child.

It's difficult to say which of these theories is the most ridiculous. The first one assumes Andrew Borden brought the lock home, which may or may not be true; no one ever reported its presence in the house after the murders. Beyond that, why would Andrew have gone to the expense of buying an envelope to protect the worthless lock instead of putting it into the pocket of his Prince Albert coat? Andrew Borden was called many things in his time but no one ever called him a spendthrift.

The legal document theory is equally implausible. For starters, there is no reason to believe that Andrew Borden ever drew up a will or deed of the type described; close associates of Andrew denied that he had done so. Then there is a difficulty with the size of the package: 5 inches x 5 inches x 1 inch. Wills and deeds come in two shapes. Today they are usually printed on a few sheets of 8 ½ by 11 paper. A century ago they were often inscribed on cylindrical scrolls. In either case it would have been senseless and virtually impossible to squash them into the small white package Mrs. Kelly described.

So what was in the package? We'll never know, but let me hazard a guess. It could well have been a small book that Andrew Borden ordered through the mail and picked up at the post office. There is some evidence for this. Bridget Sullivan said that when Mr. Borden came home, "He took a chair and sat down near the window with a book or paper in his hand." At the trial Dr. Dolan testified that near the head of the sofa upon which Andrew Borden died, there was a table with books on it. These showed up in a sketch of the crime scene shown below; look on the table left of the sofa.

Figure 7.4 Crime scene: note books on the table

WHERE MR. BORDEN WAS MURDERED

From *Lizzie Borden Sourcebook*, p. 20

A hundred years ago small hard cover books were much more common than they are today. My library in New Hampshire contains several nineteenth century books of this type. The closest in size to the dimensions estimated by Mrs. Kelly is a collection of poems by Elizabeth Barrett Browning (5" x 6" x 1 1/4"). Somehow books of poetry don't fit the image of Andrew Borden, but who knows where his literary tastes lay?

Chapter 8
THE VERDICT

The trial of Lizzie Borden started on Monday, June 5, 1893, when the jury was selected. A little more than two weeks later, on Tuesday, June 20, that jury rendered its verdict. As you can see from the chronology below, most of that fortnight was spent by the prosecution in developing its case against Lizzie. The defense presented its story in about a day and a half.

CHRONOLOGY OF THE BORDEN TRIAL

Prosecution Case

Tuesday, June 6   Opening statement by William Moody

June 6-10   Testimony by prosecution witnesses, including John Morse, Bridget Sullivan, Dr. Bowen, Adelaide Churchill, Alice Russell; Officers Fleet, Harrington, Mullaly and Medley

Monday, June 12   Lizzie's inquest testimony excluded by the court

June 12-14   Prosecution witnesses including Dr. Dolan and the Harvard trio: Prof. Wood, Dr. Draper and Dr. Cheever

Thursday June 15   Prussic acid testimony excluded; prosecution rests

Defense Case

Thursday June 15   Opening statement by Andrew Jennings

June 15, 16   Testimony by defense witnesses, including Dr. Handy and Emma Borden

Friday, June 16   Defense rests

Final Statements

Monday, June 19   Closing arguments by Robinson, then Knowlton

Tuesday, June 20   Knowlton completes closing argument
                       Justice Dewey delivers charge to jury.
                       Jury reports its verdict

Testimony in the Borden trial was completed on Friday, June 16, 1893. The weekend that followed was, in a sense, the calm before the storm. Final arguments would be presented on Monday, followed by the charge to the jury and, finally, the verdict in "the trial of the century". Meanwhile, there was intense speculation as to what the verdict would be.

The New York Herald took a poll of judges, legal officials, trial lawyers and detectives. Their opinion was almost unanimous that Lizzie would be acquitted, even though many of them were not convinced she was innocent. The response of a Brooklyn lawyer was typical: "I don't see that the prosecution has made out any case at all. No jury in christendom can convict Miss Borden on the testimony put in by the Commonwealth of Massachusetts."

Another New York newspaper, the *Recorder*, assembled a panel of twelve distinguished citizens to judge Lizzie Borden. This "jury" included Edward Everett Hale, author of *The Man Without a Country*, an ardent feminist (Lucy Stone) and Samuel Gompers, founder of the American Federation of Labor (AFL). The panel's unanimous verdict was "not guilty".

Final Arguments

When Hosea Knowlton got up to address the jury on Monday afternoon, he must have felt a little like Bob Dole in the closing days of the 1996 campaign; his task was virtually hopeless. To his credit, Knowlton rose to the occasion. There was general agreement in the press that his closing argument was the capstone of a distinguished legal career.

Figure 8.1 Knowlton sums up

"Gentlemen, it is the saddest duty of my life."—(Dist.-Atty. Knowlton's plea for the Commonwealth.

From *Emery scrapbook*, p. 90

On occasion, Knowlton was eloquent, as when he described the victims: "That aged man, that aged woman, had gone by the noonday of their lives. They had borne the burden and heat of the day. They had accumulated a competency which they felt would carry them through the waning years of their lives, and . . . they expected to go down to the sunset of their days in quiet and happiness. But for that crime they would be enjoying the air of this day."

Throughout his closing argument, Knowlton stuck to the evidence, which he presented powerfully and logically. He was even tempered, fair, and almost convincing. The press reacted less favorably to Governor Robinson, calling his final argument "disappointing." He invariably appealed to the hearts of the jury members, not to their heads. At times, his argument was absurd, as when he tried to counter the prosecution's contention that Lizzie had exclusive opportunity to commit the murders:

"In the first place, they say she was in the house [that morning]. Well, that may look to you like a very wrong place for her to be in. But it is her own home. I suspect you have a kind of an impression that it would be a little better for her than it would be to be out traveling the streets. I don't know where I would want my daughter to be, than to say she was at home, attending to the ordinary vocations of life, as a dutiful member of the household."

Non sequiturs like this led columnist Joe Howard to comment sarcastically: "Down to the opening of Governor Robinson's [closing argument], the bets were 2 to 1 in favor of an acquittal; now they are 2 to 1 in favor of a disagreement." Keep in mind, though, that Robinson was talking to the jury, not to the press; there is reason to believe that the jury members related better to his remarks than to Knowlton's.

As you might suppose, Robinson and Knowlton differed in their interpretation of the evidence presented at the trial. With regards to the note that Abby allegedly received (Chapter 5), Robinson insisted that Bridget Sullivan's testimony proved the existence of such a note. Knowlton disputed this, claiming that Bridget simply repeated what Lizzie told her. Beyond that, Robinson attempted to explain why no one came forward to acknowledge authorship of the note.

"You will find men now living perhaps in this county who do not know the trial is going on . . . they are about their own business, do not consider it of any consequence. After a lawsuit is over, it very often happens that someone will come forward and say, 'Well, if I had known that question, I could have told you all about it.' Sometimes people don't want to get into the courtroom, women especially; they have a dread of all sorts of things. [Also], the note may have been a part of the scheme in regard to Mrs. Borden. It may have got there through foul means and with a criminal purpose."

Knowlton ridiculed that argument, saying, "My distinguished friend has had the hardihood to suggest that somebody may have written that note and not come forward to say so. Why, Mr. Foreman, do you believe there exists in Fall River anybody so lost to all sense of humanity . . . who would not have rushed forward and stated, 'I wrote that.' Ah, but my distinguished friend is pleased to suggest that it was part of the scheme of assassination. How? To write a note to get a woman away when he was going there to assassinate her?"

Curiously, although the absence of blood upon Lizzie (Chapter 6) was the strongest point in the defense case, Governor Robinson (Knowlton's "distinguished friend") referred to it only briefly in his summation:

"And the murders did not tell any tales on her either. There is no blood on her, and blood speaks out, although it is voiceless. It speaks out against the criminal. Not a spot on her from her hair to her feet, on dress or person anywhere. Think of it! Think of it for an instant!"

Wisely, District Attorney Knowlton got past this point as quickly as he could:

"How could she have avoided the spattering of her dress with blood if she was the author of these crimes? . . . I cannot answer [that question]. You cannot answer it. You are neither murderers nor women. You have neither the craft of the assassin nor the cunning and deftness of the female sex."

Sometimes it seemed as though Robinson and Knowlton were competing for the role of lead male chauvinist. According to Robinson, women had all sorts of imaginary fears; Knowlton described them as cunning and sly (above).

Robinson spent some time discussing (Chapter 7) how an intruder could have come in off the street to murder first Abby and then Andrew Borden.

"Now suppose the assassin came there and I have shown he could without question; the house was all open on the north side. Suppose Lizzie were upstairs . . . or downstairs in the cellar. He passed through. Where could he go? He could go upstairs into the [guest] room . . . It was easy enough for him to go up into that bed chamber and secrete himself, until he finds himself confronting Mrs. Borden . . . He is there for murder; not to murder her but to murder Mr. Borden. Probably he is somebody that she knew . . . someone that [she] could recognize and identify, and he must strike her down . . . And when he had done his work and Mr. Borden had come in, as he could hear him, he came down at the first opportunity."

Here again, Knowlton used his favorite weapon, ridicule.

"Never mind the impossibility of imagining a person who was so familiar with the habits of that family, who was so familiar with the interior of that house that morning, to have penetrated through the cordon of Bridget and Lizzie and pursued that poor woman up the stairs to her death, and then waited, weapon in hand, until the house was filled with people again that he might complete his work."

Later on, Knowlton cited another objection to an intruder being the murderer:

"That unknown assassin . . . never would have carried away the bloody weapon with which the thing was done. He never would have gone into the streets, armed . . . with the evidence that would convict him. It would have been left beside the body of his victim."

You will recall (Chapter 7) that several prosecution witnesses cited the difference in appearance of the blood of the victims as evidence for a time lapse between the murders. Significantly, Knowlton did not refer to this in his closing argument; neither did he cite Dr. Dolan's temperature observations. He relied entirely on Professor Wood's examination of the stomachs of the victims.

"[Wood] alone was able to determine accurately the time of their death, assuming that digestion went on normally within them, and he says that in all probability the time of her death preceded his by an hour and a half; it might possibly have been a half hour less, it might possibly have been a half hour more. There was no evidence of abnormal digestion; there was no evidence of irritants that would hasten or retard it in either case."

To the surprise of everyone and the chagrin of Melvin Adams, Robinson blithely conceded the time lapse, saying:

"Mrs. Borden had died earlier. The physicians . . . put it from an hour to an hour and a half earlier than (Mr. Borden] died. That is probably correct; at any rate no issue is made about it. So, if I may be permitted to state it, she would seem to have died between 9:45 and 10:15 A.M."

Knowlton concluded his passionate argument with a solemn appeal to the jurors to do their duty to God as well as the Commonwealth of Massachusetts.

"There is no strait so hard, there is no affliction so bitter that is not made light and easy by the consciousness that in time of trial you have done your duty and your whole duty. There is no applause of the world, there is no station of height, there is no seduction of fame that can compensate for the gnawings of an outraged conscience. Only he who hears the voice of his inner consciousness, it is the voice of God himself, saying to him, 'Well done, good and faithful servant,' can enter into the reward and lay hold of eternal life."

Robinson got to his point much more quickly than the others. "Gentlemen, with great weariness on your part, but with abundant patience and intelligence, you have listened to what I have had to offer. So far as you are concerned, it is the last word of the defendant to you. Take it; take care of her as you have and give us promptly your verdict *not guilty* that she may go home and be Lizzie Borden of Fall River in that bloodstained and wrecked house where she has passed her life so many years."

Charge to the Jury

In the early afternoon of Tuesday, June 20, 1893, District Attorney Knowlton completed his closing argument. After a short recess, court reconvened and Chief Justice Albert Mason asked Lizzie Borden if she had anything to say to the jury. Lizzie arose and said, "I am innocent. I leave it for my counsel to speak for me." Her simple statement was followed by the court's charge to the jury.

The charge was written and delivered by Justice Dewey; it reflected the views of all three judges. Columnist Joe Howard described it aptly.

"The judge's charge was remarkable; it was a plea for the innocent . . . . With matchless clearness, he set up the case for the prosecution point by point . . . and knocked it down . . . He continued to the end, throwing bombs of disheartenment into the ranks of the prosecution and causing smiles of joy to play about the lips of Lizzie's friends. I doubt if ever there was such a charge before."

Figure 8.2 Judge Dewey (for the defense!)

Judge Dewey Reading his Charge to the Jury.
From *Emery scrapbook*, p. 103

Unquestionably, Dewey's charge was strongly tilted in favor of the defense. Convinced of Lizzie's innocence, he apparently feared the jury might make a terrible mistake. Many of the points he made were entirely reasonable. He told the jurors they should not be influenced by the decisions in the preliminary and grand jury hearings, which went against the defendant. Again, Dewey cautioned the jurors not to draw any conclusions from Lizzie's failure to testify in her own defense. He went on to say: "Nor is the defendant called upon to offer any explanation of her neglect to testify. If she were required to explain, others might think the explanation insufficient. Then she would lose the protection of the statute."

Sometimes Dewey argued subtly in Lizzie's favor, as when he distinguished between two different kinds of expert testimony.

"It often happens that experts testify to what is in substance a matter of fact rather than of opinion. So, for instance, Professor Wood may say, 'There are in science tests of the presence of blood . . . I have applied those tests to supposed blood stains on a hatchet and I find no blood.'

This testimony may be regarded as a matter of fact. On the other hand, if Professor Wood shall be asked to testify as to the length of time between the deaths of Mr. and Mrs. Borden, from his examination of the contents of the stomachs, his testimony must perhaps be to some extent a matter of opinion, depending possibly on the health and vigor of the two persons and constitutional differences . . . Now his knowledge and skill may enable him to form an opinion upon the subject with greater or less correctness, but the question [here] is by its essential nature different from the other. If you should accept his testimony as correct and satisfactory on the first subject, it would not necessarily follow that you should on the second."

Justice Dewey expressed this argument judiciously; everything he said about expert testimony was true, and indeed his point was well taken. Notice, however, the bias in Lizzie's favor. The absence of blood on the hatchet that Lizzie allegedly used was a "fact", while the time lapse between the murders, which made it more likely that Lizzie committed them, was only an "opinion". Certainly Dewey could have chosen a more neutral example to make his point.

Early on, Justice Dewey told the jury that Massachusetts law prevented a judge, in charging a jury, "from expressing any opinion as to the credibility of witnesses on the strength of evidence." He proceeded to violate this principle himself on more than one occasion. Consider, for example, what he had to say about Mrs. Gifford's statement that Lizzie referred to her stepmother as a "mean old thing".

"You must not separate Mrs. Gifford's testimony from all the rest, but consider also the evidence as to how they lived in the family, whether they went to church together, sat together, returned together; in a word the general tenor of their lives. You will particularly recall the testimony of Bridget Sullivan and of the defendant's sister, Emma, bearing on this subject." Dewey's clear implication was that Mrs. Gifford's testimony shouldn't be given much weight because it contradicted all the other evidence. That was hardly the case.

Then there was the matter of the note that Abby allegedly received on the morning of the murders. Dewey started by making a valid point that Robinson should have made but didn't.

" The defendant had time to think of it; she was not compelled to make that statement without any opportunity for reflection . . . She must naturally anticipate, if she knew the facts, that the question at no remote period would be asked where Mrs. Borden was . . . What motive had she to invent a story like this? Would it not have answered every purpose to have her say . . . simply that her stepmother had gone out on an errand? What motive had she to take upon herself the responsibility of [referring] to a letter or note received . . . which she might afterwards find it difficult to explain?"

Dewey proceeded to elaborate on a statement made by Robinson in his closing argument.

"But it is said that no letter was found . . . Might it not have been a part of the plan or scheme of [the assassin] by such a document or paper to withdraw Mrs. Borden from the house? If he afterwards came in there, came upon her, killed her, might he not have found the letter or note with her? Might he not have a reasonable and natural wish to remove that as one possible link in tracing himself?"

It's not an exaggeration to say that Justice Dewey made a stronger case for Lizzie's innocence than did her own counsel, Governor Robinson. Unfortunately, that's not what judges are supposed to do.

Guilty or not Guilty?

At 3:24 P. M. on Tuesday, June 20, 1893, the Borden jurors went out of the courtroom to consider their verdict. Justices Dewey and Blodgett went for a walk, spectators drifted away, and counsel moved in and out. Someone brought Lizzie Borden a bouquet of flowers. As she opened it, Lizzie smiled and her eyes grew moist, belying once again the myth that she was cold and heartless. Twice at the trial she had wept, once when the court had refused to admit her inquest testimony, again when Andrew Jennings opened for the defense.

What was going through Lizzie's mind as she waited for the verdict? Perhaps there was relief that the long ordeal was finally ending. Yet she had no way of knowing how long the wait would be; it could be minutes or hours or days. Worst of all would be a "hung jury", which some legal authorities predicted. In that case, Lizzie might well have to go through it all over again.

What happened next was described dramatically by a nameless reporter for the *Providence Journal*.

"An hour passed and the hands on the clock pointed to half past four. There was a stir in the corridor without. Someone whispered to the prisoner. The awful moment had arrived, the moment when the jury were to file into the courtroom and pass their verdict upon her. It was then that

Lizzie Borden faltered, and her form shook. Her face was a livid purple and her lips were tightly compressed."

As the jurors came in, at 4:32 P. M., they glanced at Lizzie. Chief Justice Mason went through the formalities, using the archaic language of another century: "Lizzie Andrew Borden, hold up your right hand. Mr. Foreman, look upon the prisoner; prisoner look upon the foreman. What say you?" Foreman Richards interrupted, almost shouting:

"NOT GUILTY"

Lizzie collapsed into her chair, grasped the rail in front of her (see sketch), then covered her face with her hands and broke into tears. Her sister tried to reach her, but poor Emma, ineffectual as usual, was swallowed up by the crowd. It was Governor Robinson who got to Lizzie, raising her up to press his face against hers. Andrew Jennings showed emotion in public for the first time in his life, saying "Thank God. Oh, thank God."

Figure 8.3 Lizzie reacts to the verdict

"Not Guilty," said the Foreman,
and the Prisoner's face dropped into the her hands
on the rail of the dock.
From *Lizzie Borden Sourcebook*, p. 311

Hosea Knowlton and William Moody took defeat graciously; both of them congratulated Lizzie and her counsel. When someone said to Knowlton, "Well, she's free." The district attorney smiled and replied, "That's all right." Assistant Marshal Fleet shook hands with Jennings and told him, "You have been very square [modern translation : fair] throughout the whole case. It only shows you that evidence must be strong." Marshal Hilliard, on the other hand, told reporters angrily that he would have nothing more to say about the case.

Several jurors talked freely about the verdict. The most forthcoming was the foreman, Charles Richards. He said the jury did not believe the prosecution made a strong enough case for conviction. Indeed Richards felt that when the prosecution rested the jury was unanimous for acquittal. That would seem to mean that the jury was little influenced, if at all, by the closing arguments and Justice Dewey's charge. Incidentally Richards said he was very favorably impressed by, "the clear and straightforward arguments of Robinson." Apparently, Knowlton's eloquence was wasted.

Other jurors filled in the details, noting that one of their group was so confident of a quick verdict that he made an appointment for early Tuesday evening, only a few hours after the jury got the case. Apparently they discussed the prosecution's case in the jury room for about 35 minutes before taking a single ballot. Several jurors wanted to report back immediately, but Richards persuaded them to wait another half hour to make it appear they had been reasonably deliberate. What they did during that period is unknown, but juror Augustus Swift made it clear that they never examined the handleless hatchet or other exhibits, let alone the grisly skulls of the victims.

The question remains as to whether the "not guilty" verdict was best interpreted as meaning "not proven" or "innocent". According to Juror Frank Cole, it was the latter. He said, "I am convinced that Miss Borden is wholly innocent. I believe I am agreed with the rest of the jury." The wife of juror Lemuel Wilbur put it more strongly:"I have read *The Boston Globe* during my husband's absence and if he had voted Miss Borden guilty, I should have been ashamed of him." (Now you know why juries are sequestered).

For the most part the "not guilty" verdict was popular. *The Boston Globe* polled, as they quaintly put it, "many persons, ministers, lawyers, women and others." About 90 percent of these people approved of the verdict, although many of them clearly doubted Lizzie's innocence. The remaining 10 percent were split between those who disagreed with the verdict and others who said, in effect, "Who the hell is Lizzie Borden?"

The same newspaper interviewed a series of people who had participated in or attended the trial from beginning to end. The responses of defense counsel were predictable. Governor Robinson said, a bit pompously, "Justice has been done and done promptly. An innocent woman has been freed." Andrew Jennings stated, "The verdict was the only possible one I could see upon the evidence. I do not understand how any honest man could have done anything else." Melvin Adams made an interesting observation: "The most gratifying thing about the verdict was the promptness with which it was rendered. It shows that each individual juror had fully considered the evidence and founded his opinion upon it."

Justice Dewey's comments were in accordance with his charge to the jury. He said, "I am perfectly satisfied with the verdict and, as far as I know, my opinion is that of my associates. We talked the matter over at considerable length and it was our opinion that no other verdict could justly be rendered. I was satisfied when I made my charge to the jury that the verdict would be "not guilty", although one cannot always tell what a jury may do." [So, just in case, . . . !]

Most of the reporters who covered the trial were satisfied with the verdict. Consider, for example, the comment of C. W. Taylor of *The New York World*, "It seems to me that was the only verdict that could have been rendered on the evidence . . . The government had no case." G. H. Blair of *The Boston Herald* used almost the same words, saying, "I don't think any other verdict could have been returned according to the evidence presented." Julian Ralph, the distinguished columnist of *The New York Sun* said, "From the day when I first gathered all the facts in the case, I have not believed she was guilty." A. E. Watress of the *New York Press* made a similar point, saying, "From the time Lubinsky testified to seeing Lizzie come from the barn to the house, all my doubt as to her guilt was removed."

There were, however, dissenters. J. J. Rosenfeld, who covered the trial for the *Providence Journal* said, "The verdict of the jury was not in accordance with my opinion, not in accordance with my expectations."

Then there were the editorial comments, which ranged from tongue in cheek:

Just think of those 12 jurors stepping up to the bar of the Parker House in New Bedford, with a two weeks thirst on them, and hearing

the sweet, familiar charge of the bartender, 'Well, gentlemen, what will it be?' It is safe to say there was no disagreement of the jury.
Pawtucket Times

to angry:

The police at Fall River, no matter how the trial had terminated, are on record as an ignorant, oath-ignoring set of men.
Haverhill Gazette

to philosophical:

Lizzie Borden will go out of court, if she is innocent, the victim of circumstances, suspicions and persecutions for which she can obtain neither redress nor remittance unless the actual murderer shall at some future time be found out. In that hope she must live. If she is guilty, the finding of the jury will only be a condemnation to living death. In any event, the case is as pitiable as it is mysterious, one of the horrors in actual life that outdoes in atrocity the inventions of the novelists.
Philadelphia Record

It is frequently alleged that Lizzie Borden was acquitted primarily because she was a woman. It's true that, in his final argument, Robinson played the gender card more than once. However, from the comments of the people most intimately involved in the case, particularly the jurors, there is no evidence that gender played a significant role in the verdict.

The truth is that Lizzie was acquitted for one simple reason: the prosecution did not or could not make out a strong case against her. It's interesting that a century later (September 1997) a jury of Stanford Law School alumni, faculty and students, in a mock Borden trial presided over by Justices Rehnquist and O'Connor of the United States Supreme Court, again found Lizzie not guilty for the same reason.

Lizzie After the Verdict

Where do you suppose Lizzie Borden went after her acquittal? No, not to Disney World, but you're close. She traveled to the World's Fair in Chicago, using a fictitious name to avoid reporters. She almost won a free trip to the fair in a popularity contest sponsored by the *Boston Journal*. Her second place finish entitled her to a trip to a Rhode Island amusement park, which she politely turned down on advice of counsel.

On a more substantive matter, in July of 1893, Lizzie and Emma bought a new house, in which Lizzie would live for the rest of her life. It was a fourteen room mansion on French Street in the fashionable "hill district" of Fall River. Curiously, the Borden sisters retained the house at 92 Second Street for twenty five years. Come to think of it, that place was probably difficult to unload. How would you like to buy a house where two fatal head injuries had recently occurred?

The Borden girls were involved in another property transfer in the summer of 1893. They graciously deeded all of Abby Borden's property, including her interest in Sarah Whitehead's house on Fourth Street, to Sarah and another sister of Abby, Mrs. Priscilla Fish of Hartford. Legally, Lizzie and Emma inherited all of Mrs. Borden's estate through their father, assuming (as most people did in 1893) that Abby died before Andrew. However, Sarah Whitehead and Mrs. Fish were convinced that Abby wanted all of her property to go to them. To avoid a threatened lawsuit, perhaps challenging the priority of the deaths of the two murder victims, Lizzie and Emma conceded the point. Considering the nasty things Mrs. Whitehead had to say about "those Borden girls", their gesture was a remarkably generous one.

In early September, Lizzie and Emma moved into the house on French Street shown below. The new house contained the luxuries they had been denied in the old one. For one thing, it had modern lighting and a telephone. It also had four bathrooms; at 92 Second Street there was no "indoor plumbing". For the first time in her life, Lizzie had a proper bathtub, an ornate one with legs. She had two bedrooms of her own, one for summer, the other for winter use. A glassed in porch at the back of the house made it possible for Lizzie (and Emma, if she wished) to feed the birds and squirrels unobserved.

Figure 8.4 Maplecroft
(See next page)

So far as her neighbors were concerned, Lizzie, in purchasing a new house, committed one faux pas after another. In the first place it would be unseemly for her to have started spending the inheritance she received

Maplecroft, date unknown, but while Lizzie was its occupant.
From *Lizzie Borden*, p. 282 (Brown)

so recently in such an unconventional manner. Then Lizzie committed the unpardonable sin of naming the house. She called it *Maplecroft* and actually had the letters cut into the top riser of the granite steps leading to the front door. Victoria Lincoln, a neighbor of Lizzie's, spoke for Fall River society when she said, "The naming of houses was not acceptable Fall River practice." To top it all off, Lizzie Andrew Borden started calling herself "Lizbeth A. Borden"; now she was "putting on airs".

To Fall River society, Lizzie's real crime was bringing notoriety to the city. Residents found that, wherever they went, as soon as they confessed to being from Fall River, people would ask them, "What ever happened to Lizzie Borden?" It got so bad that many natives, when asked where they came from, would simply say "Massachusetts" or even, may God forgive them, "Boston". In Fall River itself, the Borden case was not considered an appropriate topic for polite conversation. As one matron put it,"Lizzie Borden was tried, found innocent, and we really don't like to talk about it." This attitude persisted long after Lizzie was dead and gone. My first visit to Fall River came in the 1960s when I was a struggling assistant professor of chemistry at the University of Connecticut in Storrs. At the Fall River Historical Society, I talked to a delightful lady, Mrs. Florence Brigham, whose mother-in-law testified at the trial. Mrs. Brigham graciously answered my questions about the Borden case, but suggested that I might be more interested in the mills of Fall River, whose financial collapse in the 1920s brought an early taste of the Great Depression to the city. I refrained from telling her that to see abandoned textile mills I had only to go to Willimantic, Connecticut, a few miles from home. As for poverty, I could observe that without leaving my living roan.

In February of 1897 Lizzie Borden got her name in the papers again; as before, she was accused of committing a crime. The *Providence Journal* reported that a warrant had been issued for her arrest. It charged her with the larceny of two paintings from the Tilden-Thurber company of Providence.

The warrant was never served; the matter was settled out of court. Perhaps Lizzie paid for the paintings. Then again, the Tilden-Thurber company may have dropped the charges to avoid a damage suit. Many years later, a more bizarre explanation was put forward. Supposedly the store owners offered to drop the theft charges if Lizzie would admit that she did indeed murder her father and stepmother. Under pressure, Lizzie reportedly broke down and signed the "confession" shown below.

Figure 8.5 Lizzie's "confession"

This alleged confession, which surfaced in the 1950s, was shown conclusively to be a hoax. In particular, the signature was clearly a forgery; it had been traced from a copy of Lizzie's will.

The Tilden-Thurber incident apparently came as no surprise to some people in Fall River. Legend has it that "everyone" knew Lizzie Borden was a kleptomaniac. Supposedly this started long before the murders; Andrew Borden told store owners he would pay for any merchandise missing after Lizzie visited their shop. This amounted to setting up an unlimited charge account for Lizzie at every store in Fall River.

Somehow this doesn't sound like the Andrew Borden we've grown to know and detest.

Perhaps Lizzie was a shoplifter, but this story may have served a different purpose. As pointed out in Chapter 4, Fall River residents needed to believe that Lizzie was abnormal in some respect. If not insane, she must have been "queer", an adjective that could apply to shoplifters. Not that kleptomania leads to murder, you understand, but still . . . .

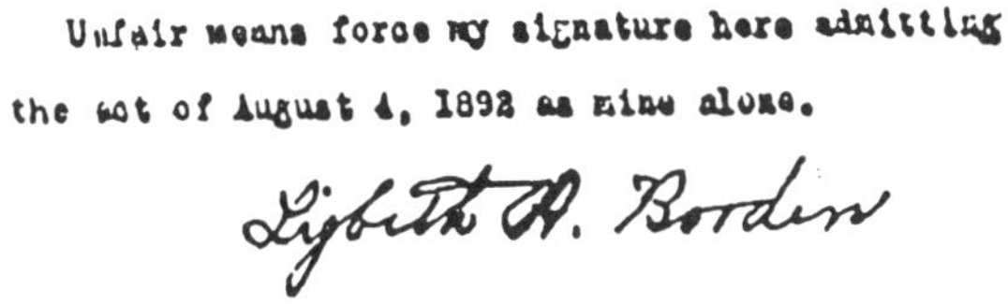

Unfair means force my signature here admitting the act of August 4, 1892 as mine alone.

Lizbeth A. Borden

From *Lizzie Borden, the Untold Story*, p. 256

Figure 8.6 Nance O'Neil

Alice Russell said once that, "Lizzie would like to have been a cultured girl." Perhaps that explains why she traveled so frequently to New York, Washington and, particularly, Boston. On her trips, Lizzie spent the day shopping and visiting museums; at night she went to the theater. She was particularly fond of tragedies. One evening in 1904 she attended a play in Boston starring the talented and beautiful tragedienne Nance O'Neil. Lizzie was so favorably impressed by Nance's performance that she went backstage to meet the actress. The upshot was that Miss O'Neil invited Lizzie to spend a few days at her home in a Boston suburb. Seldom in her life had anyone shown Lizzie Borden such kindness. No wonder she and Nance O'Neil became fast friends.

When Nance O'Neil and company came to Fall River, Lizzie received them at Maplecroft. Accounts of that occasion differ but, according to Victoria Lincoln, "Lizzie threw a tremendous

A promotional photo of actress Nance O'Neil in the earlier part of her career. (Photo courtesy of The Fall River Historical Society.)

From *Lizzie Borden Quarterly*

party. There were caterers, hired palm trees, an orchestra. The house blazed with lights from top to bottom and blared with music."

A short time later, in late spring of 1905, Emma Borden left Maplecroft and her sister, never to return. The party seems to have been the immediate cause of the breakup. Many years afterwards, Emma told a reporter that, "The happenings at the French Street house that caused me to leave I must refuse to talk about. I did not go until conditions became absolutely unbearable."

Emma's comments have sometimes been interpreted to mean that Lizzie Borden and Nance O'Neil were lovers. Certainly that would have shocked Emma and indeed all of Fall River. However, there is a simpler, more plausible interpretation. In 1905 actors and actresses as a class were considered to be hedonistic at best and probably immoral as well. To illustrate the low esteem in which they were held, consider the case of one Matthew C. D. Borden, a wealthy Fall River mill owner who was a second cousin of Andrew Borden. In his will he specifically disinherited a son because he had married an actress twenty years before!

In the long run it was almost inevitable that the Borden sisters would separate. Emma and Lizzie reacted very differently to the tragedy they had gone through. Emma, deeply mortified by the experience, never wanted to be seen in public again. She was entirely willing to spend the rest of her life atoning for the sin of getting her name in the papers. Lizzie's attitude was entirely different. She intended to stay in Fall River, stare down her accusers, and entertain whenever and whomever she pleased.

Lizzie's dream of living the good life at Maplecroft was never realized. Almost from the beginning, she was rebuffed by Fall River society. After her acquittal, she went back to the Central Congregational Church where she was a member. There was no one seated in the pews surrounding hers. When Lizzie attempted to converse with her fellow parishioners, she found that, as she put it, "Women drew their skirts away from me and men I knew turned their faces away from me." And yet proud, stubborn Lizzie Borden continued to attend that church for the rest of her life.

In 1913 a reporter for the *Boston Herald* had this to say about Lizzie: "After twenty years, Lizzie Borden lives as shut off from the world as if she were behind prison bars, condemned to solitude by barriers stronger than any prison could be . . . the silent, inexorable censure of her fellow men and women. This woman who, for two decades . . . has never by any word or sign expressed indignation at the treatment accorded her by the people of Fall River [has] no human companionship save that which she can hire." That was an exaggeration; Lizzie had some friends, but not very many.

In 1926 Lizzie entered a Fall River hospital to undergo a gall bladder operation. Reportedly, she was a difficult patient; among other things, she refused to use a bed pan. Her favorite foods, including orange sherbet, were delivered to her room from a Providence restaurant. After several weeks she returned to Maplecroft, but her health slowly deteriorated. She lost weight; her hair, once a beautiful reddish brown, turned gray. On June 1, 1927, at the age of 66, Lizzie Borden died of heart disease.

Lizzie left an estate of $300,000; today that would have a purchasing power of about $3,000,000, ten times as much. Her will listed thirty different bequests to friends, relatives, employees and charitable institutions. The largest specific bequest ($30,000) went to the Animal Rescue League of Fall River. The remainder of her estate, more than half of it, was split equally between a cousin, Grace Howe (wife of Louis McHenry Howe, adviser to Franklin Roosevelt) and a friend, Helen Leighton. To her sister Emma she left nothing; as Lizzie put it, "She had her share of her father's estate and is supposed to have enough to make her comfortable."

Helen Leighton, speaking to a reporter after Lizzie's death, reminisced about her friend:

Many, many individuals were aided by Miss Borden . . . She helped several young people to obtain a college education. Fond of good reading herself, she saw to it that many persons who enjoyed good books but could not afford to buy them were well supplied with reading matter. Very few people knew of the extent of her charities.

Miss Leighton went on to say that Lizzie, once and only once during their friendship, talked about the murders of her parents, way into the night and early morning. Lizzie said she had a theory as to what happened, but pointed out that, knowing full well how easy it is to be accused falsely, she was reluctant to accuse someone else without proof. We'll never know what Lizzie had in mind that night, but we do know that she expressed her thoughts on the murderer's identity to a reporter in August of 1892.

Figure 8.7 Lizzie's theory of the murderers

(See below)

In the second half of this book, we'll examine that theory as well as others, in an attempt to find out what really happened in Fall River on that fateful morning so long ago.

THE SISTERS' THEORY.

Think Mr. and Mrs. Borden Were Killed by Some Strange Man.

FALL RIVER, Mass., Aug. 29. — Miss Emma and Miss Lizzie Borden have a theory in regard to the murder of their parents. It is a very unsatisfactory one, but it is, nevertheless, a theory. Lizzie and Emma and Mr. Morse are absolutely certain that Lizzie did not commit the crime. They think that some strange man killed Mr. and Mrs. Borden.

They state that Mr. Borden always received his business callers between 11 and 12 o'clock in the morning. He always answered the door bell between these hours, they say. They think that the assassin entered the house between 9 and 10 o'clock, probably, and that he came in search of Mr. Borden.

This man may have wandered through the rooms down stairs in search of his intended victim, and, not finding him, have gone to the upper story by the front way. Then, hearing a noise that disturbed him, he sought a hiding place in the clothes closet at the head of the stairs, just opposite the entrance to Lizzie's room and near the door leading into the spare room.

This is as far as the family theory goes. The members of the household do not attempt to explain how or when Mrs. Borden was killed; neither can they offer any reason why Mr. Borden was murdered. They say, however, that they think the assassin could have got out of the house by the front door and escaped without detection.

From *New Bedford Evening Stnadard*, Aug. 29, 1892, p. 2

Chapter 9
IF LIZZIE DIDN'T DO IT, WHO DID?

After Lizzie's acquittal, Marshal Hilliard announced that the investigation of the Borden case was over. No attempt was made to tie up the loose ends that remained. No one ever looked for the man or men who exchanged angry words with Andrew shortly before the murders. The search for "Dr. Handy's wild-eyed man" was abandoned. Most important, no one was ever questioned further about the case, let alone brought to trial.

Several mentally unbalanced people confessed to the crime. Among them was an elderly farmer named Charles Peckham. Two weeks after the slaughter, he walked into the Fall River police station and announced that he had killed the Bordens without getting any blood on his clothing (which, as a matter of fact, he was still wearing). Peckham wanted to be hung on the spot; fortunately the police declined to comply with this request. Within a day or two he had forgotten all about his confession and wanted to know why he was in jail. His wife, when she came to take him home, told the police that his mind had been affected by his obsession with the Borden case.

Less than a year later, on May 30, 1893, another axe murder occurred in Fall River. This time the victim was a young woman named Bertha Manchester. Clearly the culprit couldn't have been Lizzie Borden, since she was residing in jail at the time. Just before Lizzie's trial started, a Portuguese immigrant named Jose Correiro was arrested and charged with the Manchester murder; he was later convicted. There was some speculation that he might have committed the Borden murders a year earlier. That ended when it was shown conclusively that Correiro was several thousand miles away in the Azores in August of 1892.

At least a dozen suspects have been accused in books and articles dealing with the Borden murders. These accusations range from the plausible to the absurd. Over the years attention has focused on three individuals: John Morse, Emma Borden and Bridget Sullivan. In this chapter, we'll look at the evidence, such as it is, for and against these three suspects.

John the Impossible

John Morse left the Borden house shortly before 9 A.M. on the morning of August 4th, while Andrew and Abby were still alive. From there, he went to visit his niece, who was staying with the Emery family on Weybosset Street, a mile and a quarter away. Morse said that he left the Emery house at 11:20 A.M. to return to 92 Second Street, where he learned that Andrew and Abby were dead. Could he perhaps have come back earlier with murder on his mind?

In the first couple of days after the crime, John Morse was the prime suspect. Newspaper headlines virtually accusing Morse of the murders had a potent effect on the frightened populace of Fall River. When Morse left the Borden house to mail a letter Friday evening, he quickly found himself in the midst of an angry mob of perhaps a thousand people. Two policemen with drawn clubs were required to escort him safely to the post office and back.

John Morse seems to have been suspected originally because of an erroneous report that he was associated with a band of itinerant horse traders out in Westport, near Fall River. Horse traders a century ago were held in lower esteem than used car dealers are today. There was, however, a more substantive reason for suspecting Morse. The unfortunate man was simply in the wrong place at the wrong time. When a guest arrives on Wednesday and his hosts are found murdered on Thursday, it's only natural to suspect a cause and effect relationship.

Closer analysis shows that John Morse's presence at the crime scene was a rather unremarkable coincidence. Prior to this trip he stayed at the Borden house once in late June and again in mid July, for a total of three times in a little more than a month. Over the period he spent roughly 1/10 of his time with the Bordens, so there was at least a 10 percent chance that he would be there when they were murdered. Ten percent may seem like a small amount, but consider an analogous situation. Suppose that, in selecting cards from a full deck, you happen to draw two hearts in succession. This might mildly surprise you, but it would hardly lead you to suspect that the deck was stacked. Yet the chance of drawing two successive hearts is a little less than 6 percent.

In the eyes of the police, Lizzie Borden soon replaced John Morse as the principal suspect in the Borden murders. Other people involved in the investigation, including at least one member of Lizzie's defense team, were not so sure. Arthur Phillips in 1892 was a beginning lawyer who acted as a "gofer" for Andrew Jennings. Half a century later he wrote a history of Fall River, including an article on the Borden case, in which he participated. Implied in the article was Phillips' suspicion that John Morse murdered Andrew and Abby Borden.

There are a couple of reasons why suspicions about John Morse have persisted over the years. First, his alibi for the murders seemed too good to be true. In describing his trip back to the Borden house that morning he showed an amazing memory for details. He was able to cite the number on the streetcar he took down Pleasant Street as well as the number on the conductor's cap. Beyond that, his behavior when he arrived back at 92 Second Street was peculiar to say the least. He seemed completely oblivious to the policemen, neighbors and bystanders milling around the premises. In his own words at the preliminary hearing:

Q. (Knowlton) "Did you see any crowds along the street when you came up?"
A. (Morse) "Nothing that attracted my attention."

One would suppose that curiosity alone would have prompted Morse to ask somebody what was going on. Instead, as he put it, "I went around the house to a pear tree to get a couple of pears." Only after several minutes did he enter the house, where Bridget told him that Andrew and Abby were dead.

Figure 9.1 Streetcar on Pleasant St., Fall River

From *Lizzie Borden Sourcebook*, p. 223

This unusual behavior clearly suggests that, despite his testimony to the contrary, John Morse knew about the murders before he returned to the scene of the crime. That could imply guilt. More likely, though, he acquired this knowledge in a completely innocent way. He boarded the street car at about 11:30 A.M., fifteen minutes after the crime was reported to the police station. As is usually the case, bad news spreads rapidly; within fifteen minutes a crowd was already gathering at the Borden house. Almost certainly there were passengers on the streetcar who knew about the crime; some of them may even have been policemen traveling to the scene. We can imagine excited conversations such as:

"Did you hear what happened to Andrew Borden this morning?"

"Slaughtered in his own house in broad daylight."

"Must have been a maniac killed him; nobody's safe any more."

John Morse's first reaction to that shocking news was probably one of disbelief; it's hard to believe that someone alive and well two hours ago is dead, let alone murdered. (Besides, there were at least four different Andrew Bordens living in Fall River at the time.) But Morse was a cautious man; he knew that if the news were true he would be suspected. To protect himself, he went about constructing a watertight alibi.

Later, when Morse came upon the hectic scene at the Borden house, he realized that the horror story he had overheard was really true. Understandably, he took a "time-out" to regain his composure and go over his alibi to make sure he had it straight. Only then did he enter the house to face grim reality. Later he told a "grey" lie, saying that he first heard about the murders from people within the house. Perhaps he felt that the simple truth would have been incriminating.

As we have just seen, close examination of the evidence against John Morse makes it melt away. Moreover there are several circumstances that argue for his innocence. What could his motive have been? He would not have gained financially from the murders; Andrew's estate went entirely to Emma and Lizzie. More important, all the evidence we have suggests that John and Andrew got along well together, both in their personal and business relationships. The frequency of Morse's visits suggests that he was a welcome and well liked guest at the Borden house.

Another fact that supports John Morse's innocence is that, of the many people who saw him at close range that August morning, no one detected blood on his clothing. When he arrived the day before he had no luggage. This means that he couldn't have changed his clothes after the murders,

It's safe to assume that he didn't go around in his underwear either; someone would have noticed.

One circumstance all by itself establishes Morse's innocence beyond reasonable doubt. His alibi, which seemed too good to be true, proved to be rock-solid. The police established to their own satisfaction that he did indeed take the streetcar he mentioned to get back to the Borden house. Furthermore Mrs. Emery told reporters that John Morse showed up at her house shortly after breakfast and stayed until some time between 11:20 and 11:30 A.M. Her account was confirmed by Annie Morse, John's niece, and by a Mrs. Kingsley, who rented an apartment in the Emery house. It's hard to believe all three women could have been mistaken. Morse couldn't have been at the Borden's when the murders were committed, and finally, we can cross his name off the list of suspects.

Incidentally, there is one puzzling aspect to Mrs. Emery's story. When asked how she established the time at which John Morse left her house she replied, "Dr. Bowen came in just as Mr. Morse left." That's impossible. At 11:20, Dr. Bowen was examining Andrew Borden's body; at 11:30 he was at the Western Union office sending a telegram to Emma. There is no way he could have gone to Weybosset Street during that time interval or anything close to it. Moreover, given the stress that Bowen was under that morning it's inconceivable that he would have taken time out to pay a house call on a sick patient at Mrs. Emery's (perhaps Annie Morse who, according to her uncle was "under the weather" when he visited her).

Almost certainly, Mrs. Emery was misquoted. (Reporters were much more careless a hundred years ago than they are now. One referred to Bridget Sullivan as Lizzie Corrigan.) My guess, for what it's worth, is that Dr. Bowen telephoned Mrs. Emery to cancel his house call and that what she really told the reporter was, "Dr. Bowen called just before Mr. Morse left." That would explain why, shortly after the murders were discovered, John Morse told a reporter for the *Fall River Globe* that, "I first learned of this affair by a telephone message when I was in a different part of the city." Morse later denied having made that statement, but the reporter stuck to his story.

Emma the Implausible

Emma Borden spent two weeks prior to August 4th at Fairhaven, a resort town on Buzzard's Bay, some fifteen miles southeast of Fall River.

There she was visiting a friend, Helen Brownell, and her elderly mother. At 11:30 A.M., Dr. Bowen sent Emma a telegram informing her of the tragedy. She returned home by train via New Bedford, arriving at about 5 P.M. Did she perhaps come to 92 Second Street considerably earlier than that, in the morning rather than the afternoon?

When the murders were committed, no one seems to have suspected Lizzie's sister. Indeed the only serious accusation of Emma was made in 1984 by Frank Spiering, a controversial true crime writer and novelist. Spiering offers no evidence whatsoever to link Emma to the crime.

Edmund Pearson, who wrote extensively about the Borden case over many years, said that "the family" (i.e., what remained of it) suspected Emma rather than Lizzie. Specifically, Colonel Louis Howe, who was married to Grace Borden Hartley, a second cousin of the Borden sisters, thought that Emma committed the murders in a "crazy spell." Do you suppose his opinion might have reflected the fact that Lizzie left his wife more than $100,000 in her will? Emma left Grace Howe nothing.

It is certainly true that Emma had a motive for the murders that was at least as strong as Lizzie's. The two of them jointly inherited Andrew Borden's estate of about $350,000. Moreover, Emma's resentment of their stepmother seems to have been greater than Lizzie's. Consider the following exchange at the inquest:

Q. (Knowlton) "Were the relations between your sister Lizzie and your [step] mother what you would call cordial?"
A. (Emma Borden) "I think more than they were with me."

This was confirmed by a friend of the sisters who testified that, "I think Lizzie talked with her stepmother more than Emma did."

While Emma had a plausible motive for the murders, she had little or no opportunity to commit them. Granted, it's only fifteen miles from Fairhaven, where she was visiting friends, to Fall River. Today the trip could be made in perhaps twenty minutes by automobile. A century ago, however, transportation was generally slow and uncertain. A fifteen mile trip could easily take a couple of hours. Emma would have had to make three trips that day, one to Fall River in the morning, another to Fairhaven around noon to receive Lizzie's telegram, and then back to Fall River in late afternoon.

To avoid detection, Emma would have been wise to travel by train. In that case the trip via New Bedford would have taken a couple of hours, assuming she walked back and forth to the railroad stations. To make matters worse, trains were scheduled only at three hour intervals. With a little bit of luck and a lot of heavy breathing, Emma might have been able to make it, but it wouldn't have been easy.

Alternatively Emma could have hired a horse and buggy for the round trip from Fairhaven to Fall River and back. That might have been faster since it involved no walking. However, it would have been risky; the driver would almost certainly have associated Emma with the murders as soon as he learned of them. However Emma traveled, she would quite likely have been recognized by her friends and neighbors on Second Street. The fact that she wasn't argues for her innocence.

All of these speculations would be superfluous if we could be sure that the police or the press verified Emma's presence in Fairhaven when the murders were committed. Did she, for example, personally sign for the telegram Lizzie sent her? All we have to go on here is a brief statement in the *Fall River Evening News* that Emma had "completely exonerated herself." How she did this is unknown; it's too late now to ask her friends, the Brownells of Fairhaven, about it.

There is another compelling reason to eliminate Emma as a suspect. All that we know suggests she did not have the kind of personality required to plan and commit murder. Emma was a spectator in life rather than a participant. She accepted adversity rather than making a concerted effort to overcome it. It was Lizzie, not Emma, who complained to her father about the primitive conditions under which they lived and nagged him to do something about it. A friend said of Emma that, "She would have felt very deeply any disparaging word from her father." You can be sure that Andrew would have had quite a few disparaging words to say if he had come across Emma chopping up his wife.

Bridget the Unlikely

Bridget Sullivan started washing windows at the Borden house at about 9:30 A.M. that morning, continuing until nearly 11 A.M. At that time she went up to her attic room on the third floor for a "liedown" prior to starting dinner. About ten minutes later, she was summoned by Lizzie's frantic call of murder. Do you suppose Bridget might have made an earlier trip to the downstairs sitting room where Andrew's body was found and the second floor guest room where Abby was murdered?

Only two people admitted to being on the premises when the Borden murders occurred. In that sense only Lizzie Borden and Bridget Sullivan had a clear opportunity to commit the crime. Perhaps that is why those who argued for Lizzie's innocence so frequently turned to Bridget as an alternative. It started with Lizzie's defense counsel. Consider, for example, what Andrew Jennings had to say in his summation at the preliminary hearing, as reported in a newspaper article (right). Despite the disclaimer, it's clear that Jennings was suggesting Bridget's guilt to get his client off the hook.

Figure 9.2 Andrew Jennings; Lizzie or Bridget?

In 1961 the distinguished true crime writer Edward Radin made a compelling argument for Lizzie's innocence in his book *Lizzie Borden, the Untold Story*. After exonerating Lizzie, he went on to accuse Bridget of the crime. Here Radin was much less convincing. His case against Bridget consisted mostly of citing instances where her story differed from that of other witnesses. Most of these discrepancies were relatively trivial, suggesting lapses in memory of the type that all of us experience. Compare, for example, Bridget's

I claim the government has excluded anybody else from committing this crime except the inmates of the house. Assuming that it was done by inmates of the house. Who were in the house? John Morse, Bridget Sullivan and Lizzie. John Morse seems to have accounted for his time to the commonwealth and is left out of the case. That brings it down to Lizzie and Bridget. Now who would be the party liable to be suspected ? Who would be the party whose clothes would be examined? Would it be natural to suppose that it was the stranger, one unconnected by ties of blood, or would it be natural to suppose that it was the youngest daughter, and that term youngest means something? It means that it was the last little head that leaned against her father's breast and called him father. If it starts up the theory that it was either of the two what then? Understand me, I don't believe that Bridget Sullivan did that deed any more than I believe Lizzie Borden did it. I don't believe either of them did it. I am showing the line of the government's theory. Was Bridget Sullivan compelled to tell how many dishes she washed, where she put them and how she laid them away? Has she been subjected to any such course of examination as this defendant has been subjected to? I would like to know if there is not something just as suspicious in her actions as there are in Lizzie Borden's? She was from 20 minutes past 10 to 15 minutes to 11 washing the upper half of one window. Did my learned friend over there try to show anything suspicious about that?

There is nothing in the evidence to warrant the government in binding her over. If Lizzie Borden had opportunity to commit the crime, so did Bridget Sullivan. Bridget says she was out doors, she says so and yet who saw her out doors? Mrs. Churchill, I believe, saw her once. I am not arguing that Bridget did this crime. I say she did not. I am simply showing the line the government is following in the case of Lizzie Borden and Bridget Sullivan. Now if Lizzie did this when did she do it, your honor? It is almost impossible to tell with any degree of certainty the temperature of the bodies by mere contact of the fingers.

From *Lizzie Borden Sourcebook*, p. 191-2

account of what happened after she got up on that fateful day to that of John Morse.

Bridget Sullivan's Account	**John Morse's Account**
6:15 Bridget came downstairs; found no one there	6:20 Morse came downstairs; found no one there
6:35 Joined downstairs by Abby Borden	6:35 Joined downstairs by Andrew Borden
6:45 Andrew came down after Abby	6:50 Abby came down after Andrew
7:15 Saw Morse at breakfast for the first time	7:00 Saw Bridget at breakfast for the first time

The two accounts differ substantially. Yet, think what you may about the guilt or innocence of these two people, can you imagine why either one should have lied about the time sequence several hours before the murders? Either Bridget or John were simply mistaken.

There were a couple of instances where Bridget's behavior seemed suspicious, at least on the surface. When Officer Doherty came to the Borden house to escort Bridget to the inquest, she started to cry, believing that she was being arrested for the murders. That seems incriminating until you realize that Doherty led off by saying, "I want you to accompany me to the police station."

Bridget as an Irish immigrant could hardly be expected to understand the intricacies of the court system in Massachusetts; few people did. Moreover, at a time when ethnic prejudice was rampant, Bridget had every reason to fear false arrest. Finally, and perhaps most important, she had been threatened with arrest the day before when she started to pack her bags, hoping to leave the Borden house forever.

Another incident, this one relating to Bridget's peculiar behavior after the first murder was discovered, is more difficult to explain. Dr. Bowen asked for a sheet (i.e., *one* sheet) to cover Andrew Borden's body. Bridget, accompanied by Adelaide Churchill, went up the back stairs to obtain the sheet from a linen closet located in a small dressing room on the second floor. According to Mrs. Churchill, Bridget asked her, "Will *two* sheets be enough?" Addie replied, "I think so; one will cover a person."

Indeed one sheet was "a-plenty" for Andrew. A few minutes later, Lizzie asked Mrs. Churchill to try to locate Abby. Specifically, she suggested looking for her in "Mrs. Borden's room." Lizzie was referring either to the dressing room or to the senior Bordens' bedroom, both of which could be reached only by the back stairs. Yet Bridget led Mrs. Churchill up the *front* stairs to the guest room, where they discovered Abby's body. Only by a macabre stretch of the imagination could that have been described as "Mrs. Borden's room."

Bridget's behavior here, acting contrary to directions given first by Dr. Bowen and then by Lizzie, suggests guilty knowledge of the second murder before it was discovered. It's difficult to come up with a simple innocent explanation of what she did. Yet it would be a mistake to put too much emphasis on one or two incriminating incidents. There is no physical evidence whatsoever linking Bridget to the crime. A host of people talked to Bridget that morning; no one reported seeing blood on her clothing or her person. No incriminating evidence (e.g., a murder weapon) was found when the police searched Bridget's attic bedroom.

Bridget, in the days after the murders, was prone to excited, emotional outbursts. Marshal Hilliard, when he questioned her the day before the inquest, found that she broke down completely, both physically and mentally. Some people have taken this as an indication of guilt (others are convinced that Lizzie must be guilty because she was so calm and unemotional; you can't win). I would suggest a different interpretation. Given Bridget's emotional instability, it seems unlikely that she could have stood up to police interrogation if guilty. My guess is that she would have confessed early in the game.

One factor alone argues convincingly for Bridget's innocence. She had no conceivable motive for the crime. (O.K., maybe she couldn't face warmed over mutton soup for dinner again, but certainly she could have disposed of that problem in less drastic ways). Bridget had nothing to gain from the murders and something important to lose: her job.

Surprisingly, Bridget was well paid compared to her peers: $4 a week plus room and board (Abby, rather than Andrew, must have hired her). Women in the mills of Fall River got $7.50 a week but they had to work twelve hours a day and find their own food and lodging. Bridget got Thursday afternoon and all day Sunday off. Her job involved no heavy lifting; she did the washing, served the meals and did a little cleaning.

Abby and, to a lesser extent Emma and Lizzie, did everything else. No wonder Bridget expressed her admiration, even her love, for Abby on numerous occasions. Granted, she never seemed to have anything nice to say about Andrew. But then, neither did anyone else.

Unhappily Ever After

For everyone who lived at 92 Second Street, August 4 1892 had to be the most horrible day of their lives. For Andrew and Abby Borden it was their last day as well. For Lizzie it ended in a nightmare that shadowed the rest of her life. The tragedy turned Emma, a shy retiring person, into a recluse. Even for Bridget Sullivan and John Morse, the murders must have inflicted emotional scars that were slow to heal. Small wonder that none of the survivors wanted to discuss the case, even with their friends.

Figure 9.3 John Morse, 1909

JOHN V. MORSE
From *Emery scrapbook*, p. 124

John Morse was detained in the Borden house by police order through the inquest. We have to wonder how he coped, since he brought no luggage when he arrived. Perhaps thinking that "out of sight is out of mind", Morse was determined to bury the bloody clothes of the victims. The man he hired to do it charged $5, which John thought was outrageous, and settled on $3. Andrew would have been proud of his brother-in-law. You can imagine how Morse must have felt a few days later when Dr. Dolan ordered that the clothes be dug up for evidence.

After the trial John Morse went back to the farm he owned in Hastings, Iowa. Every summer for nearly twenty years, he returned to the Fall River - New Bedford area where he kept a small fishing boat. He died on March 1, 1912, at the age of seventy eight.

A few years before he died Morse told a story about a gypsy fortune teller who shortly before the murders refused to predict his future, saying, "You don't want to know." In retrospect, Morse said he would give fifty dollars to know what caused the woman to behave that way. Had he made that offer on the spot she would surely have satisfied his curiosity. Indeed, five dollars might have sufficed, maybe even three.

Emma lived on at the Borden house until the late summer of 1893 when she and Lizzie moved to Maplecroft. According to the neighbors, they quarreled from time to time about one thing or another. Things got much worse when Lizzie started entertaining actresses, generally considered to be "loose women." In 1905 Emma left Maplecroft. She spent most of the rest of her life in nearby Providence, Rhode Island. Although Emma frequently visited friends in Fall River, the two sisters never saw one another again. Emma died in Newmarket, New Hampshire on June 10, 1927, only nine days after Lizzie's death. Curiously, Emma's estate was nearly twice as large as Lizzie's. Most of it went to charity; the largest single bequest was to the Animal Rescue League of Fall River. Emma was buried beside Lizzie in the Borden plot in Oak Grove Cemetery, Fall River, along with their father, mother and stepmother.

Figure 9.4 Emma, 1913

In 1913, twenty years after Lizzie's trial, Emma gave her only interview to a reporter. She was

From *Fall River Hist. Soc.* Calendar

quoted as saying, among other things that:

"Perhaps people wondered why I stood so staunchly by Lizzie during the trial. I'll tell them why . . . . When my darling mother [Sarah Morse Borden] was on her deathbed, she summoned me and extracted a promise that I would always watch over baby Lizzie . . . I did my duty at the time of the trial and I am still going to do it in defending my sister even though circumstances have separated us.

"Here is the strongest thing that has convinced me of Lizzie's innocence. The authorities never found the axe or whatever implement it was that was used in the killing. Lizzie, if she had done that deed, could never have hidden the instrument of death so that the police could not find it . . . Neither did she have the time."

Emma's qualified exoneration of Lizzie sounds strange. I would have expected her to say something like, "Lizzie couldn't possibly have murdered anyone, let alone her father whom she dearly loved." Sometimes what a person doesn't say is more significant than what she does say.

Bridget Sullivan had a morbid fear of staying in the Borden house after the murders. She spent only one (possibly two) nights there before leaving forever. At first she stayed with friends and relatives in Fall River; later she took a job at the New Bedford jail.

Legend has it that after the trial Bridget returned to Ireland, using money supplied by a grateful Lizzie Borden. The legend is wrong; Bridget did not go back to Ireland and Lizzie had no reason for a payoff. On balance Bridget's testimony was neither helpful nor harmful to Lizzie.

In 1897 Bridget moved west to Anaconda, Montana, where she married a man who was also named Sullivan. She lived there for forty five years before a nearly fatal bout with pneumonia forced her, a childless widow, to move in with a niece in Butte. Bridget died six years later on March 25, 1948.

There is an interesting story relating to Bridget's last years in Montana. When she thought she was dying, she called a childhood friend, Mrs. Minnie Green, who lived a short distance away. Bridget asked Minnie to come to her bedside; she had a secret to reveal before she died. For one reason or another, Mrs. Green delayed the trip for several days. By the time she arrived the crisis had passed and Bridget was out of danger. The only thing of any consequence that she revealed was that, half a century before, she had testified at the Borden trial. This could hardly have been the important secret that piqued Mrs. Green's curiosity, as it does ours.

Perhaps, had she come to see Bridget a few days earlier, she and we would have learned what really happened at 92 Second Street on August 4, 1892.

Chapter 10
LIZZIE COULDN'T HAVE DONE IT, BUT SHE MUST HAVE

Innocent.....Guilty

Even though the jury acquitted Lizzie, the question has persisted through the years: did she or didn't she? Was she a villain or a victim? Julian Ralph, the *New York Sun* reporter who covered the trial in New Bedford put it best:

"She is either the most injured of innocents or the blackest of monsters. She either hacked her father and stepmother to pieces with the furious brutality of the ogre in Poe's story of the Rue Morgue, or some other person did it and she suffers the double torture of losing her parents and being wrongfully accused of their murders."

In many ways the case against Lizzie today remains the same as it was a hundred years ago. Talk to anyone who believes her to be guilty and ultimately (usually sooner) they will say, "O.K., if Lizzie didn't do it, who did?" The general principle here was summarized succinctly by Sherlock Holmes: "When you have eliminated the impossible, whatever remains, however improbable, must be the truth." Applied to the Borden case this would seem to mean that, having eliminated all the suspects considered in Chapter 9, the only one left is Lizzie. Despite the weakness of the case against her, she must have been guilty.

There is a basic fallacy in this line of reasoning, which explains why juries are ordinarily warned against it. There are an infinite number of possible solutions to the Borden case, some of which haven't even been suggested yet. One such solution, based upon a scenario that hasn't been seriously considered since August of 1892, is presented in Chapter 15. I'm under no illusion that this will be the "final solution"; there will be others put forward in the future. My point is that the time will never come when Lizzie can be found guilty by elimination.

In this chapter we will examine the case for and against Lizzie. Ten items, drawn mostly from the closing arguments for the prosecution and defense, will be analyzed here. Three other crucial items which require more extensive discussion will be postponed to later chapters (11 - 14).

Throughout this chapter, in connection with each item, we'll use the symbols, INNOCENT or GUILTY on the margins to indicate my assessment as to whether, on balance, the item supports Lizzie's innocence or guilt. A question places mark places the tiem in the "damned if I know" category.

Why Did Lizzie Do It (If She Did)?

Throughout the court proceedings the prosecution claimed that Lizzie's motive for the crime was her hatred for Abby. This theory seems to have originated with Assistant Marshal Fleet. When he asked Lizzie (Chapter 5) if she had any idea who could have killed her father and mother she replied, "She is not my mother, sir; she is my stepmother. My mother died when I was a child."

In his closing argument, Knowlton made the most of this statement:

"That wicked hatchet went deep into the brain of that old woman, but . . . it never went so deep into Abby Durfee Borden as did the contemptuous refusal of the girl to call her by the name of mother. It was a living insult to that woman, a living expression of contempt . . .

"But these people day in and day out, year in and year out under the same roof, compelled to eat the same bread, compelled to sleep in the same house, compelled to meet each other morning, noon and night, yet maintain this strained unnatural hostility . . . .

"Lizzie had repudiated the title of mother. She had lived with her in hatred. She had gone on increasing in that hatred until we do not know, we can only guess, how far that sore had festered . . . ."

The testimony of Lizzie's friends and neighbors on this subject was very different from Knowlton's dark forebodings. Recall (Chapter 5) that Bridget Sullivan, who should have known more about the relationship than anyone else, testified that she never saw any quarreling between Lizzie and Abby. Dr. Bowen described the relations between the two women as "harmonious and natural." Alice Russell went a step further, saying, "In all my acquaintance, which is ten years, I never yet heard any wrangling in the family."

Curiously, the prosecution did not put on the stand the one person who was most likely to support their point of view on this issue. Sarah Whitehead, a half sister of Abby who lived only two blocks away, testified at the inquest. She was clearly hostile to both Lizzie and Emma. Although summoned as a witness at the trial, she was never called.

On balance, the frosty relations between Lizzie and Abby do not seem to go beyond the tensions that often exist between stepparent and child. My grandmother, born in the 1860s, was raised by a stepmother whom she detested. As a teenager she went halfway across the country to live with an older married sister. Lizzie Borden, thirty two years old and financially secure, might have been expected to follow a similar course rather than resorting to violence.

However Lizzie may have felt towards Abby, she seems to have gotten along well with her father. All that we know of Andrew and Lizzie suggests that theirs was the healthy, loving relationship to be expected between a parent and mature child. As a young girl, Lizzie gave Andrew a ring which he wore on his little finger for the rest of his life. More significant perhaps was the story one of Lizzie's friends told a reporter.

"As for Lizzie and her father they were, without being demonstrative, very fond of each other. I saw her at church and asked her to come [with us to Marion], but she said that she did not think she ought to. Her father and mother were going across the river where they had a farm as they had always done in the summer and Lizzie said her father, who would be in town every day and get his dinner at home, would be left alone if she went away. She felt as if she ought to stay at home, at least part of the time, to see that everything went all right. [I] told her that her father could get his dinner at a restaurant or at the hotel, but Lizzie said that there were often little things about his business in the way of writing that she could help him on."

This hardly sounds like a young woman contemplating murder. Knowlton also seems to have had doubts about Lizzie's motive for murdering her father. His closing argument contains the somewhat ambivalent statement, "There may be that in this case which saves us from the idea that Lizzie Andrew Borden planned to kill her father. I hope she did not. I should be slow to believe she did." He went on to suggest that Lizzie killed Andrew because he would have known who killed Abby and might have told the police. I would be slow to believe that Lizzie, to protect herself, murdered the father she loved.

A more plausible motive was greed. Andrew's estate of $350,000 may seem small today but this was 1892 when mutton sold for 10 cents a pound, shoes were $2 a pair, and a new lawn mower cost $3. Lizzie's share of the estate would have had the purchasing power today of at least two million dollars. Perhaps Lizzie was too impatient to wait for her inheritance until Andrew Borden died a natural death. And yet, regardless of how much she disliked life at 92 Second Street, could she have murdered the father she loved so that she could purchase Maplecroft a few years earlier?

Figure 10.1 The cost of Sunday dinner in 1892

It has been suggested that Andrew Borden was about to make a will effectively disinheriting his daughters, leaving the bulk of his estate to Abby and her relatives. Conceivably, this was what Andrew, Abby and John Morse were discussing on the afternoon before the crime. Lizzie, resting in her upstairs room, could have easily overheard them and concluded that her father no longer loved her. All of this, however, is speculation. Neither Andrew's lawyer, Andrew Jennings, nor any of

UNION MARKET !

___

BEEF ! BEEF !

Cheaper Than Ever.

A Good Sunday's Dinner

For 25c.

3 lb STEAK 25c.

Friday & Saturday's Bargains.

Come and See Us and You Will Go Away Happy.

14 North Main Street,

OPP. WILBUR HOUSE.

From *Lizzie Borden Sourcebook*, p. 157

Andrew's business associates knew anything about a will, in existence or in preparation.

The violence with which the murders were committed has spawned some bizarre theories about Lizzie's motive. Thirty years ago Victoria Lincoln, in her book *A Private Disgrace: Lizzie Borden by Daylight*, suggested that Lizzie slaughtered her parents during an epileptic fit. Never mind that there is no reason to believe that Lizzie or anyone in her family suffered from epilepsy. If you've ever seen anyone going through the agony of an epileptic seizure, you know that the last thing they could do is commit murder. Suicide perhaps, but not murder.

Recently it has been suggested that on August 4, 1892, Lizzie Borden suddenly remembered that her father had sexually abused her many years before. In retribution, she hacked his face to a bloody pulp with a hatchet. For good measure, she went on to chop up Abby, presumably an innocent bystander. The evidence for incest, like that for epilepsy, is nonexistent. Beyond that, it is almost unheard of for a victim of incest to retaliate with murder.

Could Lizzie Have Killed Andrew?

Lizzie never denied being on the premises at 92 Second Street when the murders took place. She did, however, claim that she was in the barn loft, eating pears and looking for lead sinkers, when Andrew Borden was slaughtered on a couch in the living room. If Lizzie's alibi is valid, she couldn't have killed him. If she lied about her trip to the barn, she was almost certainly guilty.

At the inquest, Lizzie testified that the sinkers were to be used on a fishing trip she had planned for the following week with friends in Marion, a resort town on Buzzard's Bay. Knowlton ridiculed her sinker story, asking rhetorical questions such as the following:

"It occurred to you after your father came in it would be a good time to go to the barn after sinkers and you had no reason to suppose there was not abundance of sinkers at the farm and abundance of lines?"

"This was Thursday and you had no idea of using any fishing apparatus before the next Monday?"

Lizzie's search for sinkers, irrational as it may have been, makes perfect sense to me. Given the dreary monotony of her life in Fall River, she must have been looking forward eagerly to visiting her friends at the shore. Part, perhaps most, of the joy of a vacation comes in preparing for it. Looking for sinkers was Lizzie's way of expressing her anticipation.

Lizzie's story about the sinkers was corroborated by two police officers, Lieutenant Edson and Marshal Hilliard. They testified at the trial that when they searched the barn the following Monday, they found a basket in the loft containing iron nails and pieces of lead. The basket was sitting on top of a carpenter's bench. This is almost word for word what Lizzie said at the inquest, except that she referred to a "box" rather than a "basket".

To disprove Lizzie's story of her trip to the barn loft, the prosecution put Inspector Medley on the stand; his testimony was cited in Chapter 5. He went out to the barn loft at about 11:50 A.M. and noticed that the floor had a thick coating of dust. Finding no footprints in the dust, he concluded that Lizzie couldn't have been there earlier in the morning.

The defense refuted Medley by putting on several witnesses who claimed to have been in the barn loft before the police officers got there. The testimony of one such witness, Alfred Clarkson, was cited in Chapter 5. His point was a simple one; if Medley couldn't see his footprints, made at 11:40 A.M., no wonder he missed Lizzie's.

Two young men, Thomas Barlow. and Everett Brown, testified after Clarkson. At one point, Barlow referred to himself and his friend as "me and Brownie", a phrase that has endured ever since. Perhaps that explains why they have always been assumed to be small boys whose testimony was unreliable. In point of fact, Barlow was sixteen years old; Brown was eighteen. Call them "young men" or "youths" if you wish, but not "boys".

Barlow testified that he went to his friend's house that morning at 11:00 A.M. and stayed about eight minutes. He and Brown took about ten to fifteen minutes to walk to the Borden house. Once there, they tried to get into the house but Charles Sawyer, standing at the door, turned them back. Undaunted, they went to the barn loft where they searched unsuccessfully for the murderer and, in the process, stirred up the dust.

Assuming it took as long as seven minutes for Barlow and Brown to argue fruitlessly with Sawyer and climb the barn stairs, they should have reached the loft at about 11:30 A.M.

11:00 + 0.08 + 0.15 + 0.07 = 11:30 A.M.

That was twenty minutes before Medley got there!

Barlow's friend, Everett Brown, was somewhat vague about time. However, he made a very significant statement: as he and Barlow came out of the barn, he saw Assistant Marshal Fleet entering the Borden house. Inspector Medley testified that he and Fleet arrived at almost exactly the same time and that he (Medley) spent ten minutes in the house before going to the barn to check Lizzie's alibi. This means that, by his own admission, Medley entered the barn loft about ten minutes after Barlow and Brown left it! In effect, Brown's testimony, all by itself, destroys Medley's credibility.

There is a very good reason why Medley couldn't see anyone's footprints (except, allegedly, his own). When you walk across a dusty floor, you don't leave footprints; all you do is stir up the dust. When Longfellow wrote,

> Lives of great men all remind us
> We can make our lives sublime
> And departing, leave behind us
> Footprints on the sands of time

he should have pointed out (probably by a footnote) that he was talking about wet sand. Footprints show up in wet cement or mud, not in dust.

As pointed out in Chapter 5, an ice cream peddler named Hyman Lubinsky supported Lizzie's claim that she came back from the barn loft to discover her father's murder. Lubinsky testified that when he drove past 92 Second Street at 11:10 - 11:15 A.M., he saw a woman walking from the barn to the side entrance of the house. Although Lubinsky couldn't identify the woman as Lizzie, he was sure it was not Bridget Sullivan, whom he knew.

The time element in Lubinsky's story was critical to Lizzie's alibi. Knowlton attacked this from both directions. A rebuttal witness, Patrolman Mullaly, testified that Lubinsky originally told him he passed the Borden house at 10:30 A.M. This was refuted by two defense witnesses who said that Lubinsky picked up the horse for his ice cream cart a few minutes after 11:00 A.M. In his closing argument, Knowlton suggested that Lubinsky might have seen the woman somewhat later than 11:15, after the crime had been discovered, in which case it could have been Adelaide Churchhill or Alice Russell. The problem here is that neither of these neighbors approached the Borden house from the barn; only Lizzie did that.

In summary, the prosecution's effort to discredit Lizzie's alibi fizzled. It's a safe bet that she did indeed go to the barn that morning. That doesn't definitely prove her innocence, though. It's possible that she could have murdered her father shortly before 11:00 A.M., disposed of her bloodstained weapon and clothing, walked to the barn without being seen by any of the neighbors, washed herself at the barn faucet, and returned to the house at 11:15. It's possible but very unlikely. For one thing, Lizzie had only about fifteen minutes to kill her father, dispose of all the evidence, bathe thoroughly, and change her clothes. She simply didn't have time to make a trip to the barn, no matter what she did there.

Figure 10.2 The Borden barn

Could Lizzie Have Killed Abby?

Many times during the trial, the prosecution was on the defensive, trying to convince the jury that it was possible for Lizzie to commit the crime. Time and again, their own witnesses made their task more difficult. The best known example of this type arose when Patrolman Mullaly "discovered" the hatchet handle that the prosecution claimed Lizzie had destroyed.

Another piece of damaging testimony from a pros-

Side view of the Borden house and barn.
From *Lizzie Borden Sourcebook*, p. 23

ecution witness came during the cross-examination of Dr. David Cheever, professor of surgery and anatomy at Harvard Medical School in Camridge, Massachusetts.

Q. (Adams) "Coming now to the injuries which you found upon the head of Mrs. Borden, I understand you to say that there are three which, in your opinion, may have been caused before she fell?"

A. (Cheever) "Yes, sir."

Q. (Adams) "Namely the one in front, covered by a flap, and the two on the crown of the head?"

A. (Cheever) "Yes, sir."

Q. (Adams) "The two upon the crown of the head, if she were standing, would they naturally have been given by a person who was taller than she, assuming that the instrument was a hatchet with a handle a foot long?"

A. (Cheever) "If she was standing upright, they must have been given by a taller person."

Robinson, in his closing argument for the defense, handled this exchange in a rather cryptic way:

"Dr. Dolan tells us that Mrs. Borden's height was 5'3" [autopsy report] and Dr. Cheever says that the wounds on top of the head were, in his judgment, caused by the assailant standing up and striking her when she stood up and he says that would come from an assailant of a greater height, who would have to strike down. Now there is no evidence as to what Lizzie Borden's height is, but you have seen her walk in and out and you have a right to say how near she comes to 5'3".

Lizzie was 5'4" tall, about the same height as Abby. You may wish to try an experiment with a victim whose height is within an inch or so of yours. Using a light rubber mallet (not a hatchet) see if you can strike your friend on the top of the head. Can't do it, can you? You have to climb up about six inches to succeed.

Which Hatchet was the Murder Weapon?

The prosecution had a difficult time identifying the murder weapon. Their first choice was a claw hammer hatchet with a 5" cutting edge. This was offered at the preliminary hearing as the likely weapon; there appeared to be blood stains on it.

Sometime between the preliminary hearing and the trial, the claw hammer hatchet dropped out of the picture. Dr. Wood, a chemistry professor at Harvard Medical School, showed that what looked like blood was really rust and/or red varnish. More important, Dr. Draper, medical

INNOCENT

examiner for Suffolk County and the city of Boston, established to his own satisfaction that the murder weapon had to have a cutting edge of 3½, not 5".

The police did indeed have in their possession a weapon with a cutting edge of 3½. This was the famous "handleless hatchet" (Chapter 6). The handle had been broken off irregularly about an inch below the blade. This hatchet was discovered on the morning of the murders by Assistant Marshal Fleet; it was resting in a box in the Borden cellar, covered with dust and ashes. Fleet, convinced that this could not be the murder weapon, put it back in the box. There it was rediscovered a few days later by Inspector Medley. It became the weapon of choice for the prosecution at the trial; Dr. Draper showed that it fit all the wounds on the skulls of the victims.

There were, however, a couple of problems with the handleless hatchet. For starters, Dr. Wood found no trace of blood on the blade or the stub of the handle. Knowlton dug his way out of that hole by suggesting that Lizzie washed the hatchet blade and then deliberately broke off the bloodstained handle. Wood agreed that, if that were the case, there need not be any blood on what remained of the hatchet.

That may be true, but Lizzie would have had a frustrating time breaking the hatchet handle by design. Try it sometime; swing a hatchet at a slightly resilient object such as a chopping block (not a skull). You will most likely take a couple of hundred swings before the handle breaks. That's about the frequency at which a baseball player like Sammy Sora or Mark McGwire breaks his favorite bat by hitting a pitched ball traveling at 90 mph.

Another reason why the handleless hatchet struck out as a murder weapon was revealed by Dr. Draper in a letter written to Knowlton about a week before the trial. He said:

"On one of the cuts in Mrs. Borden's skull near the right ear, there is a very small but unmistakable deposit of the gilt metal with which hatchets are ornamented when they leave the factory. This deposit means that the hatchet used in killing Mrs. Borden was a new hatchet, not long out of the store."

The handleless hatchet was hardly new; it was covered with rust. More important, as Draper himself pointed out, the edge of the hatchet had at one time been ground on a wheel; otherwise it would not have fit the wounds. Grinding would most certainly have removed the gilt.

INNOCENT

It's a safe bet that the handleless hatchet was not the murder weapon. Does this prove that Lizzie was innocent? Not necessarily. She grew up in that house; she possibly knew of hiding places that the police could never find. Legend has it that Knowlton wanted to tear down the house and plow up the surrounding lot in hopes of finding the murder weapon and perhaps Lizzie's bloodstained clothes as well. Quite understandably, Lizzie and Emma Borden didn't go along with that idea. For all we know, the guilty hatchet may still be hidden at 92 Second Street.

What Happened to all the Blood?

Perhaps the factor that most influenced the jury in Lizzie's favor was the complete absence of blood on her person. Six witnesses who saw Lizzie at close range that morning (Phoebe Bowen, Adelaide Churchill, Patrick Doherty, Alice Russell, Charles Sawyer and Bridget Sullivan) testified there was no blood on her hands, face or hair. Lizzie could have washed off the blood of the victims. It wouldn't have been easy though. Lizzie would have had to take what my mother called a "spit bath" using a washcloth to swab off body parts she couldn't even see.

Edmund Pearson, a famous true crime writer who was convinced that Lizzie was guilty, maintained that the murderer of Andrew and Abby Borden need not have been covered or even spattered with blood. This theory was refuted by three expert witnesses for the prosecution. Dr. Wood testified that Andrew's assailant would most likely have been spattered with blood from the waist up. Melvin Adams expanded on this theme in his cross-examination of Drs. Draper and Cheever.

Q. (Adams) "And in that situation, giving repeated blows, would not you expect it would follow that the upper portion, the head, the face, the hair, assuming it was not covered, of the assailant would be spattered with blood?"

A. (Draper) "That is reasonable."

Q. (Adams) "Would not the assailant have been spattered with blood?"

A. (Cheever) "I think he would . . . very considerably."

Why no Bloody Gloves?

In every murder trial with which I am familiar, the prosecution has come up with at least one piece of evidence linking the defendant directly to the crime. A century ago in the Maybrick trial in England, it was the fly paper from which Florence Maybrick allegedly extracted arsenic to poison her husband. Forty years later in the Lindbergh kidnapping, it was the marked ransom bills and the kidnap ladder containing lumber from his garage that sent Bruno Richard Hauptmann to the electric chair. More recently, it was the bloody gloves, the Bruno Magli shoes, the cuts on his hands, that incriminated O. J. Simpson.

INNOCENT

It cannot be emphasized too strongly that at Lizzie Borden's trial, the prosecution never produced a single piece of direct evidence linking her to the crime. Not only was there no sign of blood on her person; there was nothing to indicate how she had removed it. The police never located a bloody washcloth or towel; there was no sign of blood in the kitchen sink or any other place where she might have washed up after the crime. Several witnesses testified that her hair was neither wet nor disarranged. She left no trace at the crime scene itself; no item of clothing or piece of jewelry belonging to Lizzie was found near the bodies. Her demeanor and behavior immediately after the discovery of the crime was not what we might expect of a person who had just committed a horrible, brutal crime. Lizzie showed no trace of excitement, let alone hysteria or mania that might be expected of an axe murderer.

Perhaps most important, there was no evidence of premeditation on Lizzie's part. No one ever came forward to say that they had heard her threaten to kill her parents. Neither Andrew, Abby nor anyone else in the Borden household ever expressed fear as to what Lizzie might do to them. There is no direct evidence that Lizzie contemplated murder, let alone committed it.

Any one of these negatives by itself can be explained readily, but taken together they argue strongly for Lizzie's innocence. The greatest weakness of the prosecution's case lay in what they didn't present, not in what they did. Lizzie's lawyer, Andrew Jennings, put it well when he said:

"There is not one particle of direct evidence in this case, from beginning to end, against Lizzie Borden. There is not a spot of blood, there is not a weapon they have connected with her in any way, shape or fashion. They have not had her hand touch it or her eye see it or her ear hear of it. There is not, I say, a particle of direct testimony in the case connecting her with the crime."

The case against Lizzie rested on some suspicious things she said and did before and after the murders. In what's left of this chapter we will examine four items in this category.

Why Couldn't Lizzie Get her Story Straight?

Reportedly District Attorney Knowlton was not convinced of Lizzie's guilt until she testified at the inquest. After that he had no doubts, at one point referring to her testimony as a "confession". This reaction was based on inconsistencies between what Lizzie said at different times and to different people. First off she claimed at the inquest that she went to the barn to find lead for sinkers. In contrast, she told Alice Russell she was looking for a piece of tin or iron to fix a screen. Lizzie just couldn't seem to get her metals straight.

Again, at the inquest Lizzie said she came back from the barn to the dining room, where she laid down her hat. Only when she passed into the sitting room did she discover her father's mutilated body. According to Bridget, Lizzie told her a quite different story, saying, "I was out in the back yard and heard a groan and came in."

Then there was the question as to where Lizzie was when her father came back from downtown Fall River. First she testified she was downstairs when Bridget opened the door to let Andrew into the house. A few minutes later she changed her mind, saying, "I think I was in my room upstairs." Still later, she switched back to her original position: "I think, as nearly as I know, I think I was in the kitchen. "

Actually, these contradictions are not as bad as they sound. Lizzie said she went up to her room sometime that morning to, "sew a little piece of tape on a garment." She couldn't remember exactly when she came back downstairs, before Andrew returned or afterwards. In general, it's ridiculous to expect a person to remember, a week later, their exact whereabouts at a particular moment. If you were to ask me what part of our house I was in when my wife returned from shopping last Thursday, I wouldn't have the faintest idea.

All the inconsistencies in Lizzie's testimony are understandable considering the stress she was under. As Andrew Jennings put it:

"Is there anybody here who heard that testimony of the inquest that didn't think she was on the rack . . . ? Over and over again she was asked the same question in order to get her to contradict herself. The minutest details were gone into, and she was obliged to state the exact order of her movements that morning."

Figure 10.3 Pinkerton article

Lizzie's behavior here seems more indicative of innocence than guilt. A guilty person memorizes a story and repeats it over and over again in the same way. An innocent person, unable to remember exactly what happened when, never quite gets the story straight. This point was made eloquently by Robert Pinkerton, head of Pinkerton's National Detective Agency, in a newspaper interview reproduced above.

PINKERTON'S VIEW.

He Seems to Think the Crime Committed by an Insane Person.

Robert Pinkerton gave his views on the Borden murders to a New York reporter Saturday. He said he had not studied the case from a detective's standpoint, but only through the newspapers.

When asked if he thought the murderer an insane person, he said: "Judging from what I have read about the case, it seems to me that the person who killed Mr. and Mrs. Borden must have been insane, but I would not care to be quoted as advancing an insanity theory."

Continuing he said: "It seems strange that there are no more conclusive clues to be followed if the reports of bloodstained walls and ceiling are true. If they are in such a condition the murderer must have gone away with blood stains on his clothing. Now where are these bloody clothes? The mere fact that Miss Borden has told conflicting stories is more in her favor than if she had unhesitatingly stuck to the same tale, as an innocent person is more likely to make conflicting statements than is a guilty one."

From *Lizzie Borden Sourcebook*, p. 119

Why did Lizzie Quarrel with Emma (if she did)?

In late August of 1892, Hannah Reagan, a matron at the Fall River Police station, told of the following conversation between the Borden sisters:

Lizzie: You gave me away, Emma, didn't you?

Emma: No, Lizzie, I only told Mr. Jennings what he ought to know for your defense.

Lizzie: That is false, you have given me away and I know it. But remember, I will not give in one inch, never, never. That is all I have to say to you.

This exchange was followed by a two hour silence.

Mrs. Reagan later denied the story, even offering to sign a paper to that effect if Marshal Hilliard would let her. Hillard denied her request, saying that if she had anything to say she could do it in court. Mrs. Reagan did that, repeating her story at Lizzie's trial. The defense put on several witnesses to discredit her. For example, Thomas Hickey, a reporter for the *Fall River Globe*, stated that Mrs. Reagan told him there was no quarrel and Lizzie never used the words, "You gave me away" Hickey then said, "Mrs. Reagan, there is absolutely no truth in the story?" and she replied, "No, sir, no truth at all." The effect of Hickey's testimony and that of other defense witnesses was such that Governor Robinson devoted only about two minutes of his six hour summation to the Hannah Reagan affair.

And yet, I wonder. Why would Mrs. Reagan make up this story? Why would she repeat it under oath, particularly since she liked Lizzie? My guess is that the quarrel between Lizzie and Emma did take place, pretty much as Mrs. Reagan described it. She probably repeated it to Marshal Hilliard as an interesting bit of gossip. He took it more seriously, telling Mrs. Reagan she would have to testify in court. At that point, she may well have started backpedaling as fast as she could. Not only did she not want to hurt Lizzie but she dreaded a court appearance in which the opposing lawyer would accuse her of dishonesty. To avoid this, she denied the story; ultimately she had to testify anyway.

Assuming Mrs. Reagan was telling the truth (the first time!), does this demonstrate Lizzie's guilt? Of course not; Lizzie's statement that, "You have given me away" does not imply that Emma had confessed Lizzie's guilt. Besides, it's ludicrous to suppose that Emma went to Andrew Jennings and said something like, "Do the best you can for poor Lizzie even though she did chop up father." Even if Emma had been inclined to confess, Jennings almost certainly would have cut her off. The last thing a lawyer wants to hear is that his client is guilty.

It's interesting to speculate as to what Emma told Jennings, if indeed she told him anything at all. One thing she might have told him was that, although Lizzie didn't kill her parents, she knew who did. There were some hints from time to time that Lizzie was protecting someone. Judge Dewey in his charge to the jury asked them to consider the possibility that she might have been an accessory to the crime, even though there was no testimony to that effect. Arthur Phillips, an assistant to Andrew Jennings at the trial, made a peculiar statement many years later. He said that Jennings retained a mass of documents related to Lizzie's defense because he didn't want to jeopardize her by disclosing facts "which might by any possibility be important if the crime should be reconsidered by the District Attorney." It's reasonable for Lizzie's guilt to be reconsidered in books such as this one, but not in a criminal trial. That would be "double jeopardy" and it's illegal. So what did Phillips (and Jennings) have in mind?

Alternatively, Emma might have wanted to warn Jennings about material incriminating to Lizzie that had not been revealed at that point. That way he would not be blind sided when and if the prosecution introduced such material. This is an intriguing possibility that we'll explore later.

What Dress did Lizzie Wear When?

There was a great deal of testimony at the trial concerning the dress that Lizzie wore immediately after the murders. Was it or wasn't it the one she gave to the police for examination? Phoebe Bowen thought it was, Adelaide Churchill thought it wasn't and other witnesses weren't sure. In truth, this whole tedious discussion was really irrelevant except, perhaps, as it related to Lizzie's veracity.

Everyone who was in close contact with Lizzie after the murders said they saw no blood on her clothes. The absence of blood could have come about because:

- Lizzie was guilty, got blood on her clothes, then changed to a clean dress after the murders.
- Lizzie was innocent, got no blood on her dress, and so had no reason to change it.

Clearly the key question is not what dress Lizzie was wearing at 11:30 that morning. The important question is whether it was the same one she wore at 9:00 A.M. If Lizzie changed her dress, she was almost certainly guilty; if she didn't she was probably innocent.

Only one person was in a position to know whether Lizzie changed her dress; Bridget Sullivan talked to her before and after the murders. What did she have to say on this subject? According to the *New York Herald* of August 6, 1892: "The statement of the serving girl that Lizzie Borden wore the same dress all the morning and that upon that garment there was no spot of blood has been verified." This was confirmed in 1893 by a reporter for the periodical *Once A Week* (soon to become *Collier's*), who said, "Bridget Sullivan, a levelheaded and observing young woman, says Miss Lizzie did not change her clothes."

That might seem to settle the matter, but it doesn't. Bridget testified under oath at the inquest, the preliminary hearing and the trial. Her inquest testimony disappeared mysteriously. At the trial no one asked her the crucial question, probably because neither side knew what she might say. At the preliminary hearing, Bridget appeared to contradict what she had earlier told reporters on the subject.

Q. (Adams) "When you saw Miss Lizzie at the foot of the stairs, at that time when she gave the alarm, what dress did she have on?"

A. (Bridget Sullivan) "I could not tell you."

Q. (Adams) "What dress did she wear that morning?"

A. (Bridget Sullivan) "I could not tell you."

Ordinarily, "I could not tell you" would be taken to mean, "I do not know", but other interpretations are possible. Remember (Chapter 4) that, at the preliminary hearing, Bridget admitted she had been coached by the prosecution on one aspect of her testimony. She declined to tell Melvin Adams what instructions Knowlton gave her but did say that he read a statement of about a half dozen words. Do you suppose it was precisely five words, i.e. "I could not tell you?"

At the grand jury hearing in December of 1892, Alice Russell testified for the first time that on Sunday morning after the murders Lizzie burned a cheap cotton dress called a "Bedford cord" in the kitchen stove. She repeated her story at the trial (Chapter 6).

As you may recall, Emma Borden generally corroborated Alice Russell's account of the dress burning incident but added to it. She said that the Bedford cord dress became stained with paint when the house was painted in May. (That was confirmed by Mrs. Raymond, the family dressmaker). According to Emma, she asked Lizzie on Saturday after the crime, "Why haven't you burned that old dress yet?" Emma tried to explain to the jury that it was the custom in the Borden family to dispose of old rags by burning them, but Knowlton's objection to that part of her testimony was sustained.

The prosecution maintained that the dress Lizzie burned must have been stained with blood. However, the police searched the house thoroughly on Saturday, August 6. They never found a bloodstained dress, even though that was exactly what they were looking for (along with a bloody hatchet). It seems strange that Lizzie could have been clever enough to hide a dress so that the police couldn't find it on Saturday but stupid enough to burn that dress on Sunday in the presence of two witnesses with a policeman on patrol outside the house. Alice Russell told her afterwards, "Lizzie I think the worst thing you could do was to burn that dress." Lizzie replied, "Oh, what made you let me do it?"

Incidentally, it's possible that the dress burning incident was the one that Emma revealed to Jennings in August 1892, thereby incurring Lizzie's wrath. That's unlikely though. A few days after the "Hannah Reagan affair", Jennings said in court, "Where is the dress she had on that morning? Is there any smell of burnt clothing?" He would hardly have done this if he had prior knowledge that Lizzie did indeed burn a dress.

Why Did Lizzie Play Cassandra?

You will recall (Chapter 2) that on the evening before the murders Lizzie told Alice Russell that she was afraid something awful was about to happen in the Borden household. Like Cassandra, the accursed prophetess of Greek mythology, her prediction proved to be accurate but no one believed her.

Alice Russell was probably the closest friend of the Borden sisters, but her testimony certainly didn't help Lizzie. Her account of the conversation that evening was particularly incriminating. Miss Russell testified that:

"Lizzie said she didn't know about going to Marion, there was something coming over her and she felt as if something was going to happen. She said that her father had much trouble with his tenants; that it worried her.

"She said that she was afraid her father had an enemy, for a man had come to see him several times. She said she had seen a man hanging around the house nights and that the barn had been broken into and the house robbed in broad daylight. She had to sleep with one eye open half of the time and was afraid the house would be burned down over their heads. Then Lizzie said she didn't know but what somebody would do something."

Many people have taken Lizzie's prophetic words as an attempt to establish an alibi in advance. Alternatively, it could have been a last minute call for help. Perhaps Lizzie was trying to say, "Stop me before I do something horrible." Either way, her rambling conversation with Alice Russell suggests a guilty conscience.

As you might expect, Robinson came up with a different interpretation: "It is not for me to declare, but you will recollect that Miss Lizzie's (monthly) illness was continuing at the time and we know from sad experience that many a woman at such a time is all unbalanced, her disposition disturbed, her mind unsettled for the time being, and everything is out of sorts and out of joint and she really is disabled for a period of time."

All in all Alice Russell was probably the most damaging witness against Lizzie. Yet, after her testimony, she told a reporter for the *Fall River Evening News* that, "Neither by anything I heard in the Borden house before or after the murders was I ever made to believe that Lizzie committed the murders. I don't believe in her guilt now."

If you check the symbols in the margins in this chapter, you will find that **INNOCENT** is well ahead on points. Of the ten items considered, **INNOCENT** wins five "rounds" as opposed to only one for **GUILTY**. Four are "even", either too close to call or basically irrelevant to the question of her guilt or innocence. However, we have yet to mention three of the strongest points in the prosecution's case against Lizzie; they will be discussed in succeeding chapters.

First off (Chapter 11), we'll consider Lizzie's alleged attempt to buy prussic acid, a deadly poison. Then (Chapter 12) we'll look at the matter of the note that Lizzie claimed her stepmother received shortly before she died; the prosecution insisted that no such note existed.

Perhaps the strongest point against Lizzie was her complete inability to explain why she was unaware of her stepmother's murder. According to prosecution witnesses, Abby was killed sometime between 9 and 10 A.M. Lizzie admitted she was in the house during that time period. It would seem that at the very least she would have heard her stepmother's 200 lb body crash to the floor with a thud.

Quite clearly, the time at which Abby died was crucial to the prosecution's argument on this last point. Is it possible that their witnesses were wrong as to Abby's time of death, as we've hinted from time to time? To be specific, could she have been murdered as late as 11 A.M., at about the same time as her husband, while Lizzie was out in the barn? These questions are sufficiently important to devote two chapters (13 and 14) to them.

GUILTY

Chapter 11
THE PRUSSIC ACID STORY

Prussic acid is a water solution of hydrogen cyanide, a poisonous gas with an odor variously described as resembling that of oil of almonds, peach blossoms or maraschino cherries. In a stoppered, partially filled bottle of prussic acid, the air space above the liquid contains appreciable amounts of hydrogen cyanide. If the stopper is removed, some of the hydrogen cyanide gas escapes into the surroundings. That explains why prussic acid is dangerous to work with.

Shortly after the Borden murders, a pharmacist named Eli Bence told the police that Lizzie Borden had recently visited his drugstore, located at the corner of South Main and Columbia Streets in Fall River. According to Bence, this occurred on the morning of Wednesday, August 3, sometime between 10:00 and 11:30 A.M. Lizzie made an unusual request, asking for ten cents worth of prussic acid. The "prussic acid story" became an overnight sensation, as indicated by the headlines in the local papers (Chapter 1, p. 19).

Bence repeated his story at the inquest and later at the preliminary hearing, where he testified as follows:

Q. (Knowlton) "Tell all that took place."
A. (Bence) "I informed her that we did not sell prussic acid without a doctor's prescription. She said she wanted it, I believe, to put on a seal skin sack or a seal skin cape, I would not be certain which. I again told her we did not sell it without a doctor's prescription, that it was something that was very dangerous, and we did not sell it. I believe she said she had purchased the article before. I believe that is all that took place."
Q. (Knowlton) "Then she went out?"
A. (Bence) "Yes, sir."
Q. (Knowlton) "Is this defendant [Lizzie Borden] the woman?"
A. (Bence) "Yes, sir."
Q. (Knowlton) "Are you sure?"
A. Bence) "Yes, sir."

At the trial, you will recall, the prussic acid evidence was excluded (Chapter 5). Nevertheless, it's worth considering here insofar as the entire matter relates to Lizzie's guilt or innocence. This time around, we will focus on a single, critical question. Did Lizzie indeed attempt to buy prussic acid and, if so, what did she intend to do with it?

Did Lizzie Try to Buy Prussic Acid?

As you can imagine, the defense at the preliminary hearing tried to refute Bence's identification of Lizzie as the young lady who tried to buy prussic acid the day before the murders. Adams, on cross-examination, showed that Bence could not identify any other woman who came into the drugstore that morning. Neither could he say what they bought or attempted to buy.

Eli Bence responded that he took particular notice of Lizzie because of the unique nature of her request. In all of his previous experience, no one had ever asked for prussic acid. That makes sense; by itself, prussic acid has no medicinal use. It was kept on hand so that pharmacists could add a drop or two to a large volume of a prescription. As Bence said:

"We don't keep prussic acid in its strength; we only keep the dilute two percent. One drop of strong prussic acid has proved fatal. The dilution is as high as four drops; I have given that on prescription. We never put up four drops without first inquiring of the doctor. I would not like to give anybody five drops."

Most commonly, the prescription referred to here was for a cough suppressant or sedative. A hundred years ago, you couldn't go to the drugstore and ask for a bottle of *Robitussin* or *Benadryl*. Medicines were made up to order by a pharmacist starting from scratch.

The defense would have been on more solid ground had they challenged the way Bence identified Lizzie. The police should have asked him to pick her out of a lineup of young women with similar features. Instead, Bence went to the Borden house at 8 P.M. on August 4. There he observed Lizzie and listened to her voice. Evidence obtained this way, amounting to a yes or no identification, is at best unreliable.

There was another problem with the identification procedure. Remember, 8 P.M. was Eastern Standard Time; "daylight saving" didn't come in until World War I. The Old Farmer's Almanac tells us that sunset in New England in early August comes at about 7 P.M.; an hour later it is pitch dark. This means that Eli Bence identified Lizzie under artificial light. In the Borden house in 1892, "artificial light" meant candles or kerosene lamps. An identification made under these conditions has to be somewhat uncertain.

If the prussic acid evidence had been admitted at the trial, the defense might have used the argument just described. Beyond that they would almost certainly have brought up an item that appeared in several local papers a few days after the prussic acid story broke. The article reproduced below is taken from the *Fall River Evening News* of August 15, 1892.

Figure 11.1 Article on prussic acid incident

The poison theory, so far as actual use of the drugs by the victims is concerned, has been practically given up. The importance now attached to the alleged effort of Miss Borden to purchase prussic acid is based upon the theory that she intended to use it herself, should she be suspected of having committed the crime. This, however, is not very tenable, as Miss Borden had ample opportunity to do away with herself since these suspicions were made known to her, by other means. The fact that Inspector McCaffrey had several female agents in Fall River at the time of the murders, also leads many to believe that the identification of Miss Borden as a person who sought to buy prussic acid, is a case of mistaken identity.

"Think of the manner in which they got that drug clerk to positively identify Lizzie as the woman who bought prussic acid. Instead of bringing the two together where there were other women and asking him to point her out, they take him into her presence and ask him is this the woman. Now it turns out that several women were being employed at that time to buy poison for the purpose of testing the druggists as to whether they were fulfilling the provisions of the law in selling it. That explanation will no doubt kill off the one most suspicious circumstance weighing against Lizzie.

From: *Fall River News*, Aug. 5, 1892; *Lizzie Borden Sourcebook*, p. 100;

Lizzie Borden, p. 48 (Williams)

Apparently there was a sting operation going on in Fall River in the summer of 1892. Inspector McCaffrey, whoever he may have been, hired female agents (including his wife) to visit area drugstores and make inquiries similar to Lizzie's. If they could persuade a pharmacist to sell them a poison or restricted drug without a prescription, his license would be revoked. According to one newspaper report, McCaffrey's wife resembled Lizzie Borden.

On the other hand, there was some solid evidence behind Bence's identification of Lizzie. He said that he had seen her on the street a number of times and knew her as Miss Borden. That's reasonable; 92 Second Street is only a couple of blocks from the drugstore where he worked. Bence went on to say that he recognized Lizzie by, "a peculiar expression around the eyes, which I noticed at the time and noticed then." Looking at photographs of Lizzie, it seems to me that she does have a peculiar expression around the eyes (or somewhere).

Bence's identification of Lizzie was supported by two young men who were in the drugstore at the time. One of them, Frederick Harte, said simply that the woman he saw that day looked like the defendant at the preliminary hearing; he had never seen Lizzie Borden before. The other, a medical student named Frank Kilroy, was more positive. He said that he knew Lizzie by sight and recognized her when she came in to buy ten cents worth of prussic acid.

Lizzie denied that she tried to buy prussic acid from Bence. Indeed, in her inquest testimony, she went considerably beyond that.

Q. (Knowlton) "Your attention has already been called to the circumstances of going into the drugstore . . . on the corner of Columbia and Main Streets by some officer, has it not, on the day before the tragedy?"

A. (Lizzie Borden) "I don't know whether some officer has asked me. Somebody has spoken of it to me. I don't know who it was."

Q. (Knowlton) "Did that take place?"

A. (Lizzie Borden) "It did not."

Q. (Knowlton) "Do you know where the drugstore is?"

A. (Lizzie Borden) "*I don't.*"

Q. (Knowlton) "Did you go into any drugstore and inquire for prussic acid?"

A. (Lizzie Borden) "I did not."

Q. (Knowlton) "Where were you on Wednesday morning that you remember?"
A. (Lizzie Borden) "At home."
Q. (Knowlton) "All the time?"
A. (Lizzie Borden) "*All day until Wednesday night.*"

It's hard to believe that Lizzie didn't know where the drugstore was, since it was so close to her home at 92 Second Street. Moreover, her testimony here contradicted what she said earlier at the inquest.

Q. (Knowlton) "When did [John Morse] come to the house the last time before your mother and father were killed?"
A. (Lizzie Borden) "He stayed there all night Wednesday night."
Q. (Knowlton) "My question is when he came there."
A. (Lizzie Borden) "I don't know. I was not there when he came. *I was out.*"

John Morse arrived at the Borden house early Wednesday afternoon. All in all, Lizzie's prussic acid story was probably the single most incriminating feature of her testimony.

The likelihood that Lizzie lied about her trip to the drugstore is increased by a statement made later by a member of her defense team, Arthur Phillips, assistant to Andrew Jennings. In the *History of Fall River*, published in the 1940s, he wrote:

She was contradicted by Eli Bence concerning her attempt to purchase poison, but at the time of her trial this evidence was excluded as immaterial since there was no evidence that any poison was used or actually purchased. She had sought to purchase it for an innocent purpose.

Notice that Phillips' last sentence is a simple statement of fact. He said *she sought to purchase* prussic acid, not "she could have sought or "she allegedly sought . . . ."

It's difficult, in the final analysis, to evaluate the prussic acid story because it was never tested at the trial. Testimony there might have made it easier to decide which one of the two people, Eli Bence or Lizzie Borden, were to be believed. From the information available, my guess is that Bence's version was correct and that Lizzie lied. Quite possibly, this was the information that Emma gave to Jennings, thereby inspiring the Hannah Reagan story (Chapter 10). She may well have told Jennings: "Do whatever you can to keep Bence off the witness stand at the trial. Lizzie tried to buy prussic acid for an innocent purpose and then foolishly denied the whole story."

This makes a lot more sense than a "confession" that Lizzie committed murder. If indeed Lizzie lied about the prussic acid, it wouldn't be conclusive so far as her guilt or innocence is concerned. As pointed out earlier, innocent people sometimes lie when they feel that the truth would be incriminating. It's a foolish thing to do, but it happens. The key question is, "Why did Lizzie want prussic acid?" Did she intend to use it to murder her parents? Or did she really plan to use it on a sealskin sack or cape, as she told Eli Bence?

Why Use Prussic Acid as a Murder Weapon?

Edmund Pearson in the *Trial Of Lizzie Borden* tells the following story: "When Mr. Knowlton first entered the Borden house, he chanced to pick up a large book. It dealt with recipes, drugs and medicines. It fell open in his hand, the back was half broken, to an article on prussic acid." This incident is probably apocryphal. However, if Lizzie did read the article on prussic acid, she certainly never would have chosen it as a poison.

For starters, the active ingredient of prussic acid, hydrogen cyanide gas, is one of the easiest poisons to detect, as you may be able to deduce from the data shown below.

RESPONSES EXPECTED UPON EXPOSURE TO HYDROGEN CYANIDE IN AIR

Concentration (ppm)*   Response

Concentration (ppm)*	Response
1	Threshold for odor detection
5-20	Headache, dizziness
20-50	Nausea, vomiting, convulsions
100	Fatal in one hour
200	Fatal in ten minutes
300	Fatal immediately
10,000	Life threatening even with a gas mask

* ppm = 1 part per million = 1 molecule/1,000,000 molecules air

Notice that the odor of hydrogen cyanide can be detected at concentrations as low as one part per million. This virtually guarantees that police or other observers coming upon the murder scene will smell the characteristic odor of oil of almonds (or whatever) and identify the cause of death as cyanide poisoning. Equally important, hydrogen cyanide acts very rapidly. Notice that this gas, at concentrations as low as 300 ppm, is instantly fatal; a live, healthy person exposed to hydrogen cyanide at this concentration dies instantaneously. Anyone observing a sudden death of this type would be inclined to suspect foul play. If it happened twice in succession (Andrew and Abby Borden), they would be even more convinced that murder had taken place.

Still another telltale symptom of hydrogen cyanide poisoning is the presence of rosy-red blotches on the skin of the victim. Hydrogen cyanide is a respiratory poison; it destroys an enzyme essential to the transfer of oxygen from the blood to living cells and tissues. As a result, oxygen remains in the bloodstream in the form of its bright red complex with hemoglobin. In hydrogen cyanide poisoning, this characteristic red color appears in the veins as well as the arteries, hence the red blotches.

All of these indicators of hydrogen cyanide poisoning are described in gory detail in a book entitled *Poisons, Their Effect and Detection*, 3rd edition, published in 1895. (The spine of my copy is *completely* broken). This book points out another reason why prussic acid is almost never used in homicides. Of all poisons, it is perhaps the most dangerous to work with. The concentration of hydrogen cyanide above a dilute solution is of the order of 10,000 parts per million. Looking back to the data on page 179, you can see why Eli Bence said prussic acid was, "something that was very dangerous." Carl Scheele, the Swedish chemist who discovered prussic acid, found this out the hard way. In 1786 he dropped a bottle of prussic acid, which broke when it struck the laboratory floor. The accident was fatal. It follows that a person attempting to use prussic acid as a murder weapon might well commit suicide instead.

If Lizzie was searching for a way to dispose of her parents, the book on poisons that she allegedly consulted would have suggested several chemicals more appropriate than hydrogen cyanide. An obvious alternative would be sodium cyanide, a nonvolatile poisonous solid that looks a lot like ordinary table salt. Sodium cyanide acts on the human body in essentially the same way as hydrogen cyanide. However, since it is a solid rather than a gas, sodium cyanide is much safer to work with.

Why Did Lizzie Ask for Prussic Acid?

The judges in the Borden trial excluded Eli Bence's testimony because they concluded that Lizzie could have wanted prussic acid for some purpose other than killing her father and stepmother. In particular, she might have wanted to use it to kill moths in furs. As it turns out, they were right; for many years prussic acid was used as a general purpose insecticide and fumigant.

In 1886 prussic acid, or more exactly hydrogen cyanide, was first used as an insecticide in the citrus groves of California. A tree infested with something called "cottony cushion scale" was surrounded by a tent inside which hydrogen cyanide gas was generated. The experiment was successful (the cottony cushion scales never knew what hit them) and this application of hydrogen cyanide spread rapidly. Between 1900 and World War II (when synthetic organic insecticides like DDT were developed), hydrogen cyanide was the fumigant of choice for holds of ships, warehouses and private residences. Among the insect pests destroyed by this chemical were several different varieties of moths.

Was prussic acid used commercially by furriers in Massachusetts in 1892? Almost certainly not; one of the expert witnesses who testified for the prosecution on this subject would have known about it. Were there articles in the popular literature suggesting the use of hydrogen cyanide as a fumigant and insecticide? Indeed there were; in 1890 an article describing its use for this purpose appeared in a supplement to *Scientific American*, then as now a popular journal relating the latest advances in science. Did Lizzie read this or other related articles? Quite possibly she did. Lizzie was a voracious reader; a clerk at the Fall River library said she took out more books than anyone else in the city.

Granted, Lizzie would have been foolish to experiment with prussic acid to mothproof her furs. That would have been almost, but not quite, as dangerous as using prussic acid to dispose of her parents. Many years later, a German chemist using a Rube Goldberg like device to fumigate his clothes with hydrogen cyanide, managed to kill himself in the process.

There is, however, an important distinction between these two applications of prussic acid. Any book on poisons that Lizzie consulted would point out how lethal this substance is. An article extolling the use of hydrogen cyanide as an insecticide might say little or nothing about its toxicity to humans. Indeed, the *Scientific American* article referred to above said nothing whatsoever on that subject. The author apparently assumed that fumigation would be carried out by trained professionals, not amateurs like Lizzie Borden. As a true daughter of Andrew Borden, Lizzie would see it differently. Storing furs in a mothfree warehouse would cost a lot more than ten cents.

In summary, the evidence convinces me that:

- despite Lizzie's denial,
  she did indeed ask Eli Bence for ten cents worth of prussic acid,
- the judges were indeed correct that prussic acid could be used for an innocent purpose.
- Lizzie did indeed want prussic acid for an innocent purpose, to mothproof furs.
- Eli Bence was wise to refuse to sell prussic acid; Lizzie might well have killed herself trying to kill moths.

Chapter 12
ABBY'S MYSTERIOUS NOTE

According to Lizzie, Abby Borden told her on the morning of the murders that she had received a note concerning someone who was sick. As a result, Abby left the Borden house, presumably to visit the person who sent the note. When her father came home later, Lizzie told him about the incident to explain her stepmother's absence. Shortly thereafter, she told Bridget; later in the day she repeated the story about the note to several people.

At the inquest, Lizzie described the conversation she had with her stepmother.

Q. (Knowlton) "Tell me all the talk you had with your mother when she came down in the morning."

A. (Lizzie Borden) "She asked me how I felt. I said I felt better but did not want any breakfast. She said what kind of meat did I want for dinner. I said I did not want any. She said she was going out; somebody was sick and she would get the dinner, get the meat, order the meat. And I think she said something about the weather, and I don't remember that she said anything else. I said to her, 'Won't you change your dress before you go out?' She had on an old one. She said, 'No, this is good enough.' That is all I can remember."

The prosecution maintained at the trial that Lizzie lied; there was no note. In his opening statement, Moody said, "Mr. Borden went first to the dining room and [Lizzie] came in and asked if there was any mail and said Mrs. Borden had gone out. She had got a note from somebody who was sick. That, gentlemen, we put to you was a lie, intended for no purpose except to stifle inquiry as to where Mrs. Borden was."

Knowlton, in his closing argument, put it more strongly, "No note came; no note was written; nobody brought a note; nobody was sick. Mrs. Borden had not had a note. I will stake [this case] on your belief or disbelief in the truth or falsity of that proposition."

Was There a Note?

There are a couple of reasons for doubting Lizzie's story about the note. To begin with, no such note was ever found. Lizzie looked for it; so did Dr. Bowen. The police searched the house unsuccessfully. Alice Russell suggested that Abby burned it in the kitchen stove. Quite possibly she did. A hundred years ago, there were no "sanitary landfills" or "recycling centers". The "household garbage disposal unit" was the kitchen stove, at least for flammable material. That was true for Fall River in the 1890s as it was in the 1930s in rural New Hampshire where I grew up. (The system used to dispose of nonflammable items was even simpler, but you don't want to hear about that).

It's s more difficult to explain why neither the person who delivered the note nor the one who wrote it ever came forward. The periodical *Once a Week* offered a $500 reward for information about the note. Five hundred dollars may seem a small amount but in 1892 it had the purchasing power of several thousand dollars today.

There is another puzzling aspect of the story about the note: the idea that Mrs. Borden would go out to pay a visit to a sick person. Abby was a good woman, but she wasn't the type who took it upon herself to comfort the afflicted or visit the sick. She was a shy, retiring person with only one close friend, her half sister Sarah Whitehead. Moreover, even if Abby had gone out on an errand of mercy, she would never have neglected to change her dress. That simply wasn't done a hundred years ago in Fall River or anywhere else in this country. Alice Russell, before going over to the Borden house to console Lizzie after her father's murder, changed her dress.

On the other hand, as Judge Dewey pointed out in his charge to the jury (Chapter 8), it's hard to believe that Lizzie would have told her father an elaborate lie when a simple one would have sufficed. Instead of making up a story about a note, which could be checked and perhaps disproven, Lizzie could have said simply, "Abby went out to get something for dinner." Certainly Andrew Borden would not have questioned such a statement. Everyone who spoke on the subject, including Adelaide Churchill and Emma Borden, agreed that Abby ordinarily did the grocery shopping. Indeed, Lizzie went a step further in her inquest testimony, saying that Abby went out nearly every morning for that purpose.

Furthermore, the existence of a note is corroborated in a conversation between Bridget Sullivan and Adelaide Churchill. In her trial testimony,

Mrs. Churchill quoted Bridget as saying, "Mrs. Borden had a note to go see someone who was sick and *she was dusting the (dining] room and hurried off.* She didn't tell me where she was going; she generally does." [emphasis added]

Bridget had made it clear earlier that she learned of the note from Lizzie. However, Lizzie said nothing to Bridget or anyone else about Mrs. Borden hurrying off, leaving her chore of dusting the first floor rooms. That was Bridget's contribution and hers alone. It suggests strongly that Abby Borden left the house in response to the note, as Lizzie maintained.

One factor more than any other indicates that Lizzie was telling the truth, at least as she understood it, about the note. Andrew Borden seems to have accepted her story at face value; he made no attempt to challenge it. Yet Andrew must have known how unlikely it was that his wife would interrupt her morning chores to go out to visit a sick stranger. It seems reasonable to suppose that Andrew accepted Lizzie's story without comment because he knew the note existed.

Most likely, it was Andrew who received the note. In the period around 9:00 A.M. when the note arrived, he went outside at least twice, first to bid goodbye to John Morse and then to start off downtown. On one or the other of these occasions, he may well have intercepted the messenger, taken the note from him, and gone back inside to give it to Abby. This would explain why neither Lizzie nor Bridget saw or heard anyone coming to the door to deliver a note.

The weight of the evidence suggests that Abby Borden did indeed receive a note on that fateful morning. However, for reasons which will become clear shortly, I'm convinced that

- Lizzie misinterpreted what Abby said about its contents
- Abby went out, but not to visit a sick friend
- the author of the note had a very good reason for not coming forward.

Who Sent the Note?

All the newspaper stories about the note say that it was delivered by a boy. This information seems to have come from Lizzie. At the preliminary hearing, Dr. Dolan testified that, "I asked Lizzie if her mother had received the note; she said she had. I asked her if she had seen the note and she said no. I asked her if she knew who brought it; she said she did not know and thought it was a *boy*." [emphasis added]

In a couple of articles, the reference is to a small boy. Edwin Porter, in his *Fall River Tragedy, a History of the Borden Murders*, published in 1893, says:

While in the upper part of the house, [Lizzie] was approached by Assistant Marshal Fleet who made numerous inquiries concerning the condition of things in the house previous to the murders. She told him, as she had told others, that Mrs. Borden had received a note delivered by a boy, early in the morning, asking her to come and visit a friend who was sick. She did not know who sent the message, except that the bearer was a small *boy*.

Speculation as to who wrote the note centered upon Abby Borden's half sister, Sarah Whitehead. Robert Sullivan in his book entitled *Goodbye Lizzie* Borden wrote, "Abby Borden had few if any friends other than Mrs. Whitehead and none other than Mrs. Whitehead would be likely to write a note to Mrs. Borden in the event of sickness."

Then there is the interesting statement that Bridget Sullivan made shortly after Andrew Borden's body was discovered: "If I knew where Mrs. Whitehead [lived] I would go and see if Mrs. Borden was there and tell her that Mr. Borden was very sick." Perhaps Bridget meant only that Abby was more likely to visit her sister than anyone else. Then again, she may have implied more than that. Did Lizzie tell Bridget she thought her stepmother had gone to Mrs. Whitehead's?

Finally, there was an item in the *Fall River Globe* of August 16, 1892, which read as follows: "A report was circulated last night to the effect that a woman on Fourth Street had sent a note to Mrs. Borden on the morning of the murders." Sarah Whitehead lived at 45 Fourth Street.

Putting all these things together, it seems likely that

● the note was delivered by a small boy
● one way or another, it involved Sarah Whitehead.

What Did the Note Say?

The key to solving the mystery of the note is found in Robert Sullivan's book, referred to above. In 1972 Sullivan interviewed Abby Whitehead

Potter, daughter of Sarah Whitehead and niece of Abby Borden. (From now on, we'll refer to Sarah's daughter as "little Abby"; she was eight years old at the time of the murders, eighty eight when interviewed.) It seems that Sarah Whitehead planned to attend the police picnic at Rocky Point on August 4. This required that she find baby sitters for little Abby and her younger brother George, aged five. The plan was to send little Abby to visit with her aunt at 92 Second Street; George was to stay with another aunt (Aunt Lucy) in a different part of Fall River.

On the morning of August 4th, Mrs. Whitehead changed her mind. Little Abby never knew why, but her mother decided to send both children to Aunt Lucy's house. Abby Potter said she always regretted this change in plans; had she gone to visit her Aunt Abby, the murders might never have occurred. (Then again, there might have been three murders instead of two.)

Why did Sarah Whitehead make this switch? Many reasons are possible but one stands out as most likely. Abby Borden had been very sick for a couple of days. Beyond that, she was sixty four years of age; believe it or not, that was considered "old" a hundred years ago. (Incredibly, Knowlton referred to Abby at the trial as, "the oldest, feeblest and dullest of the whole family.") Mrs. Whitehead probably decided that, all things considered, she shouldn't impose on her sister to spend an exhausting day caring for an active eight year old. Aunt Lucy (whoever she was) would have to do double duty.

Once Sarah made this decision, she had to get the information to her sister. Today she would use the phone but that wasn't possible in 1892; the Bordens didn't have a telephone. The time-efficient thing to do was to send her son George, little Abby's younger brother, to the Borden household with a note. My reconstruction of what happened next is contained in the remainder of this section.

The five-year old boy quickly made the two-block trip from 45 Fourth Street to 92 Second Street. When he arrived, Andrew Borden recognized him, took the note, and delivered it to his wife. Little George arrived home in time to be delivered, with his sister, to Aunt Lucy; his mother went off on the excursion to Rocky Point. (Heavens knows why Sarah Whitehead went to the police picnic, but everybody agrees she did.)

Mrs. Borden opened the note and read it in the dining room where she was dusting. Lizzie was nearby, either finishing her breakfast or setting up the ironing board. Out of mild curiosity or just to be polite, Lizzie asked her stepmother what the note (see below) was all about.

Abby Borden answered Lizzie along the following lines:

> It's a note from my sister Sarah; her **little boy** brought it. The note says that my niece, *little Abby*, won't be coming to **visit** me today because I've been **sick**. That's silly; I'm perfectly capable of taking care of her. I'll hurry over to her house to catch Sarah before she leaves for the picnic and bring little Abby back with me. While I'm out, I'll get the *meat for dinner*."

Lizzie, who was only half listening to Abby, caught the key words shown in italics and bold type above and not much else. She murmured some appropriate response such as, "That's nice", and went on to more important things such as ironing handkerchiefs, picking pears and, eventually, looking for lead sinkers. Small wonder Lizzie got the story garbled when she attempted to repeat it later.

Figure 12.1 The content of the mysterious note (as deduced by the author) revealed at last:

Dear Abby:
Sorry to hear how sick you've been. Hope you feel better soon. It's too much for you to take care of little Abby. What a handful she is! I'll send her along with little George to visit Lucy; she won't mind. Then I'm off for the police picnic at Rocky Point. See you when I get back.

> *In haste,*
> *Sarah W.*

It's well-known that information given orally almost always gets distorted when it's repeated. That kind of thing happens all the time, at least in our household. When my wife leaves on an errand, to visit a friend or whatever, she usually tells me where she's going. Sometimes I'm paying attention to what she's saying, sometimes not. If someone calls for her later, I try to describe her whereabouts as best I can. Frequently I give out misinformation for which I am properly chastised later. Lizzie paid a more severe penalty for her inattentiveness.

The scenario presented above cannot, of course, be proven a century after the fact. It does, however, present a simple, logical explanation of the mysterious note that Abby Borden received that morning. For one thing, it explains why the note was delivered by a small boy, little George Whitehead. Furthermore, it shows why Andrew was not surprised when Lizzie told him about the note; he was the one who received it.

Again, this version of the note story explains why Abby Borden didn't change her dress before going out. She didn't have time. Abby wanted to catch her sister before she left 45 Fourth Street with little Abby in tow. That's why she "hurried off", as Bridget put it, without taking time to change her clothes.

Finally, and most important, this interpretation explains how the key words **visit** and **sick** got into Lizzie's story about the note. Abby wasn't going out to visit a sick person, an action which would have been completely inconsistent with her personality. Instead, she was going out to try to persuade Sarah Whitehead to let her daughter **visit** 92 Second Street; never mind that Abby had been **sick** for a couple of days. Notice that in her inquest testimony quoted at the beginning of this chapter (p. 183) Lizzie said nothing about Abby visiting a sick person. Instead she testified that the note said "somebody was sick."

Why Didn't Anyone Claim the Reward?

Once it becomes clear who wrote the note and what it said, it's easy to understand why no one ever came forward to collect the $500 reward. There are three possible explanations as to why Sarah Whitehead never acknowledged sending the note (or allowed her children to do so). First off, it's barely possible that the story was so distorted that Mrs. Whitehead didn't recognize it. That seems extremely unlikely; when she read that, "a small boy delivered the note to Mrs. Borden", she had to know what the newspaper article was referring to.

A somewhat more likely explanation is that, as a relative and potential beneficiary of Abby Borden, she didn't want to get involved. This would be plausible except that Mrs. Whitehead was already involved; she testified at the inquest and again before the grand jury. It's interesting though that she didn't testify at either the preliminary hearing or the trial, where she would have been subject to cross-examination.

By far the most likely explanation of Mrs. Whitehead's failure to come forward is the dislike, bordering on hatred, that she felt for Lizzie (and Emma). There was just no way she was going to increase Lizzie's chances for acquittal by weakening the case against her.

Sarah Whitehead's animosity toward the Borden sisters started five years before the crime, as she explained in a statement to Officers Doherty and Harrington of the Fall River police department.

This property [45 Fourth Street] was owned in part by me and [in part by] my mother. My mother wished to dispose of her interest. I could not purchase it and did not want to sell. In order that I might keep my place, Mrs. Borden, my stepsister, bought the other interest. This the girls did not like; they showed their feelings on the street by not recognizing me.

Obviously relations did not improve as the years passed. Consider Mrs. Whitehead's inquest testimony.

Q. (Knowlton) "Were you well acquainted with the daughters, Emma and Lizzie?"
A. (Mrs. Whitehead) "Well, yes, I was acquainted with them."
Q. (Knowlton) "Were you on congenial terms with them?"
A. (Mrs. Whitehead) "Well I don't know as I was. I never thought they liked me."
Q. (Knowlton) "Not on particularly friendly terms then?"
A. (Mrs. Whitehead) "No, I always thought they felt above me."

Poor Lizzie; perhaps if she had been a little more friendly when she met Mrs. Whitehead on the street, the truth about the note would have come out. Then again, maybe not. Sarah Whitehead's feeling toward the Borden girls seems to have gone beyond simple dislike. Her daughter as an adult showed a pathological hatred of Lizzie which must have been inspired by her mother. Abby Whitehead Potter told several gruesome stories about Lizzie including the following:

Lizzie Borden had company and my aunt had a tabby cat . . . The cat went in where Lizzie was entertaining and she took it out and shut the door again, and it came back so this is what she told Aunt Abby and Abby told my mother . . . Lizzie Borden finally excused herself and went downstairs, took the cat downstairs, and put the [cat] on the chopping block and chopped its head off my aunt . . . for days wondered where the cat was - all she talked about. Finally Lizzie said, 'You go downstairs and you'll find your cat.' My aunt did.

Edmund Pearson, the true-crime author who was as convinced of Lizzie's guilt as the Whitehead family was, repudiated the cat story, saying, "I speak of the [cat incident] only to express my entire disbelief. Too many people are witness to Miss Borden's almost fanatical love for animals to allow even a faint possibility of its truth." Among other things, Lizzie in her will left $30,000 to the Animal Rescue League of Fall River.

There is evidence that animosity toward Lizzie extended even to Sarah Whitehead's widowed mother, Jane Gray. In a statement to police, Mrs. Gray said that she seldom went to the Borden house to visit Abby because of the Borden girls. She went on to say that she told Mrs. Borden, "I would not change places with you for all your money." One thing is certainly true. However Lizzie may have felt towards Abby Borden, she obviously didn't get along well with Abby's relatives.

Chapter 13
WHEN DID ABBY BORDEN DIE?
(THE EVIDENCE 1892-3)

T
he enduring fascination of the Borden crime is readily explained. It is insoluble, at least if we accept the conventional wisdom concerning the facts of the murders. Only two people admitted to being on the premises when Andrew and Abby were killed: Lizzie Borden and Bridget Sullivan. As we have seen, the case against Lizzie is weak; that against Bridget is considerably weaker. Beyond that, it's almost impossible to believe that an intruder entered the house undetected, killed Abby Borden somewhere around 9:30 A.M. without alarming Lizzie or Bridget, concealed him/herself for an hour or two in a closet, and emerged at 11 A.M. to kill Andrew.

A few years ago, I guesstimated, somewhat facetiously, that there was one chance in ten that Lizzie committed the murders, one in a hundred that Bridget was guilty, and one in a thousand that an "outsider" killed the Bordens. Summing the probabilities:

$$0.100 \text{ (Lizzie)} + 0.010 \text{ (Bridget)} + 0.001 \text{ (anyone else)} = 0.111 = 1/9$$

But this is impossible. There isn't one chance in nine that somebody killed Andrew and Abby; there's one chance in one! The probabilities have to add up to one. They were definitely murdered; Andrew and Abby didn't die of heat prostration and they certainly didn't kill one another.

There are, it seems, two possible explanations of this anomaly. Maybe the murderer was fiendishly clever and/or remarkably lucky. Perhaps the Borden case was the perfect crime that everyone talks about but no one has ever observed. I prefer a second alternative. Could it be that one or more of the "facts" concerning the case, generally accepted by everyone for a hundred years, is really a myth?

One of the most important "facts" about the Borden case has always puzzled me. This is the 1 - 2 hour time lapse between the murders. In the first place, if you walk into a house and find two people slaughtered, with a hatchet no less, your natural assumption is that the murders occurred in rapid succession. District Attorney Knowlton expressed this quite well in his closing argument.

"What impresses one as the remarkable and distinguishing feature of this case is the gradual discovery of the surprising fact that these two people did not come to their death at the same time. I have no doubt that each one of you [the jurors], as you heard the stories as they came flashed over the wires, had the idea that was common to everybody who did not know anything about it, and there was nobody that did, that some man had come in, rushed through the house, killed the old gentleman, rushed upstairs and killed the old lady, and then had made his escape."

There are several other facets of the time lapse between the murders that make it highly implausible. For one thing, is it psychologically likely that anyone would commit two brutal axe murders separated by a 1 - 2 hour time interval? Assume, for example, that Lizzie was the culprit. At about 9:30 A.M., for the first time in her life, she flies into a homicidal rage and chops up her stepmother. Then, for 1½ hours, she behaves in a perfectly rational manner, ironing handkerchiefs, conversing pleasantly with Bridget and with her father. Suddenly, around 11 A.M., mania returns and Lizzie slaughters her father. In the remaining thirty five years of her life, she behaves normally. One maniacal outburst is credible; two are a bit hard to swallow. The same argument applies to Bridget and, in spades to a mysterious intruder who hides in a closet between the murders.

Another oddity is that just about everyone (e.g., Lizzie Borden, Bridget Sullivan and John Morse) had detailed alibis for Andrew's murder but not for Abby's. In particular, Lizzie said she was out in the barn looking for sinkers at 11 A.M. She never claimed to be out of the house between 9 and 10 A.M. Indeed, Lizzie could offer no explanation whatsoever as to why she was unaware of Abby's murder. Might it be that she didn't have an alibi because Abby didn't die between 9 and 10 A.M., but rather around 11 A.M., nearly simultaneously with Andrew?

Finally, of the two people killed, who do you think is the more likely victim, Andrew or Abby Borden? Considering their personalities, as described in Chapter 2, the answer should be obvious. Legend has it that Andrew was an obscenely rich miser who turned widows and orphans into the streets if they fell behind on the rent. The truth is almost certainly less damning, but the fact remains that Andrew Borden was detested by most of the people who knew him. In any fictional "whodun-it", he would be the victim.

In contrast, Abby was a pleasant, self-effacing woman who stayed close to home. Neighbors, relatives and even the *Fall River Globe* had only nice things to say about her. Someone might pity or ignore Abby Borden, but it's hard to believe that she could inspire the kind of hatred required to bring about two brutal murders. It seems far more likely that Andrew was the intended victim and that Abby's murder followed shortly afterwards in an effort to cover up Andrew's.

What Did They Say at the Trial?

The exercise in logic that we have just gone through is all very well, but what are the facts? To put it simply, they are not encouraging, at least at first glance. Reading the trial testimony, it would seem highly probable that there was a time lapse and that Abby Borden was murdered earlier than her husband. Three lines of evidence supported this conclusion. First off, six different witnesses (Francis Wixon, John Fleet, Patrick Doherty, Albert Dedrick, William Dolan and George Pettee) agreed that Abby's blood was coagulated (clotted) to a greater extent than Andrew's. This was taken to mean that she must have been dead for a longer time than her husband, i.e., she must have died earlier.

Then there was Dr. Dolan's observation that Abby's body was colder than Andrew's. For some reason, Dolan chose to estimate body tempera-ture by touch, even though he had a thermometer.

Q. (Knowlton) "Did you have with you a clinical thermometer?"
A. (Dolan) "I had, yes, sir."
Q. (Knowlton) "Did you use it?"
A. (Dolan) "No, sir."

Dolan went on to say that Andrew's body was "warm" and that, when he felt Abby's body with his hand, it was much colder than Andrew's.

The strongest argument for the priority of Abby's death came from the autopsy results. Professor Wood found that Andrew's stomach contained only about one tenth solid food mixed with nine tenths water. In Abby's case, the proportions were reversed; nine tenths of the stomach contents consisted of undigested food. From this observation, Wood concluded that Mrs. Borden must have died about an hour and a half before her husband.

From what they heard in the courtroom, two prestigious expert witnesses, Dr. Draper and Dr. Cheever, agreed that Abby must have died one to two hours before Andrew. Draper was the author of a leading forensic textbook (*Legal Medicine*); Cheever was a professor at Harvard Medical School. Their conclusion was based on their evaluation of the testimony of Wood and Dolan, not on personal observation.

Many people have cited a statement made by Governor Robinson in his closing statement as a compelling argument for a time lapse between the murders. In effect Robinson conceded the point, saying that Abby Borden probably died an hour or more before Andrew. He went on to say that, at any rate, he did not intend to make an issue of the time lapse.

This concession by Robinson is not as impressive as it seems at first glance. For one thing, the defense lawyers clearly disagreed with one another about the validity of the time lapse evidence. Again and again, Adams, in cross-examining prosecution witnesses, challenged them on this point. Consider, for example, his exchange with Professor Wood.

Q. (Adams) "Could you determine from the appearance of the stomachs, assuming that the two persons had eaten their meal at the same time, who had eaten the larger meal?"
A. (Wood) "I could not."
Q. (Adams) "In all the opinions that you have given, have they been based upon the digestion being normal?"
A. (Wood) "Yes, sir."
Q. (Adams) "And if digestion had been disturbed in the case of either of these persons, that would interfere somewhat with your opinion, would it not?"
A. (Wood) "Yes, sir, if I knew that."
Q. (Adams) "I understand you are not willing then to fix the limit absolutely in your opinion beyond an hour as the difference in time in the death of these two persons?"
A. (Wood) "No, sir.

Most lawyers would agree that, regardless of the facts, the position that Robinson took in his summation was a sound one. Disproving the time lapse between the two deaths would have been helpful to Lizzie's defense, but it was not critical. Had Robinson tried to do this, he might well have failed; the jury had to be impressed, as I was, with the array of prosecution witnesses affirming the time lapse. Had the jury disbelieved Robinson on this point, they might have inferred that he was wrong on other, more critical issues. Keep in mind that by the time Robinson gave his closing argument, on the twelfth day of the trial, the press and legal authorities were virtually unanimous in predicting Lizzie's acquittal. Like a boxer who is well ahead on the referee's scorecard, Robinson would have been ill advised to try for a knockout. He (and Lizzie) might have wound up losers rather than winners.

There may have been another reason why Robinson did not dispute the time lapse. Had he done so, Lizzie's acquittal might have suggested to a probate court that the priority of the two deaths was in doubt. If Andrew Borden died before Abby, even by a few minutes, approximately one third of his estate would have gone to his wife. Upon Abby's death, that money would have passed to her sisters, Sarah Whitehead of Fall River and Priscilla Fish of Hartford, Connecticut, not to Lizzie and Emma. At the very least, any uncertainty as to who died first could have led to a long delay in settling Andrew's estate.

What Did They Say at the Preliminary Hearing?

There were a couple of items that intrigued me concerning the time lapse testimony at the trial. First, why didn't District Attorney Knowlton ask for Dr. Bowen's opinion on this matter? Not only was Bowen the Borden's family doctor; he was the first medically trained person to examine the bodies. Certainly he would have been a more credible witness than the layman George Pettee or the physician Albert Dedrick, who didn't examine the bodies until after 2 P.M.

The question as to when Dr. Bowen thought Abby died is readily answered from his testimony at the preliminary hearing.

Q. (Adams) "Did you form any opinion as to how long these people had been dead?"

A. (Bowen) "At that time [11:30 A.M.], I supposed they had been dead only a short time."

Q. (Adams) "What do you mean by only a short time?"

A. (Bowen) "I should say a half an hour."

Q. (Adams) "Did you form any opinion as to whether there was any essential difference in the time of their dying?"

A. (Bowen) "I did not at that time."

Small wonder that Knowlton did not ask Dr. Bowen about the time of death evidence at the trial!

On another matter, there was a suggestion in Adams' cross-examination of Dr. Dolan at the trial that the medical examiner had told quite a different story at the preliminary hearing, implying that the two victims had died at about the same time. Examination of the transcript of the preliminary hearing showed that this was indeed the case. Beyond that, Dolan's testimony was a mass of contradictions.

Q. (Adams) "You said, as I understood you yesterday afternoon, you went upstairs anywhere from quarter to half past twelve to complete the view of Mrs. Borden?"

A. (Dolan) "Yes, sir."

Q. (Adams) "That was the time when you formed an opinion, so far as you could, of the time that she died?"

A. (Dolan) "Yes, sir."

Q. (Adams) "You said she might have been dead an hour, or an hour and a half?"

A. (Dolan) "Yes, sir."

Q. (Adams) "Then you would fix the time of her death from eleven o'clock until quarter past eleven, would you?"

A. (Dolan) "That would bring it."

Q. (Adams) "It has got to bring it, has it not?"

A. (Dolan) "Yes, sir, somewhere around that time."

Q. (Adams) "From eleven to quarter past eleven?"

A. (Dolan) "Yes, sir."

Less than five minutes later, Dolan changed his mind.

Q. (Adams) "What time do you say Abby Borden died, after you have testified in the way you have?"

A. (Dolan) "I should say that she died from an hour to an hour and a half before Mr. Borden." [Andrew, of course, died at about 11 A.M.]

A little later, Dolan expressed still another opinion.

Q. (Adams) "How long do you think at that time [Mrs. Borden] had been dead?"

A. (Dolan) "I say by the condition of the blood it must have been from an hour to two hours."

Q. (Adams) "Would you be surprised if it was three quarters of an hour?"

A. (Dolan) "No, sir, I would not."

Q. (Adams) "You did not see her until about twelve o'clock, did you?"

A. (Dolan) "Yes, sir."

Q. (Adams) "It was about twelve o'clock, was it not?"

A. (Dolan) "Twelve o'clock." [Dolan examined Abby's body twice, at 12:00 and 12:30]

Within less than half an hour, Dr. Dolan offered three different estimates as to when Abby Borden died:

- between 11:00 and 11:15 A.M.
- between 9:30 and 10:00 A.M.
- between 10:00 and 11:00 A.M.

Take your pick!

At the preliminary hearing, Adams also ridiculed Dr. Dolan for relying on his sense of touch to determine body temperature. The exchange between the two men provided one of the few humorous moments at the courtroom proceedings.

Q. (Adams) "Can you tell . . . by touching anybody, what the temperature is?"

A. (Dolan) "I think you can come pretty near it."

Q. (Adams) "Did you ever try?"

A. (Dolan) "Yes, sir; I do not know how many times. I try it every day of my life."

Q. (Adams) "Then compare it with a thermometer?"

A. (Dolan) "Yes, sir, not for comparison."

Q. (Adams) "Within how near can you come?"

A. (Dolan) "*Half a degree, sometimes one fifth of a degree.*" [emphasis added]

Q. (Adams) "The temperature of this room, which is not as delightful as it might be, is not more than 78°?"

A. (Dolan) "Between 78° and 80°."

Q. (Adams) "*Can't you touch it and see?*" [emphasis added]

A. (Dolan) "Can't I touch what, sir?"

Q. (Adams) "I should not have said that; I beg your pardon."

Figure 13.1 Medical Examiner Dolan

According to the *Providence Journal*, "Dr. Dolan suffered with nervous prostration after the preliminary hearing." The *Fall River Herald* went a step further, stating that, "The great nervous strain that resulted almost caused his death." That is almost certainly an exaggeration, but it's quite possible that Dr. Dolan From *Lizzie Borden Sourcebook*, p. 13-10 was plagued by nightmares in which Melvin Adams starred as Satan.

Dr. Dolan was not the only medical expert who changed his position on the time of death evidence. Dr. Frank Draper, who appeared as a witness for the prosecution at the trial, testified for the defense at the preliminary hearing. Listen to what he had to say there.

Q. (Adams) "Can you form an opinion from the coagulation of blood which has come from the body, and is found near it, as to the time of death?"

A. (Draper) "Within very narrow limits."

Q. (Adams) "How narrow are these limits?"

A. (Draper) "I should say *after fifteen minutes* [from death], *it would be unsafe to form an opinion.*" [emphasis added]

Q. (Adams) "How near, by an examination of the stomach, can you come in forming an opinion as to the time of death?"

A. (Draper) "It would be approximate only."

Q. (Adams) "And by approximate, how near, within what limits?"

A. (Draper) "I am unable to give minutes."

Q. (Adams) "Well, sixty of them?"

A. (Draper) "I should not want to."

Q. (Adams) "That is to say there might easily be an hour's variation from the fact of the appearance of the stomach?"

A. (Draper) "Yes, sir, because *stomachs differ in their digestive powers in different individuals, and in the same individual under different circumstances.*" [emphasis added]

It's impossible to reconcile this testimony with what Draper said nine months later at the trial.

"I am sure from the evidence of the digestion, of the color and its condition and consistency of the blood, and of the temperature of the two bodies, that Mrs. Borden died before Mr. Borden. As to the interval, I think . . . at least an hour passed between the two deaths."

Shortly before the trial started, Knowlton, in a letter to Attorney General Pillsbury, commented that, "Dr. Draper is coming round on our side in great shape." Indeed he was, both with respect to the priority of the deaths and the identity of the murder weapon (Chapters 6, 10). Why, you may ask? In his textbook *Legal Medicine*, Draper put it quite frankly. "If the physician accepts [an invitation to appear as an expert witness] . . . inevitably he becomes to a greater or lesser degree a partisan witness, an advocate for the party on whose side he is sitting, and by whose money he is rewarded." In plain English, Frank Draper was a hired gun, albeit an extremely competent one.

One of the several doctors who examined the bodies of the victims on the morning of the murders did not testify at either the official preliminary hearing or at the actual trial held at the courthouse. This was the well-known Dr. John H. Abbott, a prominent Fall River physician, later elected mayor of Fall River (1899, 1900). Shortly after August 4, he left for Chicago to attend a conference concerning a possible cholera epidemic. When he returned to Fall River, he talked to reporters about the Borden case. As you can see from the article reproduced on next page, Abbott disputed Dolan's testimony about the temperature of the bodies.

Moreover, for whatever reason, he was convinced that Andrew Borden died before Abby.

Figure 13.2 Abbott's opinion on time of death

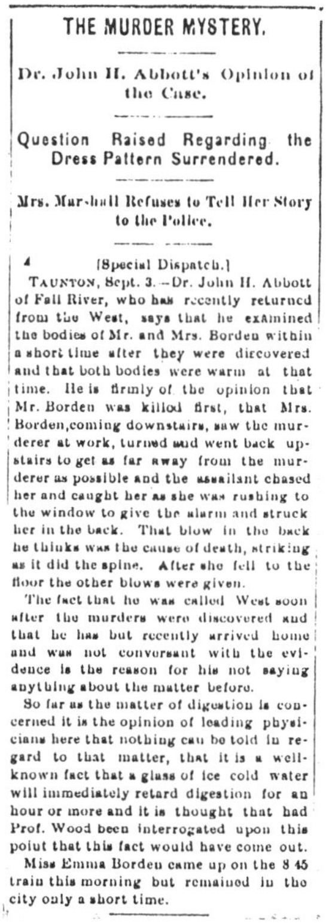

The Time Lapse; Pro and Con

This is an appropriate place to summarize what was known in 1892-3 as to when Abby Borden was killed. The trial testimony supports the thesis that she died about 1 - 2 hours before her husband. This conclusion is based upon coagulation of the blood of the victims, estimates of their body temperatures, and the relative extent of digestion.

However, at least two doctors, Bowen and Abbott, did not believe in the 1 - 2 hour time interval. Moreover, if Dr. Draper's statement about blood coagulation is correct, that evidence, cited by several police officers and two doctors, is meaningless. Finally, Dr. Dolan's conclusions about body temperature are highly suspect, in part because he relied solely on his sense of touch, but mostly because of the contradictions in his testimony.

This means that the case for the time lapse rests largely upon the autopsy evidence that indicated digestion had proceeded 1 - 2 hours further with Andrew than with Abby Borden. Keep in mind, though, that to translate this into a 1 - 2 hour time gap in the murders, you have to assume that Andrew and Abby ate essentially the same last meal at the same time. Only one person, John Morse, might have known whether this was true. This is what he had to say on the subject at the trial:

Q. (Robinson) "You and all partook of what was there [at the breakfast table] as I understand it?"

THE MURDER MYSTERY.

Dr. John H. Abbott's Opinion of the Case.

Question Raised Regarding the Dress Pattern Surrendered.

Mrs. Marshall Refuses to Tell Her Story to the Police.

[Special Dispatch.]

TAUNTON, Sept. 3.—Dr. John H. Abbott of Fall River, who has recently returned from the West, says that he examined the bodies of Mr. and Mrs. Borden within a short time after they were discovered and that both bodies were warm at that time. He is firmly of the opinion that Mr. Borden was killed first, that Mrs. Borden, coming downstairs, saw the murderer at work, turned and went back upstairs to get as far away from the murderer as possible and the assailant chased her and caught her as she was rushing to the window to give the alarm and struck her in the back. That blow in the back he thinks was the cause of death, striking as it did the spine. After she fell to the floor the other blows were given.

The fact that he was called West soon after the murders were discovered and that he has but recently arrived home and was not conversant with the evidence is the reason for his not saying anything about the matter before.

So far as the matter of digestion is concerned it is the opinion of leading physicians here that nothing can be told in regard to that matter, that it is a well-known fact that a glass of ice cold water will immediately retard digestion for an hour or more and it is thought that had Prof. Wood been interrogated upon this point that this fact would have come out.

Miss Emma Borden came up on the 8 45 train this morning but remained in the city only a short time.

From *New Bedford Evening Standard*, Sept. 3, 1892, p.6

A. (Morse) "I think so. I didn't notice what they were eating."

Presumably Morse was so busy devouring the mutton and johnny cakes that he didn't pay any attention to what was going on around him. For all he knew, Abby Borden could have eaten very little if anything for breakfast. She might then have had a substantial midmorning snack an hour or two later. That would explain, all by itself, why Abby's digestive system lagged 1 - 2 hours behind Andrew's. In this connection, it's interesting that Dr. Wood found evidence of fruit skins and other material in Abby's stomach that was not on the breakfast menu (Chapter 2).

Chapter 14
WHEN DID ABBY BORDEN DIE?
(MODERN FORENSIC ANALYSIS)

A s you have just seen, the evidence that Abby Borden predeceased Andrew, as presented at the preliminary hearing (1892) and trial (1893), is ambiguous at best. To check the validity of this important "fact" about the Borden case, I surveyed the recent forensic literature concerning methods of estimating times of death. The results were surprising in a couple of respects.

It turns out that almost all of the methods currently used for this purpose were available in 1892. A great many people have done research in this area, including Dr. Jack Kevorkian. The results have been meager; only one modern technique has been added to the classical repertoire. It was discovered about twenty five years ago that the concentration of potassium ions in "vitreous humor" (eye fluid) increases steadily for several hours after death. Unfortunately the rate at which it increases depends upon several external factors, which limits the accuracy of the method.

Modern forensic scientists have come to realize that estimating the time of death is not nearly as straightforward as it was believed to be a century ago. The following quotations taken from the recent literature illustrate this point. (I particularly like the first one!)

"The only accurate way of estimating the time of death is to be there when it happens."

"All methods now in use to determine the time of death are to a degree unreliable and inaccurate. They usually give vague or dubious answers."

"One of the popular cliches of fiction which most annoys medical men is the doctor who airily tells the police that death was (say) between one and two thirty."

"The popular conception of placing a hand on the body to determine body temperature is quite inaccurate because body temperature is an approximate, very approximate guide to the time of death."

"It would be dangerous to base an estimate on the time of death on stomach contents with regard to the amount present."

With that background, let's see what modern science has to say about the methods used a century ago to support the thesis that Abby Borden died 1 - 2 hours before Andrew.

Coagulation of Blood

Recall (Chapter 13) that several witnesses at the trial said that Abby Borden's blood was coagulated to a greater extent than Andrew's. This was taken to indicate that she died some time before her husband. However, Dr. Draper testified at the preliminary hearing that the extent of coagulation of the blood tells nothing about the time of death after fifteen minutes have passed.

Searching through textbooks and journal articles on forensic science, I found nothing dealing with the relationship between coagulation of blood and time of death. There's a simple reason for this. Draper was right; coagulation is usually complete within 5 - 15 minutes, as you may have noticed when you cut yourself. It follows that the testimony of policemen and doctors that Abby's blood was coagulated when they examined her at 11:30 A.M. or later tells us essentially nothing. At most, it means that she died somewhere before 11:15 A.M., but we already knew that.

Several witnesses testified that Andrew's blood had not coagulated when they examined him. They described his blood as "bright red", "still dripping" or "oozing from his wounds." With one such witness (Dr. Dedrick), the examination did not take place until 2 P.M., about three hours after Andrew died. A possible explanation of this anomaly involves a curious phenomenon observed in some, but not all, cases of sudden death. Often, when a person dies suddenly and violently, as Andrew did, the blood becomes uncoagulable shortly after death. No one knows exactly how this occurs or why it happens with some people but not others. It has found at least one practical albeit macabre application. In World War II, wounded Russian soldiers were given emergency transfusions using blood from their dead comrades.

Body Temperature

Dr. Dolan testified at the trial that, when he touched the bodies of the victims, Abby Borden felt colder than Andrew, indicating that she died before he did. Today, as in 1892, body temperature is commonly used to estimate elapsed time since death. Nowadays, though, pathologists and police officers do not rely on their sense of touch to determine temperature. Instead, they use a thermometer inserted into the body, usually the rectum or the liver. Moreover, they take a series of temperature measurements over time rather than a single reading.

Temperature measurements are virtually useless as a predictor in the first few hours after death. You can see why by referring to the graphs shown in the figure below. Notice that in the cooling curve shown at the top for an inanimate object such as a metal cylinder, temperature drops off sharply with time. This makes sense; cooling is fastest at the beginning, when the temperature of the cylinder is much higher than that of the surroundings. As time passes and the temperature of the cylinder approaches that of the surroundings, the rate of cooling decreases. Eventually the two temperatures become equal and cooling stops.

Figure 14.1 Cooling curves

FIG. 1.1. Graph showing fall in temperature when a small inorganic body cools from a temperature of 98.4°F. to atmospheric temperature (see text).

FIG. 1.2. Graph representing the way in which a dead body cools to atmospheric temperature. The graph incorporates the initial post-mortem temperature plateau (see text).

From, Shapiro + Shapiro, *Forensic Medicine*, pp. 6-7

The cooling curve for a dead body, shown at the bottom of the figure, is quite different. Here temperature drops very little if at all during the first few hours. This "plateau" was discovered about thirty years ago. In part it reflects the fact that heat conduction in a human body is a much more complex process than in a metal cylinder. Moreover, the decomposition reactions that take place immediately after death give off heat and hence tend to maintain a nearly constant temperature.

The elapsed time before body temperature starts dropping steadily after death varies from one to six hours; two to three hours is most common. In some cases, the temperature actually increases in the early postmortem period. A study carried out at Johns Hopkins University with eleven subjects found that, on average, body temperature three hours after death was about 1°F higher than before death occurred.

It's a safe bet that Abby Borden died sometime after 9 A.M. on the morning of August 4, 1892 (that's when she was last seen alive at 92 Second Street). This means that when she was examined by Dr. Dolan at noon, her temperature was almost certainly in or close to the plateau region of the graph shown above. In other words, it differed only slightly from the normal value. Had Dolan used a thermometer rather than relying on his sense of touch, the chances are that he would not have found any significant difference in temperature between the two bodies.

State of Digestion

When he carried out autopsies on the victims, Professor Wood found very little solid food in Andrew Borden's stomach. In contrast, Abby's stomach contained a large amount of undigested solids. On this basis, Wood concluded that Abby must have died 1 - 2 hours before Andrew, assuming they both ate their last meal at the same time and that they both ate essentially the same meal. The time required for food to clear the stomach depends upon the composition of the food. If you have a cup of coffee and a couple of cookies for breakfast, the "gastric emptying time" (hereafter referred to as GET) will be an hour or less. If, heaven forbid, you choose to eat cold mutton, johnny cakes, bananas and mince pie, the GET may be as long as six hours.

Wood also had to assume that digestion occurred normally in both cases. The stomach disorder that the Bordens suffered about thirty six hours before the crime could drastically increase the GET. Emotional stress, fear and pain are expected to have a similar effect. The GET can be shortened by vigorous exercise or cigarette smoking (probably not relevant with Andrew or Abby!)

In 1892 very little research had been done on gastric emptying time with live subjects. Until quite recently, the only technique available was something referred to as "intubation-aspiration." Suffice it to say that this involved the use of a stomach pump; the details are better left to the imagination. Neither the principal investigator nor the subject enjoyed this kind of research, so not much was done.

About twenty five years ago, a new method was developed to study gastric emptying time. The subject eats a meal consisting typically of chicken liver, beef stew and orange juice. A tiny amount of a radioactive tracer is incorporated into the chicken liver. Using an instrument capable of detecting and measuring radiation, it is possible to follow the passage of tracer through the digestive system. The availability of this technique has made it possible to study the effect of all kinds of factors on GET.

As you might expect, one of the first factors to be studied was gender; gastric emptying times were compared for women versus men. A 1984 study showed that, on average, women had GETs almost twice as long as men. This could explain why Abby Borden's stomach contained so much more undigested food than Andrew's.

However, later studies found that longer GETs were shown only by young (premenopausal) women or by older women who were taking female sex hormones such as estrogen. (Why sex hormones should favor the retention of food in the stomach I have no idea, but apparently they do.) Abby Borden at age 64 was certainly not premenopausal. Neither was she taking sex hormone supplements; the word "hormone" does not appear in Webster's dictionary for 1892 or for many years thereafter.

Another factor which has been studied extensively is obesity. This is an area where Abby and Andrew Borden differed considerably. Abby, 5'3" tall, weighed over 200 pounds; Andrew was tall and thin. Studies of the effect of obesity on gastric emptying time fall into three categories:

● those showing that obese people have longer GETs. That seems to make sense, at least to me. The longer food is retained in the digestive system, the more likely elements of it are to be retained in the body.
● those showing that obese people have shorter GETs. This makes even more sense. If food clears your stomach quickly, you feel hungry and eat more. That's how people become obese.

● those showing no difference in GET between obese and thin people. This makes the most sense of all. Why in the world should obesity have anything whatsoever to do with gastric emptying time?

All kidding aside, there's a basic difficulty common to all experiments in which the subjects studied are human beings. Men and women do not necessarily follow the natural laws that govern the behavior of tennis balls and chemicals. There is a basic law of chemistry which states that all samples of a pure substance behave in exactly the same way in an experiment. That doesn't hold for human beings. Two people who appear to resemble each other closely in every respect (gender, age, height, weight, . . .) may and frequently do behave very differently in an experiment.

Figure 14.2 Graph with scattered points

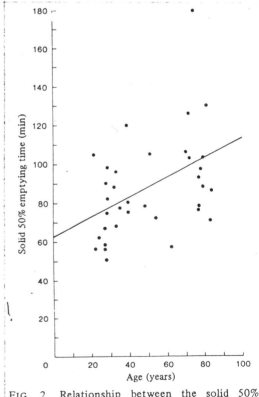

One way to describe this situation is to say that in any experiment involving human beings as subjects, large deviations from "average" behavior are the rule rather than the exception. An extreme example is shown at right. The graph is supposed to indicate that gastric emptying time increases with age, but notice the enormous scatter of the points. It wouldn't be hard to draw a line with a downward slope through the data, which would suggest that GET decreases as you grow older. A graph

FIG. 2. Relationship between the solid 50% emptying time and age in 35 subjects ($r = 0.42$, $P < 0.01$).

Horowitz, *Clin. Soc. 67 216*, (1984)

like this would never appear in a physics or chemistry journal. This doesn't mean that physicists or chemists are better experimentalists than medical scientists. It simply means that results are much more reproducible when you're dealing with inanimate objects as opposed to human beings.

The large uncertainties associated with gastric emptying times lead to major disagreements as to how they should be interpreted. Consider, for example, what happened in the murder of a young girl in Canada several years ago. She was known to have eaten supper (white turkey meat, brown turkey skin, potatoes, peas, celery, onions, pineapple upside down cake) at about 6 P.M. Based on the analysis of stomach contents, four different experts estimated the time of her death as follows:

1. Between 7:15 and 7:40 P.M.
2. Between 9:15 and 9:45 P.M.
3. Between 6:45 P.M. and 4:45 A.M. the next morning
4. Between 3:15 and 7:15 A.M.

So much for Professor Wood's opinion that Abby Borden died 1 - 2 hours before Andrew!

O. J. Simpson Revisited

This chapter may have given you the impression that determining the time of death in a murder investigation is a very imprecise science. Indeed it is. A statement to that effect appears in every modern textbook of forensic science. In TV dramas a police officer may tell you that he believes the victim died at 9:30 A.M., but in the real world the situation is very different.

This point came up repeatedly in the trial of O. J. Simpson for the murders of Nicole Brown Simpson and Ronald Goldman. The crime must have taken place sometime between 9:40 P.M., when Nicole talked to her mother on the phone, and midnight, when the bodies were discovered. The prosecution favored a time period between 10:15 and 10:30 P.M., when O.J. Simpson had no alibi. The defense preferred a time closer to 11 P.M., when O. J. was in a limousine on his way to the airport. Moreover, they maintained that if the Los Angeles Police Department had contacted the coroner promptly, a precise time of death could have been established.

The prosecution disagreed, claiming that there was no way the time interval could have been narrowed down by forensic evidence. Prosecutor Marcia Clark, in her opening statement, put it this way:

"The coroner can never really be precise. A coroner can usually . . . bring it down to a range of within three hours, between 9 P.M. and midnight, between midnight and 3 A.M. If you want to pinpoint the time within a minute, ten minutes, a half hour or even an hour or two hours, a coroner solely by his examination of the body cannot do it."

Later (March 7, 1995) Detective Tom Lange spoke to this issue at the trial.

Q. Marcia Clark) "In your experience, sir, and based on the prior homicide experience you've had, what is the most narrow time frame you've been able to be given by a coroner based on the analysis of stomach contents?"

A. (Lange) "As to time of death, I've never known time of death to be [given to closer than] two or three hours."

Shortly afterwards, Lange made the same point again, saying, "No matter whether he calls [the coroner's office] now or calls them three or four hours from now, they're still not going to be able to give a better range than two or three hours."

The last words on this subject at the Simpson trial were spoken on June 14, 1995, by Chief Coroner Sathyavagiswaren. A summary of his testimony, taken from the *Los Angeles Times* of June 15 is given in the box below. Peter Arenella, a UCLA law professor covering the case for the Times commented:

"Today's lesson in forensics: determining time of death is an imprecise science with a three-hour time estimate being about the best that can be done. The chief coroner insisted that if everything had been done correctly as soon as the victims were discovered, he still would not have been able to tell whether they were killed at 10:15 or close to 11 P.M."

Figure 14.3 Coroner's statement

L. A. Times, June 15, 1995
Sathyavagiswaren said Wednesday that he cannot be sure exactly what time the victims were killed except to say that it was between

9:40 P.M., when Nicole Simpson spoke to her mother on the tele-phone, and 12:13 A.M. the following morning, when a police officer found the two bodies.

While explaining that medical evidence only can produce a range of possible times, Sathyavagiswaren testified that jurors should be wary of any defense expert who produces a more precise time. Citing half a dozen forensic textbooks which a prosecutor stacked imposingly on the government team's table Sathyavagiswaren stressed that estimating time of death depends on a host of variables such as body temperature, muscle rigidity and pooling of blood inside the body.

The trouble with those measurements is that each of them is inexact, and even when taken together, only a range of possible times can be confidently predicted.

In fact, the medical methods of determining time of death are so crude that they cannot narrow the time of death in the Simpson case to less than almost four hours, the coroner said. The narrower window was established by nonmedical clues such as the telephone records showing when Nicole Simpson spoke to her mother and the last known sighting of Goldman, as he left work at a nearby restaurant.

Conclusions and a Challenge!

It should be clear from what has been said in this chapter that neither Professor Wood, Dr. Dolan nor anyone else in 1892 could say that Abby Borden died 1 - 2 hours before Andrew. The time lapse between the murders, taken as an article of faith for a century, is just another facet of the Borden legend that has no basis in fact. All we know is that Andrew Borden was killed close to 11 A.M., while Abby Borden was killed somewhere between 9 A.M., when she was last seen alive, and 11:30 A.M., when her body was discovered.

As pointed out at the beginning of Chapter 13, I believe that Andrew Borden's death was the centerpiece of the crime, that he was killed first, and that Abby's murder was an afterthought, required to prevent identification of the murderer. That's a reasonable hypothesis which will be expanded upon in Chapter 15; let me admit here and now that I can't prove it.

Dropping the idea that Abby Borden must have died between 9 and 10 A.M. on August 4, 1892, demolishes what is perhaps the strongest argument for Lizzie's guilt. She couldn't explain how she was unaware of her stepmother's murder for a very good reason. She wasn't there when it happened.

This makes the case against Lizzie Borden even weaker than it was before. Having furnished a reasonable explanation of the note Abby received (Chapter 12), all that is left to incriminate Lizzie is:

● the prussic acid story (Chapter 11)
● her strange conversation with Alice Russell on the eve of the murders. (Chapter 10)

Overbalancing these mildly incriminating items are the arguments for Lizzie's innocence referred to in Chapter 10. In order of increasing importance:

● her motive for the murders was weak at best
● the evidence indicates she was in the barn when Andrew was murdered
● Abby's wounds suggest that her assailant was a considerably taller person
● the weapon used was neither identified nor connected in any way to Lizzie
● no one saw blood on her person or clothing
● there was not a single piece of physical evidence linking her to the crime.

In Chapter 9 we considered and essentially eliminated three other suspects: John Morse, Emma Borden and Bridget Sullivan. In Chapter 7, we pointed out how difficult it would have been for a "mysterious intruder" to have come into the house to kill first Abby and then Andrew Borden.

This would seem to eliminate the entire human race so far as culpability in the Borden murders is concerned. Yet if you think about what has been presented in the last six chapters (particularly Chapters 13 and 14) there is one and only one logical solution. Can you see what it is? (You might find it helpful to consider how the elimination of the time lapse between the murders affects the case against each possible suspect.)

Chapter 15
FALL RIVER, AUG. 4, 1892:
WHAT REALLY HAPPENED?

T he elimination of a significant time lapse between the murders of Abby and Andrew Borden dramatically strengthens the case against one individual. As you have probably deduced by now, that person is the "mysterious intruder", someone with a grudge against Andrew, who came off the street to commit the crime.

In the first few days after August 4, it was generally assumed that the murderer was indeed an outsider. The case against the mysterious intruder faded away when it appeared that Abby Borden died a considerable time before her husband, probably shortly after 9 A.M. In that case, he would have had to enter the house undetected by three women (Abby Borden, Lizzie Borden, Bridget Sullivan) and, most likely, two men as well (Andrew Borden, John Morse). Then he would have had to kill Abby without alarming either Lizzie, who admitted to being in the house at that time, or Bridget, who was washing windows within a few yards of the guest room. Finally, the stranger must secrete himself with his bloody hatchet somewhere within that house for a couple of hours, patiently waiting for Andrew to come home so that he can complete the massacre.

Consider, though, how the picture changes if we eliminate the time lapse between the murders. Let us suppose that the intruder enters the house shortly before 11 A.M. Lizzie has just gone out to the barn to look for sinkers and gorge herself on pears so that she won't have to eat mutton for dinner again. Bridget has retired to her third floor bedroom to rest before preparing dinner. Andrew, resting on the sofa in the sitting room, has just put down the book he was reading and dozed off. Abby . . . we'll get to later; for the time being, let's just say that she is out of the way. The coast is clear!

Under these conditions, it was entirely possible for an intruder to enter the house, commit the murders, and escape undetected. This point was made in several newspaper articles dealing with the Borden case. The famous detective Robert Pinkerton was quoted as saying, "It would be quite possible for a person to enter the house and commit the crime without being seen." A veteran policeman (not a member of the Fall River police force!) commented as follows to a reporter for the *Providence Journal*:

"Broad daylight is the best time to commit certain crimes. A man may walk slowly away from a building in a populous section in morning or afternoon and escape observation. It is expected that people will come and go in the daytime; [butchers], grocery men, errand boys and the like. If no great amount of blood was spilled, spots on his clothing would not interfere with his escape."

As pointed out in Chapter 7, the visibility of an intruder would have been considerably reduced by the wooden fences, trees and outbuildings that surrounded the Borden property. The fence fronting on Second Street is shown in the sketch below; it appears to have been about four feet high. Similar fences shielded the Borden house and yard from neighbors to the north (Mrs. Churchill) and south (Dr. and Mrs. Kelly). At the back of the property, toward Third Street, there was a somewhat higher fence topped with barbed wire.

Figure 15.1 Jurors behind the Borden fence

THE JURY GOES TO FALL RIVER TO VIEW THE BORDEN PREMISES

From *Lizzie Borden Sourcebook*, p. 218

In 1893 a reporter for *Once a Week* gave a dramatic demonstration of how easy it would have been for an intruder to have escaped undetected from the Borden house. He spent a couple of hours wandering through the Borden property and the neighborhood without anyone noticing him. As the reporter put it, "If the murders were committed by a stranger, there would be no difficulty whatever in his escape, no matter how many people were about the building at the time."

At the trial the prosecution put on the stand several neighbors, workmen and bystanders who were near the Borden house that morning and swore they saw no suspicious strangers. However, as pointed out earlier, they were in no position to see what was going on at the Borden house during the crucial time interval, 11:00 - 11:15 A.M. Moreover, most people are too absorbed in their own affairs to pay attention to what's going on elsewhere in the neighborhood. Only one person (Mrs. Churchill) testified to seeing Andrew Borden leave the house at 9 A.M. Only Caroline Kelly saw him return later; she met Andrew coming along Second Street. Perhaps more significant, no one said they saw the "stranger" John Morse leave the house that morning. For that matter, no one seems to have seen him arrive the day before, not even Lizzie!

The defense produced several witnesses who claimed to have seen a potential "mysterious intruder" near the Borden house. For the most part their testimony was either vague or irrelevant, but there was one notable exception, Dr. Benjamin Handy. As a doctor, his observations should be more reliable than most. He drove past the Borden house in a carriage sometime between 10:20 and 10:40 A.M. on August 4, 1892. There he saw a man who was acting very strangely. Dr. Handy's testimony on this subject was presented in Chapter 7.

Handy said the man he saw was medium sized, relatively young (estimated age = 24) and was well dressed in a light suit of clothes with collar and necktie. Most important, he appeared to be mentally agitated, pacing up and down with his eyes on the sidewalk, and *had a very pale complexion.* Beyond that, Dr. Handy said he thought he had seen this individual on Second Street a few days before.

A reporter christened this individual as, "Dr. Handy's wild-eyed man." The phrase has a nice ring about it but no basis in fact; Handy said nothing about the nature of the man's eyes, wild or otherwise. A more apt description would have been, "Dr. Handy's pale-faced man." It was this aspect of his appearance that Handy emphasized every time he told the story. At one point he told a reporter:

"I see a thousand people on the street every day whom I never notice or give a thought to, but this man was most extraordinary and had a face that is impressed upon my memory now as plainly as when I saw him . . . There was not a mite of color in it and it looked completely bloodless. He was moving along slowly but in a suspicious manner, not as one would stroll who had no definite object in view . . . I think it will be shown that this man was, at the time I saw him, *just nerving himself to go in and commit the crime.*" [emphais added]

Dr. Handy's pale-faced man was never identified. The best the police could come up with was a derelict called "Mike the Soldier" who was recovering from an alcoholic binge somewhere on Second Street that morning. He didn't remotely resemble the man Handy described.

The Murderer

The remainder of this chapter amounts to a reconstruction of what I believe really happened at 92 Second Street on the morning of August 4, 1892. It covers the crucial period between about 9 A.M., when Abby Borden was last seen, and 11:15 A.M., when Andrew's body was discovered. One caveat: the times listed in this chronology should be taken as approximate, accurate at best to five minutes in one direction or the other.

There were five people who played major roles in the horror story that evolved that morning. The activities of three of these, **Andrew Borden**, **Lizzie Borden** and **Bridget Sullivan** can be deduced from evidence presented at the several court hearings on the Borden case. We will rely particularly on Lizzie's inquest testimony and Bridget's testimony at the preliminary hearing and trial.

We can only speculate on the activities of the other two players. For more than a century it was assumed that **Abby Borden** died 1 - 2 hours before her husband. As we've seen, there's no evidence for that. Most likely Abby died sometime around 11 A.M., at about the same time as Andrew. What did she do between 9 A.M and 11 A.M.? I'm convinced that she spent most of that time at Sarah Whitehead's house at 45 Fourth Street. She went there in response to her sister's note; she returned home to 92 Second Street just in time to meet the murderer.

The villain in this drama (there was no hero) was of course the "mysterious intruder" who came in off the street to commit murder. From now on we'll refer to this person as **Nemesis** (which he certainly was, for

Andrew and Abby Borden at least). It's likely that Nemesis was Dr. Handy's pale-faced man. He may also have been the man Lizzie overheard talking to her father. Remember, Dr. Handy said he thought he had seen him on Second Street before.

What kind of person was Nemesis? We'll have more to say on that subject in Chapter 16. However, it's safe to say that Nemesis must have been someone who had good reason to hate and/or fear Andrew Borden. Perhaps he was a disgruntled former employee, business associate or tenant of Andrew. There is still another intriguing possibility. Nemesis could have been a dishonest bank officer who had embezzled money from one of the banks with which Andrew Borden was associated. In that case, Andrew might have been pressuring Nemesis to return the money, possibly even blackmailing him.

To remind you that the reconstruction of what Abby Borden and Nemesis did that morning cannot be based on sworn testimony or hard facts, their activities will appear in italics. The paragraphs following each italicized section cite the evidence, such as it is, for the roles these two people played.

Nemesis Approaches: 9 A.M. - 10:45 A.M.

At about 9 A.M., Andrew Borden left 92 Second Street to go downtown. His first recorded stop was at 9:30 at the Union Savings Bank of which he was president. Leaving there at about 9:45, he proceeded to the First National Bank, where he spent perhaps ten minutes. He was next seen at 10:20 by Jonathan Clegg, who dealt in "Hats and Gentlemen's Furnishings." Clegg, an English immigrant, had arranged to rent a store from Andrew in the A. J. Borden building on South Main Street. Two carpenters, Joseph Shortsleeves and James Mather, were busy remodeling that store. Andrew went there, walked upstairs and may or may not have put something in the pocket of his Prince Albert coat (a long coat with voluminous pockets). He then came downstairs, picked up an old lock, and left for home at about 10:40 A. M.

There are a couple of gaps in Andrew's schedule. One of them was probably spent at Pierre Leduc's barber shop, where Andrew frequently indulged himself in the luxury of a shave. (In the "good old days" before razor blades were invented, shaving at home with a straight razor could be downright uncomfortable, even bloody). Some time while he was downtown, Andrew must have gone to the post office, located at the far north end of Second Street. There he mailed a letter Lizzie had written to Emma (it was later returned). Then he picked up his mail; there was none for Lizzie that day.

Lizzie Borden's morning was pretty much of a fizzle. She had set herself the task of ironing eight to ten handkerchiefs, which should have taken her twenty minutes if everything went well. It didn't. The wood fire in the kitchen stove kept smoldering or going out completely. Consequently, Lizzie's "flats" (flatirons) never got hot enough to use. It should perhaps be pointed out that old-fashioned flatirons were a lot simpler than modern irons. In particular, they didn't have electric cords attached to them; wall plugs had not yet been invented!

Besides her misadventures with the flatirons, Lizzie reread an old *Harper's* magazine, which she apparently found more interesting than Thursday's *Providence Journal*. At some point, Lizzie carried some clean clothes up to her bedroom and "basted a loop on a garment" (whatever that means). She also made one and only one trip to the toilet in the cellar. This was a typical morning for a 32 year old spinster living in urban America a century ago. What a godawful life Lizzie and a few million other women of her era must have led.

Bridget Sullivan had a more productive morning. Her major task was to wash the downstairs windows; Abby Borden told her they were "awful dirty." Starring at about 9:30 A.M., Bridget finished her sixth outside window somewhere around 10:20. At that point, she went into the house to wash the windows on the inside.

When last heard from in Chapter 12, Abby Borden was on her way to Sarah Whitehead's, leaving 92 Second Street around 9 A.M. As she approached #45 Fourth Street, her sister's house appeared deserted. Sure enough, when she unlocked the door and entered the house, it was empty; Sarah and her children, George and "little Abby", had left. Mrs. Borden was disappointed; she would have enjoyed her niece's company that day.

To relieve her frustration, Abby Borden decided to indulge in a midmorning snack. She drew a glass of milk from the bottle in her sister's ice chest and cut a slice of mince pie she had baked for Sarah and her family a couple of days before. Sitting down in a soft, comfortable chair, Abby slowly consumed her snack, enjoying every morsel. Then she fell asleep.

According to their sworn testimony, neither Lizzie Borden nor Bridget Sullivan saw Abby after about 9 A.M., at which time she was dusting downstairs. Lizzie clearly believed Abby left the house in response to the note she received; however, Lizzie did not say that she saw her stepmother leave. Bridget, on the other hand, did; she told Mrs. Churchill that Abby "hurried off" without saying where she was going. As pointed out earlier (p. 186) Bridget assumed her destination was Sarah Whitehead's house on Fourth Street.

Like most overweight people, Abby almost certainly ate between meals. Years later, Sarah Whitehead's daughter recalled her aunt's frequent visits, which suggests that she would have had a house key. Often Abby Borden brought food with her; little Abby particularly enjoyed the mince pies that her aunt sprinkled with rosewater.

No one seems to know how mincemeat for mince pies is made nowadays, which is probably just as well. However, a hundred years ago it was made by mixing finely chopped meat with suet, apples, raisins and spices. Such a mixture is entirely consistent with the contents of Abby Borden's stomach, as analyzed by Dr. Wood. He found considerable amounts of meat, fatty material and fruit residues, which he tentatively identified as apples. Who knows; maybe Abby had a couple of pieces of mince pie!

Some time after 9 A.M., Nemesis left his place of employment to travel to the Borden house. Perhaps he took a carriage; more likely he walked. He arrived at about 10:30 A.M. for an 11 o'clock appointment with Andrew Borden. To himself Nemesis muttered, "Somehow I have to persuade the old b . . . . . . to stop persecuting me. How the Hell can I do that?" As the minutes passed, the tension rose within him, and Nemesis started to pace back and forth nervously.

I've assumed here that Nemesis was Dr. Handy's pale-faced man. Andrew Borden ordinarily "held court" at his home between 11 A.M. and noon; anyone wanting to see him on business could call during that period. One such person was Jonathan Clegg, who had talked to Andrew at least twice that week at 92 Second Street. Beyond that, Clegg said he had planned to come again on Thursday until he met Andrew downtown that morning.

Nemesis Enters: 10:45 - 11:00 A.M.

Andrew Borden arrived home at about quarter to eleven. At that point, Bridget was washing a sitting room window on the inside. Lizzie was either eating a pear in the kitchen (a tremendous quantity of pears must have been consumed that day), or basting a garment in her room upstairs, or standing at the top of the stairs; she couldn't remember which. It really doesn't much matter; contrary to the legend, there weren't any dead bodies in the house at that time.

Andrew tried to enter the house through the screen door in the kitchen, but Bridget had hooked that when she came inside. He then went to the front door which, to his frustration, was triple locked. Bridget, with some difficulty, let Andrew in. While doing so, she uttered some kind of expletive which made Lizzie laugh.

A few minutes after entering the house, Andrew Borden sat down in a chair in the sitting room. He started reading; according to Bridget he was reading a thin book. Lizzie spent a few minutes talking with Andrew. Among other things, she told him about the note Abby had received.

Shortly after Andrew came home, Bridget decided she'd washed enough windows for one day. Her only remaining duty was to cook dinner; on Thursday she had the afternoon off. Lizzie suggested to Bridget that she might want to check out a sale of dress goods at Frank Sargent and Co. that afternoon. Bridget expressed interest, but right now she was heading for her third floor bedroom for a brief "liedown."

Figure 15.2 A sale at Sargent's

THE DRESS-GOODS SALE AT SARGENT'S WHERE LIZZIE PLANNED TO SHOP

Monday	Monday	Monday
THE FRANK	E. SARGENT	COMPANY.
GREAT	EST OFFERIN	G YET.

From *Lizzie Borden Sourcebook*, p. 48

Shortly afterwards, Andrew decided that he too might benefit from a short nap. He took off his Prince Albert coat and put on his "reefer" (a short coat of thick cloth). Lizzie claimed her father took off his shoes when he moved from chair to sofa in the sitting room. He didn't. Andrew made himself comfortable on the sofa, at which point Lizzie headed for the barn to eat some more pears. She left what was to be the scene of the crime at about 10:55 A.M.

Bridget and Lizzie have now left the stage; Andrew plays only a silent role in the ensuing drama. From this point on, we'll concentrate on the two people who played major roles: Andrew's wife Abby and his enemy, Nemesis.

Abby Borden, taking a nap in an easy chair at #45 Fourth Street, awoke suddenly. A glance at Sarah Whitehead's mantle clock told her it was 10:45 A.M. It was too late to go shopping for meat for dinner, bring it home, and have it cooked by noon. John Morse, Andrew Borden and Lizzie would have to eat warmed over mutton for dinner, like it or not.

Abby tidied up, washing her milk glass and pie plate. Then she started to walk home, which was only a few blocks away. When she arrived at 92 Second Street, it was about 10:55. Entering by the front door, she heard the screen door in the kitchen close; Lizzie was on her way to the barn. Bridget had gone upstairs a few minutes before. The only person remaining downstairs was Andrew Borden, and he was about to fall asleep on the sofa in the sitting room.

No one came forward to say that he/she saw Abby on the street that morning. Then again the police never looked for witnesses. Early in the game they convinced themselves that Lizzie was the murderer. As a result, they never checked on any item that would tend to exonerate her. The police never seriously considered the possibility that Abby Borden left home that morning, even though Bridget's comment to Mrs. Churchill indicated that was exactly what happened. Along the same lines, the police never searched for the author of the note that Abby received. Neither did they look for the Englishman who came to the door to talk to Andrew about a store at 9 A.M. that morning.

Recall that after Andrew's body was discovered, Lizzie asked that someone look for Abby; she thought she heard her return. That must have happened after Lizzie's last conversation with Andrew; otherwise she would have mentioned it to him. This in turn means that Lizzie's exit and Abby's entrance were nearly simultaneous; Lizzie went to the barn immediately after talking to Andrew. Bridget left before Lizzie; she was ascending the stairs to her room when Lizzie told her about the sale at Sargent's.

As 11 o'clock approached, Nemesis became more and more convinced that Andrew Borden would never grant his request. He contemplated flight, from 92 Second Street, from the city of Fall River, from the state of Massachusetts . . . leaving friends and family behind. As he saw Abby entering the house, he changed his mind again. Perhaps this pleasant looking lady would intercede for him. On impulse he hurried to the front door and knocked. When Abby let him in, he explained to her that he wanted to see Andrew on business. Abby nodded, waved him into the sitting room, and discreetly withdrew to the upstairs guest room. There she started tidying up, a task postponed two hours earlier when she went to Sarah Whitehead's in response to the note.

Much of this is, of course, speculation. It's worth noting, though, that it was Abby's custom to withdraw when Andrew was discussing business in their home. She must have gone to the guest room; that's where her body was found. At about 9 A.M., Abby told Lizzie she still had work to do in that room.

Nemesis Strikes: 11:00 - 11:15 A.M.

With Abby on her way upstairs, Nemesis was left alone to deal with his enemy, Andrew Borden. To make things more difficult, Andrew had fallen asleep. Nemesis steeled himself to wake the old man so he could plead his case. Then he noticed a shiny new hatchet partially concealed near the sofa. A macabre but tempting idea occurred to Nemesis in his desperation. With that hatchet, he could put an end to Andrew Borden, the only person who knew his secret. Murder was a way out of his dilemma; Nemesis could think of no other.

Moving quickly lest he lose his nerve, Nemesis positioned himself at the end of the sofa where Andrew's head rested. Horrified by the awful thing that he was about to do, Nemesis closed his eyes and started swinging blindly. Ten times the hatchet fell silently except for an ominous crunching noise. Nemesis, convinced that his task must have been accomplished by now, opened his eyes. The carnage he saw was far worse than anything he had imagined. Andrew's skull had been smashed in, his face was obliterated by blood, and an eyeball, hanging out of its socket, had been cut in half.

"At least it's over", Nemesis said to himself. His secret was safe now that Andrew Borden was dead. Then, with a sinking feeling, Nemesis

realized that it was far from over. The old lady who let him in and looked him in the face still lived; he could hear her moving about upstairs in the guest room.

Silently and swiftly, Nemesis did what he felt he had to do; eliminate the woman who could identify him. He climbed the front stairs with the bloody hatchet clenched in his hand. When he reached the guest room, Abby was facing away from him toward the window. He struck her in the back with a glancing blow. Wounded, bleeding profusely, poor Abby turned to face her assailant. In her terror she spoke only one word: "Why?" Nemesis answered by striking her twice on top of the head. Abby crashed to the floor, unconscious and dying. There was no one but Nemesis to hear her. In a maniacal frenzy, he straddled her body and struck blow after blow to the back of her head.

Now at last it was over, or nearly so. Nemesis, drained of emotion, returned downstairs, passed through the sitting room where his first victim lay dead on the sofa, and left by the kitchen door. Then he realized that he still had the hatchet in his hand. "Why am I holding on to that?" he thought, and threw it as far as he could. By happenstance, the murder weapon landed on the flat roof of John Crowe's nearby barn, where it would remain undetected for nearly a year. That done, Nemesis turned left, passed through the yard between the Borden and Churchill houses, opened the gate in the fence fronting on Second Street, and walked away from the slaughter into oblivion.

In mid August of 1892, between the inquest and the preliminary hearing, references appeared in several different newspapers to a hatchet that Bridget supposedly found "half-hidden" in the sitting room where she was washing windows that morning. The periodical *Once a Week*, which gave extensive coverage to the Borden case, went a step further. It alleged that Bridget testified to the existence of this hatchet at the inquest. Since her inquest testimony has disappeared, there's no way this claim can be checked.

Some of the articles dealing with the half-hidden hatchet state or imply that Lizzie put it in the sitting room, presumably in preparation for the second murder. That makes no sense. Even assuming Lizzie's guilt, why would she put the hatchet in the one place where it could most easily be seen by the intended victim, Andrew Borden? More likely, Andrew picked up the hatchet while he was downtown, rummaging around upstairs in Clegg's store. He could then have brought it home in his coat pocket and laid it down in the sitting room pending a trip to the cellar, where the hatchet belonged.

A way to account for the large number of hatchet blows received by the victims is to assume that the murderer struck them with his eyes closed and wanted to make sure that the victims were dead. Put yourself in the position of Nemesis, "forced" to commit murder. How would you kill a human being with a hatchet? Could you watch what you were doing?

The wounds described above are those reported by Medical Examiner Dolan. The medical authorities, Dolan, Draper and Cheever, disagreed as to the sequence of the hatchet blows suffered by Abby; the order followed here seems reasonable. Abby did indeed fall on her face; Dr. Dolan found bruises there. Lizzie and Bridget were too far away to hear her fall; so, in a sense, was Andrew.

Most likely, Nemesis left by the kitchen door; Lizzie found it wide open when she returned from the barn. He could have turned to the right and exited to Third Street. To do that, though, he would have had to scale a fence and cross a yard where several men were working. It would have been easier to turn left and walk out through the gate into Second Street. Mrs. Churchill, who lived on that side of the Borden house, was downtown buying meat for dinner, so it's unlikely Nemesis would have been seen if he took that route.

On June 14, 1893, as the prosecution was nearing the end of its case against Lizzie Borden, a fourteen year old boy named Arthur Potter, while looking for a lost ball, found a shingling hatchet on the roof of John Crowe's barn. The hatchet must have been new when it came to rest on the roof; its blade showed evidence of the gilt coating applied by the manufacturer. Recall that Dr. Draper found traces of gilt on Abby's skull.

If Nemesis went out the kitchen door, he could have thrown the hatchet to the place where it was found. By doing so, he increased his chances of escaping detection. A pedestrian on Second Street might have been suspicious of a man carrying a bloody hatchet, particularly if closer examination showed blood stains on his clothing.

Figure 15.3 Newspaper article on Crowe's hatchet
(See next page)

John Crowe told reporters that, to the best of his knowledge, no one had been working on the roof of his barn for more than a year. Arthur Potter said that he had made a similar trip to the barn roof, for the same purpose, about a year before. At that time, he saw no hatchet. Taken separately, these two statements are not particularly significant but, putting them together, we conclude that *somebody must have thrown the hatchet onto the roof between June 1892 and June 1893.*

Convinced as they were that Lizzie was guilty, the police showed little interest in this particular hatchet. So far as we know, its blade was never tested for the presence of blood. Neither did anyone check to see whether the blade fitted the wounds on the skulls of the victims, even though its cutting edge, 3¾", was very close to Dr. Draper's estimate (3½") for the murder weapon. When last heard from a hundred years ago, this hatchet was in the possession of Caleb Potter, Arthur's father. Where it is today is anybody's guess.

The Discovery

A few minutes after Nemesis left, probably around 11:15 A.M., Lizzie came back from the barn. She went into the house through the open kitchen door and entered the dining room, where she laid down her hat. When Lizzie opened the sitting room door, she discovered her father's mangled body. Stunned, she cried out to Bridget, who was resting upstairs: "Come down quick Maggie. Father's dead. Someone came in and killed him."

Indeed, as we have seen, Lizzie was right. Someone did come in and kill Andrew Borden and Abby as well. But this is where we started; we have come full circle (recall p. 1). Only one question remains: who was Nemesis?

"I HAVE FOUND

LIZZIE BORDEN'S HATCHET"

A NEW SENSATION.

Boy Playing Ball Discovers a Hatchet on John Crowe's Barn In the Rear of the Borden Estate.

During the game of the boys, the ball was knocked, or thrown, upon the roof of the main barn, and Master Arthur. Potter, 1 years old, son of Caleb C. Potter, of the Water Works office, sca'ed the bai'ding in quest of it.

Near the northwest corner of the main building,—about six feet from the west and four feet from the north line of the structure,—on the northeast corner of the roof, he found a hatchet, of ordinary size, lying with the head toward the southeast, the handle towards the north west corner.

He forgot the ball and he rushed for the hatchet, and then rang out his salute to the boys below:

I've Found Lizzie Borden's Hatchet.

The hatchet is an ordinary shingle hatchet with a blade 3½ inches in length. It was covered in rust and part of this was scraped off by the boy when found. It has the appearance of having been comparatively new and but little used.

The handle, which is 13½ inches long, looked weather-worn as if it had been long exposed to air, sun and storm. The under side of the handle had few slight stains but nothing that resembled spots. Near the head of the hatchet, these stains were more pronounced.

The boys were much excited over the find and it was given to Mr. Potter, the father of the finder, who now has it in his possession. He at once notified the police and tried to find Mr. Jennings, but in this was unsuccessful.

If the murderer of Andrew J. Borden and his wife, escaped from the Borden premises by the rear, and it was a very easy way for him to so escape, he could easily have thrown the hatchet to the place where it was found.

So far as is known no man has been of the roof within two years. Mr. Crow knows of none; all telegraph, telephone, electric light wiremen, roofers and several photographers agree on this. The police did not visit it in their thorough search.

The police have been carefully examining the hatchet this morning. They though they could tell whether there had been blood on it or not. They confess that they are baffled.

But one of them, who has been an important witness in the Borden case, admits that with this new find and the exclusion of the Bence story

Everything Has Gone Up

for the government so far as a possible conviction of Lizzie Borden is concerned.

The defense has opened its case. Now look for important and vital contradictions of government testimony.

About 7 o'clock last evening a number of boys were engaged in playing ball on Third street, in front of John Crowe's barn, which is nearly in the rear of the Borden estate, the north side of the barn serving as a fence between Dr. Chagnon's orchard, which is directly in the rear of the Borden house, and the Kelly lot, on which the barn stands.

The barn is a flat roof structure about 18 feet high. In the rear is an ell, the full width of the main building, but not more than 12 feet high. Still extending to the west and toward the Borden estate is a narrower flat roofed ell, about 9 feet high. A six foot fence runs diagonally and southeasterly from the north line of the first ell to the second ell, so that it is very easy to scale the roof.

From *Fall River News*, June 15, 1893, p.8

Chapter 16
WHO WAS NEMESIS?

At one level, this question is easily answered. Nemesis was the Greek goddess of retribution who punished extraordinary crimes. She also seems to have had something to do with fertility. In Greek mythology, Nemesis was pursued by Zeus. To escape him she turned herself into a goose but, in the form of a swan, he caught her. The fruit of their union was an egg, from which, supposedly, Helen of Troy was hatched. Somehow I doubt it.

Quite possibly, that wasn't the answer you were looking for. In that case, you're probably going to be disappointed. A hundred years after the fact, I can't tell you for sure who murdered Andrew Borden and his wife. All I can do is offer three possible choices, starting with a bank employee who has never been mentioned, let alone suspected, in the Borden case.

The Frightened Embezzler

In 1882 a young man named Henry Palmer, a recent high school graduate, went to work as a messenger for the Fall River National Bank. Palmer, highly intelligent and a hard worker, moved up the ladder quickly. Within ten years, he had become a bank teller earning $900 a year (equivalent to an annual salary of perhaps $15,000 today).

Henry Palmer had a virtually perfect record of attendance at the bank; he never asked for or took a vacation. As a result, his superiors were puzzled when he failed to show up for work on Monday morning, March 20, 1893. They contacted his wife at 30 Hanover Street to check on his whereabouts. She told them that she had no idea where he could be and that she was frantic with worry. It seems that Palmer had left home Sunday afternoon on an errand, telling his wife he would be home for dinner. He never showed up.

The bank officers were worried too and, like Mrs. Palmer, they were a mite suspicious. That afternoon the cashier of the bank informed the directors, who happened to be gathered for a meeting, of Palmer's disappearance. The directors initiated an examination of his records and found, as they had feared, that something was seriously wrong. It turned out that over a fourteen month period starting in January, 1892, Palmer had embezzled (i.e., stolen) several thousand dollars from the Fall River National Bank.

The system Palmer used was deceptively simple. When a large depositor added, let us say, $10,000 to his account, Palmer would give him a receipt for that amount. However, he would pocket perhaps $2,000 and enter $8,000 in his own deposit book. At the end of the day, his account would tally very nicely with the amount the bank actually received. The scam was unlikely to be detected as long as Palmer showed up every day to cover his tracks, unless a depositor spotted the discrepancy.

As the days passed in Fall River and Palmer didn't appear, his reputation went downhill in a hurry. A newspaper report accused him of trying "to accumulate money so he could lavish it on the frivolous things of life." A friend of Palmer's wife went a step further, suggesting that he devoted too much of his time and energy to habits "foreign to the best interests of a well regulated home." His home life was not based on "absolute danestic felicity" and he drank occasionally. As if that wasn't bad enough, Palmer also lost money in the stock market. *The Fall River Globe* put it quaintly: "It is a peculiarity of stocks to behave queerly and turn on those who invest in them."

On April 17, 1893, four weeks to the day from the time he disappeared, Palmer showed up in Fall River and surrendered to Assistant Marshal Fleet. A friend said he had been in St. Louis and returned to face his accusers only because of his love for his family. The police were inclined to believe that he had been in or around Fall River all the time.

At any rate, on the advice of his lawyer, Andrew Jennings, Palmer went to court and pleaded not guilty. Jennings was not nearly as successful here as he was in a much more famous case a couple of months later. Unlike Lizzie Borden, Henry Palmer was found guilty and sent to prison. At that point, his name disappeared from the headlines and he seems to have faded into anonymity.

As you may have guessed by now, Henry B. Palmer was the embezzler referred to in Chapter 15 as a candidate for Nemesis, the person who came in off the street to do in Andrew Borden. Why Palmer? Well, in the first place, the dates check. The Bordens were murdered in August, 1892, about half way through Palmer's embezzling career, which stretched from January, 1892, to March, 1893.

More important, Andrew Borden was in a good position to detect Palmer's thefts and call him to account, perhaps even blackmail him.

Certainly Andrew frequently deposited large amounts of money in all the major banks of Fall River, including Palmer's. His deposits came not only from his own funds but from those of the mills and real estate holdings in which he had a controlling interest. All in all, Andrew must have had many opportunities to come across discrepancies in Palmer's accounts. Moreover, Andrew Borden was suspicious by nature, always on the lookout for fraud that threatened his financial interests.

There is one reason above all others why Henry Palmer is a good choice for Nemesis. *He matches almost exactly the characteristics of Dr. Handy's pale-faced man*, who was pacing anxiously in front of the Borden house shortly before the murders. Consider what the Fall River Globe had to say about Palmer's appearance:

"It is believed that his chalklike complexion will lead to his arrest. It is sure that it will attract attention." (March 21, 1893)

"He had the same pallor that characterized him before his disappearance." (April 18, 1893)

In the *Fall River Evening News* of April 17, 1893, we read that, "The pallor about his face has always been noticeable; it is now intensified. This would have assisted more than ever in his [i.e., Palmer's] apprehension."

Clearly a chalklike facial appearance was the outstanding characteristic of both Henry B. Palmer and Dr. Handy's pale-faced man. In other, less important ways, they resembled one another also, as indicated in the comparison below. If only Dr. Handy could have been in the courtroom when Palmer was arraigned!

Characteristic	Dr. Handy's pale-faced man	Henry B. Palmer
Age	estimated to be 24	30
Mustache	yes	yes
Height	medium	5'9"
Dress	well dressed, grey suit	"always neatly and quietly dressed"

There is an obvious weakness in the case against Henry Palmer. There is not a single piece of physical evidence linking him to Andrew Borden, alive or dead. In Chapter 10 it was pointed out that an analogous situation applied to Lizzie Borden; there was no physical evidence linking her to the murders. However, there's a big difference between the two cases. Lizzie was thoroughly investigated; Palmer was not even considered as a suspect. It is entirely possible that if we could find out, a hundred years after the fact, what Henry Palmer was doing on August 4, 1892, the Borden puzzle might be solved. Then again, Palmer might be completely exonerated.

There is an interesting footnote to the Palmer story. Legend has it that Andrew Jennings, after Lizzie's acquittal, never discussed the Borden case again, even in the privacy of his own family. As is so often the case, the legend is wrong. In June of 1894 Jennings granted an interview to a reporter for the *Fall River Daily Herald* in which he said that at one point he found a clue which looked like it might lead to a solution of the Borden case. Jennings went on to say that he pursued that clue for a couple of months in the summer of 1893, but got nowhere. Do you suppose that the clue related to something Palmer revealed to Jennings, who defended him against embezzlement charges shortly before Lizzie's trial? Did Jennings notice the striking resemblance between Palmer and Dr. Handy's pale-faced man? Maybe; maybe not.

The Disgruntled Employee

On July 15, 1893, a dentist in Rome, N.Y., found a letter in the street which read as follows:

My Dear Husband:
Lizzie has been acquitted and I don't think they can do anything with you now. I want you to come home to spend the Fourth. The papers give a description of the man seen over the fence on the morning of the murder. Can you prove where you were on the morning of the murder?
Annie

The letter was addressed to "Joseph W. Carpenter, Jr., Albany N.Y." It was mailed from Fall River on June 22, 1893.

Annie Barney Carpenter, who lived at 152 North Main Street in Fall River, freely admitted having sent the letter to her husband. She said that he had not been home since Memorial Day of 1892. His failure to return to Fall River was explained, at least in part, by the fact that Joe Carpenter had been an early suspect in the Borden murders.

In 1873, when Carpenter was eighteen years old, he was hired as a bookkeeper by the firm of Borden and Almy. Andrew J. Borden and his partner, William M. Almy, dealt in furniture (including coffins) and funerals. Four years later, when the partnership was being dissolved, an auditor found that Joe Carpenter had embezzled $6,000 from the firm. Borden and Almy agreed not to prosecute if Carpenter made restitution for the money he had stolen, which he did. It turned out, however, that much of the money Carpenter returned to the firm was in the form of mill stock which became worthless when the mill failed.

At that point Andrew Borden, against the advice of his partner, insisted that Carpenter be arrested. That turned out to be a mistake. In his years with the firm, Carpenter had unearthed some unsavory business practices of Borden and Almy. In particular, Andrew Borden had a habit of selling expensive caskets to grieving relatives of the deceased and then substituting cheap wooden boxes. Threatened with exposure, Andrew dropped charges against Carpenter; the two men parted angrily. Andrew Borden went on to make a fortune in banking and real estate. Joe Carpenter left Fall River to become a "drummer" (traveling salesman) for ink, pens and stationery in upstate New York.

Shortly after the murders, Marshal Hilliard sent Officer Philip Harrington to Albany, New York, to investigate the Carpenter connection. Given that Harrington was thoroughly convinced of Lizzie's guilt, it's perhaps not surprising that his investigation was perfunctory. Carpenter's account book showed that he sold a bottle of ink to a customer in Albany on August 5, 1892; two days earlier he helped another drummer sell a billiard table in nearby Troy, New York. There was no entry for August 4, but Harrington convinced himself that Carpenter must have been in the Albany area on that day as well.

Joe Carpenter swore in an affidavit that he had spent every night between July 18 and August 13, 1892, in a rooming house in Albany. His landlady said that, to the best of her knowledge, Carpenter was telling the truth. Harrington was willing to take these statements as convincing evidence of Carpenter's innocence. He returned triumphantly to Fall River to report that another false lead in the Borden case had been exploded. Do you suppose he would have accepted an affidavit from Lizzie Borden that she was in the barn when her father was murdered? Not likely!

At least two people claimed to have seen Joe Carpenter in Fall River in early August of 1892. A barber, Peter Driscoll, insisted that he shaved Carpenter on August 1. A man named Dean, identified only as a schoolteacher, claimed that Carpenter was in Fall River on August 4 and left the next day with his wife (Carpenter's not Dean's), presumably for Albany.

So much for the case against Carpenter or, if you wish, the case for identifying Carpenter as Andrew Borden's Nemesis. Now let's look at the other side. It's difficult to understand why Joe Carpenter would have committed murder in 1892 because of a dispute, no matter how acrimonious, with Andrew Borden fifteen years earlier. There is no evidence that the two men were in contact with each other after Carpenter left Fall River.

Beyond that, Carpenter does not match up well with Dr. Handy's pale-faced man. For one thing, he was thirty seven years old in 1892; Handy estimated the age of the man he saw to be twenty four. None of the newspaper articles describing Joe Carpenter say anything about his having a "chalklike complexion" or anything of that nature. The *Fall River Globe* went a step further, saying that Carpenter did not resemble Dr. Handy's man.

The Tenant Who Talked Too Much

Henry Palmer and Joseph Carpenter, the first two candidates for the role of Nemesis, were mentioned for the first time in this chapter. In a sense, that's unfair to you, the reader; there's no way you could have deduced their involvement in the Borden case. (Neither was there any way in which they could logically have been introduced in earlier chapters.)

The third candidate is in a different category. He has been mentioned several times in this book, although never as a potential murder suspect. This person had something in common with Lizzie Borden; he behaved strangely, almost irrationally, shortly before the crime. Put simply, he talked too much. We refer to Jonathan Clegg, a prospective tenant of Andrew Borden. He described himself as a merchant dealing in "hats and gent's furnishings."

Jonathan Clegg was born in England in 1842; thirty years later he emigrated to the United States. He came to Fall River in 1876. At the trial, Clegg said he had known Amdrew Borden for about fifteen years. It follows that Andrew must have been one of the first people Clegg met when he came to Fall River. Most likely the two men conducted business with one another. In fifteen years, Clegg probably got to know members of Andrew's family, perhaps including his wife Abby.

And what, you may ask, was strange about Clegg's behavior prior to the crime? Well, for one thing, he testified to four lengthy conversations with Andrew Borden within 48 hours of the murders. According to Clegg, all of these discussions involved "making arrangements" for the store he wanted to rent in the A. J. Borden building.

Clegg first went to see Andrew Borden at 92 Second Street on Tuesday, August 2. Their first meeting apparently took place between 11 A.M. and noon, when Andrew was ordinarily "at home" for business purposes. That same afternoon, at the store he occupied on North Main Street, Clegg had a long conversation with Andrew. It was at this point, Clegg testified, that he made final arrangements to rent a store from Andrew Borden.

For meeting #3, Clegg returned to 92 Second Street on Wednesday morning. This was at a time when Andrew Borden was too weak to leave the house, having suffered an attack of indigestion the night before. Their final meeting, according to Clegg, took place on Thursday morning in downtown Fall River. This time Clegg hailed Andrew Borden from across the street; he "especially wanted to see [Andrew] that morning."

Why was Jonathan Clegg so insistent about meeting with Andrew Borden shortly before the murders? What was so urgent about the "arrangements" they were making? Couldn't the matter have waited until Andrew was feeling better? Beyond that, it's curious that Andrew seems never to have mentioned these discussions to John Morse, to his daughter Lizzie, or, as far as we know, to anyone else. Was the topic of their extensive conversations something more sinister than renting a store? Remember, we have only Clegg's word for it that this was what they talked about.

But wait, there's more! Almost certainly, there was a *fifth* meeting between Jonathan Clegg and Andrew Borden. Recall (Chapter 7) what Lizzie Borden told Assistant Marshal Fleet about the man who came to see her father on the morning of the murders. She said *he spoke with an English accent and talked about renting a store.* Who could that have been other than Jonathan Clegg, the Englishman obsessed with making arrangements to rent a store from Andrew?

It is significant that Clegg never mentioned this meeting, which took place at about 9 A.M. on Thursday, August 4. Perhaps he thought it would put him too close, in time as well as place, to the scene of the crime. It might have led to speculation about a sixth meeting between the two men in Andrew Borden's sitting room a couple of hours later.

It's also interesting that Clegg mentioned casually at the trial that, prior to their meeting downtown, he had planned to come to 92 Second Street to talk to Andrew Borden that fateful morning. Was he perhaps preparing a fall-back position in case somebody saw him in the vicinity of the Borden house?

Another question: was the man who came to the Borden house the same one Lizzie overheard, a week or two earlier, arguing loudly with her father about renting a store? If so, Jonathan Clegg would be the leading candidate for the role of Nemesis. However, there is nothing, either in Lizzie's testimony or in Fleet's, that establishes such a connection. Indeed, it seems unlikely; had Lizzie recognized the stranger's voice as one she had heard before, she would most likely have said so. On the other hand, Lizzie did refer to the earlier conversation as being loud. That could be explained by Clegg's deafness (Chapter 4); Andrew would have had to speak loudly to make himself understood.

If Clegg was indeed Nemesis, he must have followed Andrew home after talking with him downtown on Thursday morning. In that case he was most likely the man Dr. Handy saw anxiously walking back and forth near the Borden house a half hour before the murders. Clegg fits the description of Handy's "wild-eyed man" in a couple of respects, as indicated in the comparison below. Certainly Clegg was agitated; otherwise he wouldn't have pestered Andrew Borden so many times.

Moreover, he had been at the Borden house at least twice earlier in the week. On the other hand, there is no reason to suppose that Clegg had an unusually pale complexion; no one ever mentioned that. Finally, Jonathan Clegg was much older than Dr. Handy believed his man to be.

Dr. Handy's Wild-eyed Man Versus Jonathan Clegg

Handy's description	*Clegg's appearance*
Agitated, nervous	Yes!
Thought he'd seen the man recently on 2nd street	Yes!
Well dressed	Probably, a businessman
Medium height	Maybe
Very pale complexion	Not as far as we know
Young, age about 24	No! Age = 50

How likely is it that Jonathan Clegg, as opposed to Henry Palmer or Joseph Carpenter, was the man who came in from the street to murder the Bordens? Let's start with the negatives. Certainly Clegg didn't share Palmer's striking resemblance to Dr. Handy's palefaced man. So far as we know, he had no grudge against Andrew Borden, as Carpenter did.

On the other hand, Clegg is the only one of the three candidates who can be located with reasonable certainty at 92 Second Street on the morning of the murders. Beyond that, Clegg spent more time with Andrew Borden in the two days prior to the crime than did anyone else (except perhaps Abby!) Finally, Abby Borden would most likely have recognized Jonathan Clegg, a man who had known her husband well. She wouldn't have hesitated to let him enter the house, an act of kindness that cost poor Abby her life.

Had the police not made a "rush to judgment" as to Lizzie's guilt we would know more about the role, if any, played by Clegg. At the very least, they should have looked for the man Lizzie heard talking to her father on the morning of the murders. That search would almost certainly have led them to Jonathan Clegg. Further investigation might have made Clegg a leading suspect; alternatively, it might have exonerated him completely.

A Postscript

So ends the account of what I believe really happened in Fall River, Massachusetts on August 4, 1892. Is this the "final solution?" Is it time to say, "Goodbye, Lizzie Borden?" Of course not. No one can solve, once and forever after, the puzzle that has fascinated mystery writers for more than a century. What I hope to have done is to change the ground rules for solving the Borden case.

Quite simply, there is no reason to suppose that there was a time lapse between the two murders. (It's amazing that no one has pointed this out before). This makes it much more likely that the murderer was an intruder who came in off the street to kill first Andrew and then Abby Borden. Was this person Henry Palmer? Joseph Carpenter? Jonathan Clegg? Perhaps so, perhaps not. I look forward to other suggestions concerning the identity of "Nemesis."

On a related topic, I am convinced that Lizzie Borden was innocent. By offering rational explanations for the three most incriminating pieces of evidence against Lizzie (the note, the prussic acid story and her whereabouts when Abby was murdered), I believe that what was already a weak case against her has been demolished. It is certainly true that there is no direct physical evidence linking Palmer, Carpenter or Clegg to the murders. The fact is, however, that anyone who maintains Lizzie's guilt has to argue against the evidence.

Let me close by quoting the piece of doggerel that has been associated with the Borden case for a century more or less. No one knows when or where it originated, but everyone recognizes "the rhyme":

Lizzie Borden took an axe
And gave her mother forty whacks;
When she saw what she had done
She gave her father forty one.

Purists have complained that the murder weapon was actually a hatchet, that Abby was actually Lizzie's stepmother and that the numbers of whacks were actually nineteen and ten respectively. All of these objections are trivial; they fall well within the poetic license of the unknown author. (How many words can you think of that rhyme with "hatchet" or "nineteen"?)

There are however two far more serious errors in the rhyme. First, it wasn't Lizzie who swung the axe (the hatchet, whatever). Most important, the order of the deaths is wrong; Andrew was murdered at least a few minutes before Abby. Clearly it's time for a new rhyme that tells what really happened. It won't be easy to compete in popularity with the original version, but why not take a whack at it? I invite you to send your rhyme and any comments you have about this book to: [William L. Masterton, 1 Ridge Road, Storrs, CT 06268.]

Index